Holy Horr

Holy Horror

The Bible and Fear in Movies

Steve A. Wiggins

McFarland & Company, Inc., Publishers
Jefferson, North Carolina

ISBN (print) 978-1-4766-7466-7
ISBN (ebook) 978-1-4766-3371-8

LIBRARY OF CONGRESS CATALOGUING-IN-PUBLICATION DATA

BRITISH LIBRARY CATALOGUING DATA ARE AVAILABLE

Front cover: poster art from *Carrie*, 2013, featuring Chloë Grace Moretz
(Sony Pictures Releasing / Photofest)

Printed in the United States of America

*McFarland & Company, Inc., Publishers
Box 611, Jefferson, North Carolina 28640
www.mcfarlandpub.com*

To Kietra, Kay, Kelly, Jim, and Jeff

"It's impossible for words to describe what is necessary to those who do not know what horror means. Horror... Horror has a face... And you must make a friend of horror. Horror and moral terror are your friends. If they are not, then they are enemies to be feared."

—Col. Kurtz, *Apocalypse Now*

Table of Contents

Acknowledgments

A number of people contributed to this book without knowing it. My wife, for instance, by allowing me to indulge my fascination with horror movies, and eventually watching some with me. My daughter put up with my obsession while writing this book to the exclusion of our usual, more pleasant, discussion topics of a literary nature. She also designed the website. My brother-in-law, Neal Stephenson, showed polite interest as I discussed the very early thoughts behind this book with him in a serendipitously named restaurant in New York City. My big brother Ben could be counted on to do what big brothers do, fueling my interest in monsters and always being willing to chat about them. He still knows how to scare me with the most innocent of comments.

The colleagues who had conversations with me concerning monsters, and those who showed up to hear the paper that started this idea in book form, didn't realize the creature they were helping create. My students from my teaching days inspired me in ways they likely never realized. While I no longer have the opportunity to teach, much of this book developed in the classroom. Students not only watched clips from some of these movies, but also suggested many of them to me. As usual, the young lead the old.

Among academic colleagues specifically I would like to thank James Watts of Syracuse University for starting the conversation. Although I met him as an editor hoping for a book from him, he gave me a book idea instead. He encouraged me through difficult times and even, without knowing it, gave his imprimatur to this project. Diana Walsh Pasulka of the University of North Carolina, Wilmington, helped me think through the early stages of the project and encouraged me at several points. She was a consultant on the actual movie of *The Conjuring*.

Even earlier Deane Galbraith asked me to review a book on Satanism for *Relegere* (an Australian open-access, peer-reviewed journal), that slowly started the wheels turning. Deane also supported my work on my blog when many other religionists didn't understand what I try to do there.

My interest in monsters lay still in its coffin until I learned that Kelly Murphy of Central Michigan University, Esther Hamori of Union Theological Seminary in New York, and Joseph Laycock of the University of Texas at Austin shared this fascination. At various meetings of the American Academy of Religion and Society of Biblical Literature we talked about monsters and how to move ahead with them. Kelly has been especially encouraging regarding this book. Others joined the conversation as well: Rhiannon Graybill of Rhodes College, Christopher Meredith of St. Mary's University, and Denise Buell of Williams College. Matthew Ketchum, who like me has been kept on the life-support of adjunct work at Rutgers University, talked to me about ghosts when I was in need of some haunting. Andrew Mein of Durham University, and a colleague from Edinburgh, encouraged me to chase Cthulhu. It became clear that monsters and horror had a quorum among biblical scholars and those teaching religious studies.

Jennifer E. Porter and Scott Daniel Dunbar, the editors of the *Journal of Religion and Popular Culture*, accepted an academic paper on the subject for publication, thereby convincing me that it was more than a chimera worth pursuing. My colleagues in the publishing industry have taught me more about writing books than they'll ever know.

Playwright David Koslow kindly encouraged my work along the way despite our never having met. David Alff at McFarland has been quite understanding as an editor as I've transitioned from a writer of technical monographs to an author. Even editors require other editors! I acknowledge his help in making the book better than it was when he first saw it. Keith Bodner of Crandall University remains a personal booster.

Jeffrey Kripal of Rice University has been a source of undying support in recent years through what has proven to be a strange and unsettling career. Unlike many scholars he has taken a personal interest in my story and provided more resources than I had any right to expect. I have learned much from him. Not all hauntings are fiction and laughter isn't always the best way to look at the strange.

For those I have left out, please don't take it personally. Mistakes and errors that remain in this book are my own, in any case. Even with all the eyes staring from the forest, the trembling hand of this author bears full responsibility for such lapses.

Preface

"Danny!" Jack Torrance shouts, limping through the snow, axe firmly in hand. Winifred's trapped in the Overlook Hotel. Danny races through the maze, aware he's leaving telltale footprints. His father's going to kill him. He slips. Falls. Jack's closing in. Suddenly he realizes if he steps back in his own tracks, he'll buy some time. His father won't stop until he's dead.

* * *

Come on in. Don't be frightened. What are you afraid of? No, seriously—what sends chills down your spine? And why are so many of us willing to pay good money to go into a large, darkened room filled with strangers and expose ourselves publicly to our fears? Whether our terror's inspired by sharks just off a sunny beach or haunted dolls that come to life during a stormy night, movies that scare us have one thing in common—they tend to do very well at the box office. When we're safe, we like to be scared.

If something invisibly affected you every day in ways both subtle and important, would you want to know about it? What if that something was so much a part of the background noise that it could blend in like Predator so that you wouldn't even see it? And what if that thing could harm you? Would you want to know about it?

This book is about these two things—horror and something hidden. The hidden thing is often in plain sight, like Poe's purloined letter. We'll talk more about it later. Right now let's consider what scares you. You see, what makes us afraid differs from person to person. We all share fear. What's really frightening is we often don't know exactly what it is that's scaring us.

Trailers

Fear lurks in the darkened rooms of our minds, waiting to spring upon us. That spider suddenly spotted when you're in the shower, naked and vul-

1

nerable. That creepy guy you didn't hear coming to your isolated bus stop before the sun comes up. Fear comes in many varieties, giving horror wide scope. Movies play on that undefined field of dread.

What is horror? It's difficult to say. For one thing, it means different things to different people. At the very least horror must contain some frightening or disturbing elements. For movies, at one extreme are the gruesome bloodbaths such as slashers, splatter films, and torture porn. At the more genteel end stands Tod Browning's 1931 film version of *Dracula*, the first horror film. Between there are reanimated corpses, giant spiders and snakes, zombies, monsters, aliens— you name it. If it scares people, there's a movie about it.

Horror comes in many varieties. Here's just a quick hit list:

- Action Horror
- Body Horror
- Comedy Horror
- Disaster Horror
- Drama Horror
- Gothic Horror
- Natural Horror
- Psychological Horror
- Science Fiction Horror
- Supernatural Horror
- Slasher
- Splatter
- Thriller

One of the things you're sure to notice is that these categories overlap and aren't always easy to separate from one another. Another thing to notice is that they can all cause fear.

Let's consider just a couple: psychological horror may contain little or no blood at all, yet might still be terrifying. Remember *The Innocents* (1961, based on Henry James' novel *The Turn of the Screw*) or *The Haunting* (1963, based on Shirley Jackson's novel *The Haunting of Hill House*)? Psychological horror may also show sheer graphic brutality, while being nearly naturalistic. Lars von Trier's *Antichrist*, for example, shows an erect phallus ejaculating blood after being smashed by an unbalanced wife, as well as her self-inflicted un-anesthetized clitoridectomy with rusty scissors. Although these are both surely horrific images, they remain within the realm of possibility. (This assessment overlooks the talking fox, for obvious reasons.) The torture porn of *Wolf Creek* and the remake of *The Hills Have Eyes* (2006) showcase almost unbelievable brutality but are for the most part stories that could—allowing for a bit of supernatural in the latter—take place.

Natural horror, on the other hand, including movies without supernatural elements, satisfies some viewers. Others have an incredulous reaction to having *Jaws* classified as horror. "Really? It's just a movie about a shark!" *Sharknado*, with its inherent campiness, is on the other hand clearly horror in the way a particular fan may think of the genre. Flying sharks in tornadoes are scary beyond measure. The point is that different things scare us. "Horror film" isn't a fixed genre. Thrillers frighten some people more than monsters.

Horror is in the eye of the beholder. One analyst of horror films suggests that horror is finding your own path and defining it according to your own purposes. Writing a book like this necessarily requires that "horror" be defined by the author's understanding of it. Some of the movies treated here may be more a tour of personal neuroses than what necessarily frightens every reader. That's the nature of the beast. Horror reflects our fears. Fear is a good thing—it keeps us safe from danger. Like flying sharks.

Shutter Island—horror or not? *Rocky Horror Picture Show*—horror or not? *Deliverance*—horror or not? The horror label has been applied to films from mainstream drama such as *Black Swan* to more obscure fantasies such as *Tideland*. Horror films are notoriously difficult to pin down. Genre's an opinion, and never a fact. What's horror without a few surprises?

Some of the cinematic choices in this book might startle you. Many genre standards are here, such as *Psycho, Carrie, The Fog, Clive Barker's Hellraiser, Rosemary's Baby, The Omen,* and *The Exorcist.* Others may seem a strange fit. Any movie with monsters counts as horror in this nightmare. What scares you may not scare everyone. It's like visiting another person's nightmares. The scariest films may be where you never see the hidden thing.

The Hidden Thing

Horror loves religion. Even if it's just the subtle supernatural, horror frequently invokes religious belief. Sometimes the overlap's explicit—even secular movie critics notice it. Other times it's subtle. Religion and horror feed off each other.

If something invisibly affected you every day in ways both subtle and large, would you want to know about it? Consider the Bible.

The Bible occurs unexpectedly often in horror. Although it may be a prop, it's never *only* a prop. When you see the Bible, there's something uncanny going on. That's why this book is necessary. Don't worry, this isn't a religious book. In fact, the observations of this book apply no matter what you may personally believe. It's simply bringing something from the shadows into the limelight. It's a shift of focus, not a matter of belief. The Bible's here, like that monster right behind you, whether you've noticed it or not.

How were the movie choices made for this book? Cole Sear sees dead people. Other people see Bibles. Seeing Bibles in movies is often the result of growing up in a Fundamentalist family, like Max Cady's. There's a kind of Bible radar that develops when children are taught that eternal salvation depends on it. Using movies while teaching biblical studies also helps. Each appearance of the Bible in cinema convinces you that there are probably more, like finding a couple pennies on the sidewalk. You grow accustomed to looking for more examples. The selection offered here wasn't systematically chosen. The movies presented represent a lifetime of watching, and noticing. Hush, the preview's starting.

Preview

"Danny!" Jack Torrance shouts, limping through the snow, axe firmly in hand. As the crazed father chases his only son through the maze, we know the boy gets away because we've seen *The Shining* dozens of times, but we still can't look away. Will Danny escape this time? Will the son be sacrificed? What can stop the possessed Jack Torrance? Hit "pause."

The story is somehow familiar, isn't it? Where've we seen this before? A father obsessed with a singular idea. In an isolated area with his son. He raises a sharp instrument to slay the boy because of the voices in his head.

The story of Abraham and Isaac in the biblical book of Genesis clearly serves as an inspiration for this horror scene. Alone on Mount Moriah, Abraham binds his only son Isaac to the altar, intent on sacrificing him. Killing your own child is so horrific that we all naturally cringe. Yet we can't look away. The Bible is a book of horror. Movies freely borrow from its stock footage.

One of the dynamics at play between Scripture and celluloid is how open the categories are. "Horror" and "Bible" can both mean many things. What scares us is personal, like approaching that door in the house that's always remained shut and nobody will tell us why. If you were raised with the Bible, you already know horror. This book just makes it explicit.

Intertitles

What you're about to see is a true story.

This book isn't intended to be comprehensive. Nobody's seen every horror film ever made—who has the time? The selections here begin in 1960, the year of *Psycho*. Horror films had been around for about three decades at that point, but appearances of the Bible start to take on a new urgency from this time forward. (Not coincidentally, it's just after the era of McCarthyism.) *Psycho* was a kind of bellwether for how the Bible could be treated and it took a director of Alfred Hitchcock's stature to move horror into mainstream respectability (if it has ever had such respectability. And what is a bellwether anyway? It is, appropriately, the ram that leads the flock of sheep—the one wearing a bell around its neck, the "bell wearer." It's all there in *Zootopia*. Unfortunately the sheep of *Silence of the Lambs* don't ever reference the Bible so it won't be discussed in this book).

You don't have to watch the movies under discussion to make sense of this treatment. For the most part fairly detailed descriptions are provided so that viewing the films isn't necessary, unless, of course you want to watch. You don't even have to read the Bible. It all makes sense without it.

This book shows how scary movies reflect various American views of the Bible. All films in which the Bible appears do this to some extent. The focus here is on North American cinema because the question at hand is how horror reflects American views of the Bible. You'll find only a few foreign films here. It's not that foreign horror movies don't count, but the Bible's noticeably absent in many of them. The Bible doesn't bear the cultural weight abroad that it does domestically. Arguably, many foreign films are made with affluent American viewership in mind. *The Others*, for example, was shot in English although filmed in Spain. American devotion to the Bible seeps into all aspects of life. In other cultures it doesn't appear to be the same trigger for horror as it is here.

Everyone knows sequels are a hallmark of the horror genre. In the interest of not letting the size of this book get out of control like the Blob, sequels had to be sacrificed here. There are good reasons for this. If sequels were included we'd be here all night. Also, story lines often change with subsequent development. For example, Laurie Strode becomes Michael Meyers' sister in subsequent chapters of *Halloween*. In the original they're unrelated. While *Halloween* doesn't use the Bible, in many instances that do—such as *The Evil Dead*—subsequent installments complicate things. (For example, *The Evil Dead II* renames *Naturom Demonto* as the *Necronomicon Ex-Mortis* in the voice-over introduction. Raymond Knowby's tape within the film, however, still refers to it as *Naturom Demonto*.) Such complications, while fun to explore, tempt us to go back and adjust the first film in the light of the sequel. This book deals with first impressions. The impact of an original is difficult to match. Going back after having viewed the next installment would get tedious on a walk in the dark like this. With one exception, we won't be screening any sequels.

Remakes, on the other hand, are important to watch when it comes to the Bible. Engage in this practice and you'll notice that Scripture often becomes less or more important in a remake than it was in the original. The way the Holy Writ is presented in both always differs. One version always has more of it than the other.

Like the Bible, movies come in many versions—directors' cuts, unrated renditions, with deleted scenes, alternate endings. With easy access to multiple versions of films, the observations here are limited to theatrical releases. Since people like to talk about movies after the show's over, what's described here is what you'd see if you paid your money at the box office. Reference isn't made to on-disc commentary either. This book is main lining the films only.

Television programs aren't viewed. Made-for-television movies have a different set of parameters than theatrical releases, and the focus here remains on the latter. You won't find the TV versions of *Carrie*, *Children of the Corn*, or *The Exorcist* here. Horror and the Bible on television will have to wait for another book.

Thanks for coming in. If you like being scared, there's no better combination than horror and the Bible. Let's mix them together and see what happens.

Introduction:
America's Magic Book

Apparently it's the apocalypse. An environmental disaster has just struck, and the locals have crowded to church for guidance. Suddenly an old man breaks out in a prophetic warning. "Horrible things are going to happen!" he shouts. As he spells out the cryptic signs of God's coming judgment, a little girl turns to her father and begs him to do something. Homer Simpson flips through the pew Bible and cries, "This book doesn't have any answers!"

*　*　*

Thus opens *The Simpsons Movie*. Critics long ago noted that Fox's long-running animated program was exceptionally biblically literate. While not horror, *The Simpsons* quite often makes asides about the Bible and even has episodes entirely based on it. *The Simpsons Movie*, however, captures in this one moment a snapshot of how the Bible is viewed by Joe Sixpack. Apart from those who regularly read, mark, and inwardly digest Scripture, the average cultural Christian assumes that the Bible is some kind of spiritual manual with answers to life's difficult questions. In fact, if you know how to use it, you can recite certain passages to ensure specific results. Sometimes it's like magic.

This introduction is like a director's commentary, only it's recommended that you read it before viewing what comes after. Before we bring the Good Book and horror together, we have to sort out what the Bible is. Or at least what we think it is. This book suggests that movies tell us just that. To understand America's magic book we have to go back long before the movie camera was invented. We start this commentary with fears of witches and devils in Salem, Massachusetts.

Magic Books

Try to imagine American life in the 1690s. New England. A good place to start might be the movie *The Witch* (treated in Chapter 5). Meticulously researched and designed, this movie based itself on historically accurate details in every regard. Salem, a small town that would grow to great importance in Massachusetts history, housed families well-known to each other. There were many land squabbles between them. An accusation of witchcraft—believed in with deadly seriousness—flew and soon many women and men were jailed and 19 people were officially, "legally" executed. We might have felt justified if we had lived then. Our small community had to be kept safe from the Devil. These tragic events highlight the American fascination with magic.

We now know that the Salem Witch Trials were an unfortunate miscarriage of justice. We understand that the 20 victims (one man was pressed to death for refusing to enter a plea) who were legally murdered were thought to be something that, in reality, simply didn't exist—people who attended witches' sabbaths, had sex with the Devil, wrote their name or mark in his book, and cast evil spells on young girls. They were thought to be astral projectors, accomplished at leaving their bodies at night. Rebecca Nurse was a particularly sad case, as she was an old woman at the time she of her trial. Hard of hearing, she probably couldn't even understand the charges against her. At Gallows Hill she was hanged as a threat to society—a society that sincerely believed in magic.

Although more than three centuries have passed, the fascination remains. The 2014 horror movie *The Conjuring*, based on a true story involving Ed and Lorraine Warren, took the spooky tale of a haunted house and added magic. A descendent of one of the Salem "witches" was hanged from the tree in the yard. The implication is clear—the Salem 20 were actual witches. The film's use of this concept is a horror trope that goes back as far as H.P. Lovecraft.

In real life, Ed and Lorraine Warren were well-known paranormal researchers who actually did investigate the haunting of the Perron family in Rhode Island. They also found, in an unrelated case, an allegedly possessed doll, Annabelle. The movie introduces Salem into the plot. We all know there were no witches in Salem, but still…. *The Conjuring*, as a movie that draws many of these themes together, will be treated in detail later in this book (Chapter 6). The melancholy history of Salem doesn't mean, however, that belief in magic ceased in America, at least in people's minds. Far from it.

Imagine a long, dark night in rural Massachusetts in 1692. A deeply religious community tending toward Puritan sensibilities. Riven with all the disagreements and jealousies that attend unequal distribution of goods and affections. Unexplained happenings occur. The Enlightenment is underway in Europe, and these are no colonial rubes with unsophisticated leadership. Some of the clergy, at least, have Harvard educations. Cotton Mather himself calls on the village. Communal biblical literacy runs high and is reinforced by regular attendance at worship. Witch trials in Europe ended nearly a century prior to this, and yet the fear lingers on the frontier. It's difficult to distinguish between miracles and magic when weird things are happening. The Good Book offered answers to the horror.

Communal biblical literacy doesn't necessarily refer to the personal reading of the Bible by everyone, but rather to a level of base knowledge about Scripture in a society. Puritans, for example, would know the Ten Commandments and would be able to identify major biblical figures and stories, even if not everyone could read. Their culture was suffused with the Good Book.

What average early Americans actually believed about the Bible is difficult to know, due to the lack of personal records on how Holy Writ was privately understood. Knowing the demographics of various denominations certainly gives us an idea of official teachings on the Bible. Private beliefs are less certain. Personal diaries rarely survive to preserve thoughts on how the Bible was interpreted, if anybody actually journaled on that topic. We do know, however, that the belief in magic persisted. Puritans didn't see magical beliefs as necessarily inconsistent with Christian teaching. The Bible, after all, condemns witches, but not magic specifically.

In the popular imagination magic and the sacred are very similar. Fine distinctions separate the miracles (for which the Bible is famous) from magic. Moses, for example, performs the miracle of turning his staff into a serpent. Pharaoh's Egyptian magicians perform the exact same wonder by using magic. This also applies to turning water into blood and multiplying frogs. By the time of Jesus water is being turned to wine. Thus sayeth the Bible. Salem was a community with a dilemma. Holy Writ lauds miracle workers, but loathes practitioners of magic.

In Salem, beginning in the house of a Puritan minister, Samuel Parris, witchcraft and the Bible would meet. The folk "magic" of Parris' slave Tituba was associated with the dark powers of Satan. A social insanity broke out leading to hysteria in this small community. The Bible declares, "Thou shalt not suffer a witch to live." The Good Book clashed with long-established folk magic with catastrophic results. The mix, however, of Bible-aware colonials who also believed in magic survived the Witch Trials. It continued in American culture, and continues right down to the present day.

Fast-forward to the 1980s. America's mind hadn't really changed that much on the subject of magic. It was often called something else, but it was still there. Witches still existed. They weren't those of Halloween or from the movies, but Wicca had entered the public consciousness. It was more widespread than Reagan-era Americans wanted to believe. Satanic panics were starting to break out and otherwise rational people would go on witch hunts for the neighborhood Satanists. Behind it all was a lurking fear that maybe some of this talk of magic could be real. Fundamentalism played into this as well since the Bible says witches shouldn't be permitted to live. If the Bible said that, didn't it imply witches were real? (We'll see this conflation, by the way, in *Rosemary's Baby*, which came out just before the satanic panic.) Who knew witches still existed? Bible believers did. Belief in magic had gone hand-in-hand with Bible-reading culture from the beginning. And belief in magic was still thriving in the 1980s.

One of the natural tendencies of every era is to project current assumptions over the past. Today science presumes no divine presence in the physical world. It's easy to suppose that earlier generations would have come to the same conclusions once science took hold. The evidence of history, however, offers a more subtle scenario.

Over the last couple of centuries the Bible has come to be seen as irrelevant by many. At the same time, the indirect influence of the Bible in America has at least remained constant, and, it could be argued, has increased. The specific place that we'll look for confirmation of this is in popular culture. Popular culture still allows for magic. Harry Potter—what more needs to be said? Popular culture also allows for the Good Book.

Nobody wants to be thought of as naive. Publicly we recite the creed that there's no such thing as magic. Magical beings exist only in the imagination. But remember the Satanism scares of the 1980s; the very idea of people worshiping the Devil scared otherwise rational people straight. Cool-headed investigation eventually revealed this was a panic not unlike Orson Welles' broadcast of *War of the Worlds*. We'd been there before. When we all gather together we frown, shake our heads and say "Of course there's no such thing as magic. Or the Devil!" Once we shut the door at home what we really believe creeps out. The polls show this to be true. Many Americans believe in an actual Devil. The power of magic remains.

Magical thinking is still alive and well, if hidden. How many times have you gone into a high-rise, stepped into the elevator and noticed that there's no thirteenth floor? Of course there's a thirteenth floor. It's numbered 14. This is the power of magic. Doesn't such widespread practice say something about what people believe? Rationally there's no reason not to have a floor numbered 13. Still, pressing that elevator button with 14 feels so much more comfortable. Just in case.

It doesn't really help that "magic" isn't easy to define. Books on magical thinking indicate that such thought isn't at all rare. We still wonder about the truth of urban legends. Do you flash your headlights at that car driving at night without them? We all know superstitious people. Who doesn't hesitate, for at least a second, before walking under a ladder? Or doesn't throw spilled salt over a shoulder once in a while? Or doesn't carry around a personal talisman, no matter how passé?

Magic is defined, for the purpose of this book, as a non-physical causal connection. Einstein's famous "spooky action at a distance." There should be no way, given what we know of the universe, that a person could move an object, no matter how small, by using the power of her mind only. The trajectory of a black feline perpendicular to your path should have no impact on how well your day turns out. It doesn't matter where the sun, moon, or planets were the day you were born—they can't influence your life. Right, Mr. Reagan?

Measuring magical beliefs is problematic. Anthropologists have a difficult time distinguishing magic from religion in the first place. Even if a poll's anonymous, many adults wouldn't want to admit to holding non-rational outlooks. Surveys have repeatedly shown that religious beliefs strongly persist, and American religion is based on the supernatural. But believing in magic? That's just not something respectable people would confess. So what proof do we have that people are still secretly fey?

One bit of evidence, beyond the anecdotal, is the sheer number of secret societies and occult groups in America. These collectives are thriving. Vampire societies, Wiccan covens, and cosplay gatherings occur with large numbers of participants. (Comic-Con, out in the open, is a mainstream venue for allowing magical thinking, if we're honest about it. We defend ourselves by saying it's only pretend.) These groups meet a very deep need. "Occult," strictly speaking, may not be synonymous with "magic," but both admit of a hidden world of power not evident to the untrained or uninitiated. That's a large part of their draw. And people come to occult gatherings.

Magical thinking survives in America alongside the Bible. There's no wall separating them. Magical thinking has always been a part of who we are. But what does all this have to do with the Good Book?

The Mysterious Bible

The Bible's famous enough that anyone can recognize it, like a movie star. Like a star it has a hidden inner life that few actually see. Filmmakers have become a main source of authoritative information when it comes to the Good Book. A culture with high Bible awareness and low Bible literacy depends on popular media to tell them what Holy Writ says. The paid experts have left the building and nothing's as scary as the unknown. We gather information where we can.

It doesn't help that the Bible can be a scary book. Or can be involved in violent situations. Consider a pre-satanic panic movie where it features— *The Cross and the Switchblade* (1970) which, inexplicably had a GP rating. Not exactly horror, such a film can terrify children. A "Christploitation" movie by Don Murray, it was made with Christian intent, and therefore is not discussed in detail in this book. In the movies, even knife-fighting gang-bangers recognize the Good Book. Scripture's no stranger to cinema. *The Cross and the Switchblade* had it in spades. Or blades. The same is true of many secular films. Before we go to the movies, though, we have to have a talk about the Good Book. Can we get an expert opinion?

Biblical studies is an odd field. It's one of the very few where "experts" are routinely and expectedly ignored by practitioners (clergy, average Bible readers). One of the reasons for this is that in American culture anyone can claim to be a Bible expert. Biblical scholars spend years learning dead languages in order to read ancient texts. What they say about all this studying matters very little to the average Bible reader. Movies, however, provide *hoi polloi* with much more information about the Bible than any scholarly monograph. And movies tell us that Holy Writ is magical.

Many calm, respectable Bible-believing Christians—mostly regular American Protestants—harbor magical beliefs about their Bibles while holding down challenging, even technical, jobs. Doctors, computer programmers, lawyers, police officers. The make-up of Bible-believing Christian groups, like those who claim to have seen UFOs, is a mix of education levels and backgrounds. You know this is true when you visit a doctor and have the Bible quoted to you. The Good Book is pervasive in American culture.

Believers recognize that the Bible is something different. Unique. Something more than any other book. This outlook toward the Bible is deeply embedded in American consciousness. While many don't read the Bible, the expectation that it's not like other books remains. It's somehow magical.

Sociologists have conducted studies that demonstrate, via polls and statistics, that Americans revere (and some even still regularly read) the Bible. Scripture's pervasive, and—although we don't often think about it—it continues to influence public policy and opinion every single day. The Good Book appears in many more subtle guises as well, particularly in popular culture. Although this book considers movies, references in other media could easily fill a study like this. You need only consider the novels of Margaret

Atwood or the songs of Bruce Springsteen or the apocalyptic worlds of many video games to find numerous biblical references. They may be unorthodox, for sure, but such sources share origins with Cecil B. DeMille's *The Ten Commandments* and Ridley Scott's *Exodus: Gods and Kings*. Who interprets Holy Writ in a world of Nones? Popular culture.

The Bible itself, however, is doing fine. A fading star perhaps, but it still has wide public recognition even though it's not as prominent as it once was. As a book, it's difficult to understand. Those who don't attend religious services see it in the media. The media gives definite impressions of how Holy Writ should be understood. And you don't even have to open the book.

Any discussion of the Bible adds to its interpretation—its meaning. Movies interpret the Bible for us. Since we live in the post-modern period we know that the "meaning" of a text comes as much from the reader as from the writer. Simply put, anyone can interpret the Bible. Movies do so all the time. Think of *The Book of Eli* (discussed in Chapter 4). The entire film is based on media perceptions of Scripture.

Movies reach massive audiences, across religious traditions. Media stars are the modern intellectuals. How else can we explain Ronald Reagan, Jesse Ventura, Arnold Schwarzenegger, or Donald Trump? For large numbers of people, the portrayal of the Bible in film is just as valid, if not more valid, than those impenetrable books scholars write for each other. Or what some minister says in a quickly forgotten Sunday morning sermon. As you'd expect, scholars have a fancy name for this. It's "the iconic Bible."

The Iconic Bible

This book isn't technical, but understanding how an iconic Bible works is necessary for what follows. It'll be relatively painless—that's a promise.

A few years ago some biblical scholars began noticing that the Bible serves in culture more as a symbol than as a book that's actually read. The phrase they used to describe this is "the iconic Bible." An example would be laying your hand on a Bible to swear to tell the truth. Or an evangelistic preacher hitting someone with the Bible to heal them, or to cast out a demon. These kinds of actions aren't recommended in the pages of the Bible itself. In fact, the Bible is seldom even open when these things happen. Such actions use the Bible as a symbol—that's an iconic book. What's an icon, anyway?

Before icons were computer symbols, they were religious paintings. Specifically, they were paintings of Christian saints, done in a rigidly precise style—very popular in the early church. The style requirements were so conventional that the painter was said "to write an icon," not to paint one. In Eastern Orthodox Christianity, icons still hold a place of honor near that of the Bible. Icon came to mean "essential symbol."

When the Bible's an icon it's an established object. The exotic German phrase for this is "*Ding an sich*," or "thing in itself." Such a *Ding* is ultimately unknowable, unexplainable. It may help to think of it as an idea that exists fully formed in your head. Love, for example. We all know what love is but we have a difficult time spelling it out. Love is a *Ding*, just like the Bible is a *Ding*.

Since "*Ding*" captures the idea of the Bible in American culture so well, and is less cumbersome than repeating "established object" all the time, (and more fun to read—*Ding!*) it'll be used here to describe the Bible as an established object. The Bible is a *Ding*.

This doesn't imply that God made the Bible as a *Ding*, but rather that humans have designated it as one. (This book doesn't presume to speak on behalf of any deity.) With a magical view of the world, we've created the concept of the Bible as a *Ding* with which to be reckoned. People place their hands on the Bible to swear an oath in court, regardless of their personal belief. The Bible is a *Ding* and all we can do is interpret it since it can't be further broken down.

The "iconic Bible" means that the Bible represents a *Ding*. As such, it's an immediately recognizable object. People don't need to read the Bible to know what it is. They already know. This is what is meant by the phrase "iconic Bible." This book focuses on the iconic Bible as a *Ding*. We won't be going down to "chapter and verse" level unless a secular movie does. The focus will be the iconic book, the *Ding*. Sunday school this is not.

The idea of the Bible (regardless of its contents) has taken hold and can't be dislodged. Consider how in an otherwise scientific and technological culture it still holds sway over elections and even, to some extent, what might be considered moral behavior (one man plus one woman and all that nonsense). This is characteristic of a *Ding*.

Iconic books aren't neutral; they affect things. The most obvious way this happens is when a book is read and it makes someone do something. The book has performed a function. There are other ways for books to perform, too. Think about a presidential inauguration (if you dare). A hand is laid on a book, often the Bible. The physical object is performing the function of making a man honest (so it is believed). Attentive readers will have noticed that we've slipped from "iconic Bible" to "iconic book." We'll come back to the reasons for this in just a moment.

A major role the iconic Bible performs is salvation. In popular culture, the Bible saves. That's part of its role as an iconic book. And books beyond the Bible function as iconic Bibles in this role as well. When they do, they too save. You can trust iconic books.

Not only is the Bible an iconic book that saves, it's also somehow magical. Not literally, but in the world of popular media the Bible has supernatural abilities. Magic, as will become obvious below, has never fully left American popular consciousness. And that belief in magic, as we've seen, goes back to the beginning.

Often in movies the mere presence of the Good Book conveys a message. It's more pervasive than you might think. Obviously, many movies don't show the Bible. There's not even any paper at all, for example, in the *Star Wars* franchise. Nevertheless the Bible surfaces frequently enough to demand attention. You just need to keep an eye out for it. Sometimes it's disguised.

This is another feature of the iconic Bible; sometimes it's not actually the Bible. Viewers may know what sacred texts are, but they have trouble distinguishing between them. Just as the Bible is iconic, other books may be iconic in different ways. *War and Peace*, for example, is iconic of a really long novel. In popular imagination the Bible is an old, leather-bound book. Visually, at first glance, any book fitting this description suggests the Bible to a viewer's imagination. In other words the books of the biblical canon (a fancy word for a collection of books) is open. It's a loose canon. Other books may stand in for the iconic Bible. We'll see this from time to time in horror. An Elvis impersonator works because he makes you think of Elvis.

Why might a film director or writer use a "stand-in" for the Bible? Sometimes the Bible just doesn't say what you want it to say. For movie-makers this can be quite a problem. Since many people don't distinguish ancient books from the Bible others can "stand in" for it. Fortunately, there are many old books that look or sound a lot like the Bible.

Starting in about the 1870s explorers and missionaries—followed by archaeologists—began discovering other ancient documents in the Near East (or Middle East, depending on how you divide it). Many of these ancient texts are even older than the Bible and, since they come from similar cultures, sound kind of biblical when they're translated. These texts don't visually look much like the Bible—many of them are written on clay tablets—but they sometimes raise ideas that fit horror movies spectacularly well. These "books" aren't the Bible, but in the minds of denizens of a biblical culture, they act like the Bible. Examples will be seen in *The Evil Dead* and *Stigmata*.

Old, leather-bound books sometimes stand for the Good Book. So do other religious books. Sometimes they even have gilt-edged pages. Such books act like the Bible in popular imagination. Grimoires function this way. In possession movies so does *The Roman Ritual* (as we'll see in Chapter 6).

By far the majority of examples presented in this book involve the actual Bible. It's important to realize, however, that once this iconic Bible has been planted in the mind of the viewer, other books may be substituted for it. It's not cheating to include those books—that's how iconic books work. The original iconic book is the Bible. But whose Bible is it?

Bibles—Protestant, Catholic and Jewish

The Bible is a scary book. In 2015 it landed on the list of banned books. The Bible surely can be a "text of terror." It's full of horror movie moments. All the people in the world, except eight, drown only six chapters in. The protagonist (God) demands that a man sacrifice his only son on an altar. A woman is gang-raped and then her body is dismembered so it can be sent throughout the nation to show the evil in it. And we haven't even got to the nation of Israel yet. If you're Catholic, a woman is forced to watch her sons being fried to death in a huge frying pan. For Christians, Jesus is given *The Passion of the Christ* treatment before being gruesomely crucified. Rape, murder, eyes being gouged out, and all kinds of mayhem occur in these pages of terror.

Why single out Catholics when mentioning Holy Writ? Doesn't everyone have the same Bible? No, not exactly. The Jews were the first to collect sacred texts together. Their Bible wasn't even finished before Christians started adding their own books. And not all Christians agree on which books belong. (This may be one reason the iconic Bible's often held closed!)

Think back to Salem again. In the early days, before large influxes of Catholics into what would become the United States, the Bible American people recognized was the Protestant Bible: Old Testament, New Testament, *tout court*. There were early Jewish immigrants (as well as Muslims) in early America. Their Bible, of course, had no "New Testament." The Bible as an American icon clearly grew out of its Protestant heritage, however. Jews and Catholics tended not to present themselves as "Bible believers." Both groups had long and rich traditions in which the Bible was interpreted. Protestants, on the other hand, had only one source of salvation: the Good Book. They even had their own theological term for this situation—*sola scriptura*, "Scripture alone." Only the Bible could lead to salvation for Protestants. This also played into magical thinking about it. Such a powerful book was a magical book.

The first Europeans to settle permanently in the English colonies were Protestants. Instead of a Pope or Magisterium to guide them, they had a book. By the time other religiously oriented colonists joined the young nation, the Bible was already deeply established as America's book. Love of the Bible had its roots in England where the monarchy existed in a strange tension with the religious sensibilities of the common people. There was, however, also magic in the air even there. When the nonconformists became colonists, the magic came with them. It's been here ever since.

As mentioned above, the Catholic Bible is different from the Protestant Bible. It's bigger. Its "Old Testament" has some books that the Protestants left out. These books are called "the Apocrypha" by Protestants and "the Deuterocanonical Books" by Catholics. Both the Protestant and Catholic Bibles are larger than the Jewish Bible. So whose Bible are we discussing here? Broadly speaking the iconic Bible is a Christian Bible. In very general terms, it's Protestant (that is, it doesn't have the Apocrypha in it) although this isn't an absolute. Often the Bible isn't even opened, so it's kind of hard to tell.

Protestants were the first to believe that the Bible alone leads to salvation. If that's all you need, everyone can interpret it for her or himself, right? Well, not exactly.

The preaching tradition soon brought Bible specialization back to the clergy. Ministers learned what they knew from biblical scholars. Biblical scholars no longer corner the market on interpretation. In this world of Nones and evangelicals who don't read the Good Book, Bible interpretation is frequently left to popular media. Nobody speaks for God. Churches—far too many to count—no longer hold the sole authority. And who takes theologians seriously? They write about things that can't even be seen. The Bible's in the public domain. The Bible's a *Ding*. It's generally a Protestant *Ding*.

Possession movies (see Chapter 6) especially will challenge this convention. We'll see an instance of the Jewish Bible in *The Possession*. Most explicitly Catholic horror movies seldom show the Bible—*The Exorcism of Emily Rose* does but we don't get close enough to see if it's a Catholic translation. America's iconic Bible tends to be the Protestant Bible.

The Reluctant Star of the Show

American culture is a strange chimera with a religious heart. We're a nation enamored of the Bible but unsure of what it says. The Bible's a book that requires considerable effort to comprehend. It's a big book and we're pressed for time. We leave knowing the content to our clergy. They know all about obscure things such as the book of Hezekiah. (There is no such book in the Bible, but you knew that.) We can't tell if quotes come from the Bible or not. "Early to bed, early to rise"? What about "God helps those who help themselves"? Or "Do or do not. There is no try"? As a culture we often find ourselves at the mercy of the filmmakers. Blessed are the filmmakers—biblical, no?

In general people visually recognize sacred books when they see them. They're a *Ding*. If recognition of the canonical Bible is a bit vague, as noted above, other magical books might just do. Sometimes the Bible's reluctant. Here's where stand-ins can help. Some fans of H. P. Lovecraft suppose the *Necronomicon*, a fictional book invented by Lovecraft, actually exists. Lovecraft was no great lover of multiculturalism, and the *Necronomicon* was written by the "Mad Arab" Abdul Alhazred. It's a book of magic so powerful as to be evil. Lovecraft himself was an atheist, but he found use for a sacred, or perhaps anti-sacred, text in many of his stories. The *Necronomicon* is but one instance of how an iconic book functions (see Chapter 4). Books that aren't the Bible can inform us how sacred Scripture is understood in a culture that is biblically illiterate but open to magical books, especially in films reluctant to use the Good Book.

A classic, non-horror example is the *Book of Armaments* from *Monty Python and the Holy Grail*. While not the Bible, the way that the *Book of Armaments* is handled (protected by a priest, processed out with incense and chanting, and read solemnly in public) invokes the image of the Bible in the viewer's mind. It's not the Bible, but it is. That's what we're talking about as the reluctant star.

We'll meet a variety of such variations as Anti-Bibles, false Bibles, and even implied Bibles. It's safe to say that the Good Book occurs in widely divergent iconic roles. As a *Ding* the Bible is an effective, magical book of salvation. Salvation may be understood in many different ways, but at a minimum there's some element of deliverance involved. We'll see examples where the fallback *Ding* image just doesn't work. We'll encounter actual Anti-Bibles—the effective, magical book that leads to the opposite of salvation.

So if the Bible's reluctant, why put it in the same room with horror if it doesn't want to play? It's like forcing a scared child into a room where he can plainly see a spider. "Why do it?" Sergeant Howie asks the girl who's tied a beetle to a nail in Rowan's empty desk. There's a catharsis here. The Bible and horror have more in common than anyone might suspect. Horror, like that beetle with that nail, gets closer and closer to the Good Book as it goes along. Until they meet.

When Horror Met Scripture

Lots of horror movies don't have the Bible in them. Most, in fact, don't. Too much shouldn't be read into this. Not all stories have room for the Bible.

Every once in a while, however, the bug meets that nail. The juxtaposition of the Good Book and horror may strike you as a little odd. Uncanny, even. Horror and Christianity are often cast as natural enemies. If you google the terms "horror," "movie," and "Bible" together, the top results address whether it's okay for Christians to watch horror or not. Kids like to watch monster movies. Fat kids, skinny kids, kids raised in conservative Christian homes. Many of the last category are forbidden to do so.

Evangelical Christian culture prefers well-lit rooms and wholesome themes. Horror suggests monsters, demons, and the Devil. Dusk and approaching nighttime. Listening to the wrong kind of music, like that of Alice Cooper, might open you to the demonic. Or horrors such as cross-dressing. Even Barnabas Collins in Tim Burton's *Dark Shadows* was confused by a male Alice. Such dark themes don't fit in a well-ordered world. Evangelicals are the ultimate champions of the Good Book. The bizarre and grotesque, however, are more troubling to adults than to children. Alice Cooper even featured on an episode of the *Muppet Show*. And, lo and behold, he turned out to be a conservative Christian himself.

Religious sensibilities can be found all over the place. In Alice Cooper's music. On television. In all kinds of movies. Horror included. Horror especially.

Enter the Bible. The Bible is so well known as a *Ding an sich* (an "iconic book") that it may be slipped into horror films without anyone batting (or poking out) an eye. So how does the Good Book play with bad movies, once that beetle's string runs out?

Like a movie star, Scripture appears in many different roles. We'll see that the Bible is a book tinged with magic, but not always so. It's a book of immense power, and yet it often can't save people. The Bible is a reminder, a hollow book, and a weapon. These are all valid views of Holy Writ. They're the views we'll see on the horror screen.

In the late-night screening that follows there will be some necessary overlap of biblical functions. Appropriate to horror, the categories morph into one another. Monsters, after all, tend to be unholy mixes. It's to be expected that different films will have somewhat different expectations of Holy Writ. It's a buyer's market when it comes to interpretation. Simply put, since the Bible's an iconic book that means the fact that it *is* the Bible takes precedence over what the Bible actually says. "The Bible" becomes an icon, an image that conveys a message. *Ding!*

There are several ways that the Bible shows up in cinema: it's shown visually; it's read; it's quoted from. It's thematic. Entire stories may be based on it. These usages can be quite distinct or they can blend together. In some instances the Bible appears in films for "verisimilitude"—the Bible makes a movie seem more real. We'll see that a time or two. More often, however, we'll see that it's unusual for the Bible to be treated neutrally in horror. Scripture may be a "visual metaphor." The Good Book suggests—or even stands in for—God from time to time. The Bible and horror play uneasily together. Let's briefly consider the three ways the Bible might show up and then we'll go to the movies.

First, the Good Book may be shown visually. A character pulls out a Bible and you know something serious is going down. The ultimate confrontation of good and evil. Without opening the book, and without reading a word, the Bible possesses a kind of magical power. One thing we'll see repeatedly is that the Bible functions as a magic book in the American imagination. Often in horror, this is done without even having to read it. Most of the movies here will have a visual Bible, but not all.

The second way Scripture appears—the vocal way—is with a character reading or quoting from Holy Writ. The Bible may or may not be shown. This function of the Good Book here is often magical too, but the more general word is "performative." (Apologies for the shop talk, but this one's kind of necessary for this commentary.) "Performative" means that the Bible has an effect on its movie world. Sometimes there's an effective use of the Bible as an unopened book, but to get the force flowing reading aloud serves especially well. Think of it like Harry Potter casting a spell. Just saying it makes it happen. That's performative. Hearing the Bible read tends to function like this.

The third way, thematic use of the Bible, is necessarily more tenuous to identify. Did the director or writer intend for a resurrection scene (itself almost a sacred commandment for horror) to be biblical? Many Christian analysts of movies look for biblical themes. This book only addresses them when they encompass an entire horror movie. The Bible has had a tremendous influence on American cinema. Thematic uses may or may not show the Bible but the entire premise of the story may be based on a concept that derives from Scripture. Among examples explored here are *The Seventh Sign* and *The Reaping*.

The observations made in this book need not have been intended by the writers and directors to be true. An idea doesn't have to be intentional for viewers to see it. In other words, those who create entertainment may not be trying to make statements about the Bible but if they use the Good Book at all they are making a statement, intentional or not. Iconic books are like that. They're never neutral.

Entire movies can also be based directly on the Bible, of course, with biblical characters in biblical times. These are "Bible movies" (think *Noah*, or *Exodus: Gods and Kings*). They aren't discussed here. Mel Gibson's *The Passion of the Christ* might be classified as horror for all its violence and blood. It's also a Bible movie so it's best to leave it to the many books already devoted to those. We will, however, look at secular movies that take their hook from the Bible. These aren't simply retelling biblical stories, or "Bible movies." Films where the Devil is the monster, or the Antichrist arises, for instance, fall into this category. Possession movies as well.

This book looks at what happens when horror and the Bible come together. The beetle meets the nail. Some of the films are religious in theme (*Stigmata, The Omen, The Reaping, The Exorcist*, for example) and others aren't. This study considers how they use the Bible. Or a stand-in for it. The Bible, it should be remembered, has some pretty scary stories of its own. It can be its own brand of holy horror.

It's time to be afraid. Very afraid. You've done your homework—you've viewed the commentary—now let's go to the movies together.

1

Popcorn

"And I gave my heart to know wisdom, and to know madness and folly: I perceived that this also is vexation of spirit. For in much wisdom is much grief: and he that increaseth knowledge increaseth sorrow. For God shall bring every work and every secret thing into judgment, whether it be good or whether it be evil." Standing on the ice, Captain Robert Walton reads from Ecclesiastes while Frankenstein's monster stands weeping in the Arctic snow. A bier with the dead scientist awaits the final torch. The ice suddenly breaks up, throwing men into the freezing water. The creature, having had enough of humans, grabs the torch and immolates himself along with his creator and his ill-fated journal.

*   *   *

This scene from *Mary Shelley's Frankenstein* is but one example of how the Bible slips, almost unnoticed, into horror. Think about movie popcorn. What comes to mind? The irresistible scent? The crunching of multiple kernels? The buttery goodness? The price? Popcorn isn't the movie, but it prepares our senses for the experience. We see and hear the film, but we touch, taste, and smell the popcorn. Popcorn's not uniform. Some pieces have more butter than others. Some may be burnt. There may be unpopped kernels. It's the experience of this mixing that makes popcorn what it is. This chapter's like that.

The Bible shows up surprisingly frequently in horror cinema. There are both large-scale uses of the Bible on the silver scream and movies where the Bible plays a small but crucial role. This chapter begins with the latter as a bucket of popcorn, a figurative sampling of the Good Book. We'll look at movies where the Bible is largely—almost completely—in the background. These films show just how little it takes to insinuate Scripture into horror. We start, innocently enough, with *Psycho*. Horror analysts frequently designate *Psycho* as the first stab at modern horror. The Bible appears in it, very briefly. Here's a case, however, where a remake brings Holy Writ a bit more into focus.

Psycho was the American reawakening of horror after the troubled slumber of the 1950s when the genre was largely represented by Hammer Studios productions from England. No Hammer movies are directly addressed here since primarily American reactions to the Bible are being explored. One of the exceptions to this "America first" approach, however, is addressed here for a specific reason: *The Wicker Man*.

The Wicker Man is useful for comparison with *Psycho* because of its remake. It's one of only two British horror films included in this book. The original uses the Bible for the exact same function that Alfred Hitchcock did. Horror handled the Good Book gently at the beginning, as we'll see. As with *Psycho*, the remake of *The Wicker Man*—which requires some commitment to watch—also changes the way Scripture is presented.

In many ways it could be argued that Stephen King invented the horror novel that begs for movie adaptation. Please don't take that statement literally. For the purposes of this book, King's name will be sufficient to bring a movie into consideration. King, as his readers know, brings religion into his stories with some regularity. *Pet Sematary* has the Bible appear visually only very briefly, but its implications loom large over the entire plot. Thematically it's quite significant.

Not all pieces of popcorn have the same amount of butter. Although often classified as a thriller, *Memento* has a brief but important shot or two of the Bible. Taken in a handful with the other pieces, you'll hardly notice. *Van Helsing* also has one brief, significant showing of the Good Book, so it's also included with the popcorn. There are many ways the point of this particular scene could have been made, but the Bible was chosen amid the monsters. It adds a little salt to the bucket.

Pirates of the Caribbean is an on-going collection of films based on a Disney theme park ride. The only sequels discussed in this book are in this franchise. Horror fans may dispute the use of a family-friendly, mainstream adventure series in a treatment such as this. It might break the mood! Sprinkling them among the popcorn emphasizes that not all pieces are the same size. Remember, some pieces may even be burnt. We eat them anyway, after paying that much. The *Pirate* films themselves may not be horror, but they do have monsters. And even Adam Rockoff states in his popular treatment of horror films that a Disney movie (*The Watcher in the Woods*) is the one that scares him the most.

Popcorn isn't the point of the movie, of course. It can still enhance the experience. These movies show how, in very small amounts, the Bible flavors horror. Let's start snacking.

Psycho (1960, 1998)

How can a book about horror films not have at least a passing mention of Alfred Hitchcock's groundbreaking 1960 contribution, *Psycho*? Often considered the beginning of modern horror, it makes sense to begin here, although the Bible is nearly buried in the movie. The remake notices this, demonstrating how remakes shift perceptions of the Good Book.

The hippie heart of the 1960s was still in the future when *Psycho* was released. Up until then horror movies had featured creatures we all knew weren't real. Who actually believed in Godzilla? Norman Bates (Anthony Perkins), however, was as authentic as any person we might know. Horror had moved in next door.

Although the public expressed shock at such a movie from Hitchcock, *Psycho* redefined American cinematic horror overnight. Suddenly the genre was resurrected after a decade of dabbling with science fiction and cowering under the dominance of Hammer Studios. Hitchcock was a trusted suspense and noir director. His previous thrillers hadn't prepared viewers for anything as graphic or disturbing as this. The studios smelled blood in the water.

The 1950s, however, weren't exactly a time of freewheeling use of the Bible for non-religious purposes. The Good Book was serious business. The word of God was not mocked. This was so much the case that it's easy to overlook the very brief scene with the Bible in *Psycho*. You have to look for it. Sam Loomis (John Gavin; "Loomis" will dedicate his surname to *Halloween*'s detective/psychologist and establishes a pedigree stretching far into horror's future) and Lila Crane (presumably no relation to Ichabod; played by Vera Miles) have visited Sheriff Chambers (John McIntire) about their missing girlfriend/sister, Marion (Janet Leigh). The reports from Detective Arbogast (Martin Balsam) have mysteriously stopped after he learned that Marion spent a night at Bates Motel. The Sheriff suspects that someone has run off with the money, but murder? Hardly likely in Fairvale. This is, after all, the 1950s. After waking the Sheriff in the middle of the night, the couple meets him outside Fairvale Church on Sunday morning. They talk as the faithful stream out of worship, greeting the minister. One man walks by with a Bible clearly tucked under his arm. That's it.

What does this scene tell us about the Bible? Hitchcock never allowed extraneous images in his films. It was all about *mise-en-scène*. What appears is what he wanted there. The use of the Bible in horror films prior to this is rare. So was a flushing toilet. The industry watchdogs had little tolerance for anything seemingly un–American. With godless communists everywhere, the Bible was a sure pledge of allegiance. It couldn't be anything but respectable.

This is perhaps an instance of verisimilitude, which is to say, the Bible is used as a touch of realism. Respectability. Utterly conventional. This will change radically over the coming decades. The Bible stands here as a marking point. There is a subtle subversive element, however.

Bible-reading Americans like Sheriff Chambers really have no idea what's going on. The sinful Sam—shown in the opening scene making love to a woman who's not his wife—and the pushy Lila have already deduced something's wrong. Chambers supposes Norman Bates to be normal, if a bit of a hermit. The death of Bates' mother and her lover on the same day was simply a murder-suicide. Case closed. But the truth perverts all these assumptions. Norman is, well, a psycho. Button-down, Bible-reading America is wrong. Worldly people will lead to the arrest.

It must've felt like tempting fate to follow up Hitchcock's classic with a remake, which Gus Van Sant did in 1998. Reviews indicated that the new film was a slavish, shot-by-shot reproduction of the original, mostly. What could be different? The Bible.

Like the original, the 1998 *Psycho* understates religion, but it's clearly there. Interestingly, not in Norman Bates (Vince Vaughn). Bates is played pretty much as Anthony Perkins played him. The difference is in Sam Loomis (Viggo Mortensen), the lover of Marion Crane (Anne Heche) and investigation partner of her sister Lila (Julianne Moore). In the opening shot in a tawdry hotel, Sam is shown wearing only a cross on a chain around his neck. The banter between Marion and Sam is similar to the original and no mention is made of the obvious religious symbol worn by a naked man.

After Marion checks into the Bates Motel, however, and seeks to hide the stolen money, she pulls open the nightstand drawer to reveal a Gideon Bible. There's no Bible visible in the Hitchcock original of this scene. Gideons have been placing Bibles in hotel and motel rooms since 1908. Where the original left the Bible out (as we'll see several times in films with cinematic remakes) the new version has added it in. Marion, of course, doesn't survive the night.

When we see Sam in his apartment behind the hardware store in the remake, religious imagery is obvious. A heavy crucifix hangs on the wall, as well as a picture of the Last Supper. A Bible doesn't appear, but we get the sense that Sam is honest. Or at least religious. When Sam and Lila visit Sheriff Chambers (Philip Baker Hall), a last supper image also hangs on his wall. Notably, however, the church scene—the only one in which the Bible shows up in Hitchcock's original—isn't included in the slavish, shot-by-shot remake. Sam and Lila head out to Bates Motel after their late-night call on the Sheriff. On their drive we see Sam has a cross hanging from his rear-view mirror.

At Bates Motel, as Sam and Lila are searching cabin 1, Sam pulls open the nightstand drawer. He pauses, pulls out the Gideon Bible and gives it a significant pat before setting it reverently on the stand. That's the last we see of it. The Bible imagery in this horror movie is spare (remember popcorn) but different from the original. Sam is also presented as a somewhat opportunistic lover. He kisses Lila in his shop—on the cheek, but rather forward for a woman he's just met and whose sister he's been sleeping with. At the motel, he and Lila pose as a married couple. The suggestion is there that he'll take Lila if Marion is gone. And he's the one who finds and appreciates the Bible.

Lest you think all of this is too subtle, consider that either version of *Psycho* would easily stand without the Bible at all. It's there nevertheless. *Psycho* is a good test case for how a remake tends to differ in its use of Bible imagery. Some such differences will boldly stand out below.

Before we go there, however, consider the Gideon Bible. Ostensibly placed in hotel and motel rooms to make Scripture available to those "in need," it has become a big screen fixture. Motel rooms have always been known as venues of potential illicit sex. The Bible reminds the would-be sinner to, in the words of ET, "be good." A flushing toilet was challenging in 1960 cinema. A Bible in a drawer suggests something by its absence. In remaking *Psycho*, the updating of the Good Book says something just by being pulled from a drawer. The same subtly reappears in our next handful of popcorn.

The Wicker Man (1973)

Robin Hardy's *The Wicker Man*, although it initially suffered from serious distribution problems, has become among the most respected of British horror films. Both following on from and departing from the horror established by the famous Hammer enterprise, *The Wicker Man* stunned critics by its depth, intelligence, and social commentary. In the tradition of many classics, the film came close to being lost to posterity, but it has survived in a cut that is now more or less the canonical version.

There are three reasons to include *The Wicker Man* in this bucket (apart from the simple presence of the Bible): one, it shows how the Bible continued into the 1970s as a symbol of respectability. Two, the remake leaves the Good Book out completely. And lastly, this minimal use of Holy Writ compares instructively with *Psycho*, the feature we've just watched. Surprisingly enough, also like *Psycho*, *The Wicker Man* is naturalistic—the supernatural is absent in a way many horror movies would find restrictive.

Like *Children of the Corn*, to be discussed in the next chapter, *The Wicker Man* is premised on a religion that takes itself very seriously—perhaps too seriously—and which is based on agricultural concerns of the locals. Police Sergeant Neil Howie (Edward Woodward) undertakes an investigation of a missing child in the remote Scottish Outer Hebrides, on Summerisle. A devout Christian (presumably Anglican), Sergeant Howie quickly becomes disgusted by the lewd paganism he discovers as the denizens of Summerisle prepare to celebrate May Day. Highly sexualized and based on worship of the old gods, this religion offends the officer to the point of rudeness and disrespect toward the locals.

Deceived from the start, Sergeant Howie has been set up to be sacrificed in a wicker man, a giant wickerwork statue to be burned to propitiate Celtic pagan deities. Along the way, in an effort to confirm his status as a virgin, Willow MacGreagor (Britt Ekland), the daughter of the island innkeeper, dances naked in her room next door, inviting him to come on over. Although sorely tempted, Sergeant Howie feverishly imagines, in intercut scenes, his time in church, trying hard to maintain his continence. The flashback sequence shows him, significantly, reading the New Testament lesson during mass. Not simply any Bible portion, the passage he reads is about the institution of the Eucharist. The comparison of being consumed, as Howie literally will be in the belly of the wicker man, is surely intentional. Although Scripture here is intended to be salvific, it's foiled by the pagan religion of Summerisle. Keep a lookout for this horror standard—the Bible is intended to save, but fails to do so. We'll see this screened time and time again. As with Hitchcock's use of the Good Book, the Bible signals respectability here.

Scripture appears in two vocal instances in *Wicker Man* as well. One is performative (it has an effect), the other is incidental. The incidental scene goes back to when Howie is still trying to solve the riddle of the missing girl, Rowan Morrison (Geraldine Cowper). Growing more and more upset by the heathen practices of the locals—including naming children after trees— Howie demands the local death register from the librarian (Ingrid Pitt). Skimming the list, he notes that the previous generation included the names Benjamin and Rachel, "Names from the Bible," he muses, gazing into the middle distance. "Yes," the librarian counters, "they *were* old." Once again a Bible intended to save has lost its power—it's an outdated book.

The effective quotation of the Bible comes in the disturbing death scene where Howie is inside the wicker man with the flames climbing up around him. He begins to sing out, "The Lord is my shepherd," a hymn based on Psalm 23. Here the Bible is again intended to be salvific, but is subverted by the heathens of Summerisle. The intention of the Bible is clearly to provide salvation, but the magic just isn't there. Howie dies as a pagan sacrifice with the words of the Bible on his lips. The expectation of salvation is present, but in *The Wicker Man* it fails to come. Indeed, there is no Bible shown on the island.

Cultural sensitivities, although flaunted a bit by the very premise of the movie, would likely not permit a deeper engagement with the Bible this early in the 1970s. As the decade progressed, and chiefly across the Atlantic, the Bible boldly entered cinema as a potential source of evil. This salvific expectation always remains, but Scripture—perceived as a magical book—may have been starting to lose its power. This will become thematic in a number of movies based on Stephen King novels in particular.

Curiosity compels the viewer to wonder what the 2006 *Wicker Man* remake by Neil LaBute will do with this upright character. Over three decades have elapsed. Will we see more Bible or less? Remakes often contain important differences regarding presentation of the Bible. This isn't the place to critique the movie—others have done a fine job of that—but it is significant that the Bible does not occur in it at all.

As we'll see in *Carrie*, *The Fog*, and *The Blob* below, it isn't at all unusual for a remake to add the Bible to new scenes or to the plot as a whole in horror films. This may be done for a variety of reasons that fit under the general rubric of the Good Book being scary. The treatment goes the other way in *The Wicker Man*. The Hardy version has a pious, Bible-reading man as the eventual victim. The LaBute version has a profane police officer (Edward Malus, played by Nicholas Cage)—who curses, beats women, and is never shown with a Bible—entrapped by a female cult in Puget Sound. The only snatch of an iconic book we see is an old tome called *Rituals of the Ancients* in Dr. T.H. Moss's office. Even this isn't leather-bound and doesn't appear to be anything more than part of the trap set to catch Malus. In that sense it's an effective text, but the rites it prescribes aren't factual. They describe how a girl is to be sacrificed while it is in reality a grown man who must fill that role. If the movie were sophisticated enough this could be considered deceptive scripture (see Chapter 5).

Ironically, this is an instance where a British film contains the Bible and an American one doesn't. We shouldn't make too much of this, but American viewers can handle the Good Book with their terror. In fact, it often enhances the experience. It was one mistake, among many, to leave it out here. But moving on to redder pastures…

A traditional source of horror movies has been the film based on a novel. Indeed, the earliest films generally classified as "horror" (*Dracula*, and *Frankenstein*, both 1931) were based on the novels sharing their titles. Perhaps the most recognized contemporary name when it comes to horror fiction is Stephen King. Four of the movies based on his works are treated in this book. The first of these films, *Pet Sematary*, has only a very brief (kernel of popcorn) use of the Bible. It does, however, show how universes built on a biblical theme can fill the bucket.

Pet Sematary (1989)

Pet Sematary (based on the Stephen King novel of the same title), directed by Mary Lambert, revolves around the inherently terrifying religious concept of resurrection. Since the screenplay was written by King himself the movie follows the book fairly closely. The Bible acts both visually and thematically in this particular film, although its visual appearance is quite brief. *Pet Sematary* also introduces King as an author who inherently belongs in a book about horror (even when his stories may be classified as something else).

The visual Bible in *Pet Sematary* is iconic, but very brief. Thematically it's omnipresent. The story revolves around the Creed family. The name already suggests religious issues, as a "creed" is a formal statement of belief. Selecting a new home along a dangerous road in Maine, the family's set up for disaster. Trucks barrel along here far too fast. Louis Creed (Dale Midkiff), the father of the small family, learns of a mysterious pet cemetery (deliberately misspelled as "sematary") where local people have been burying their animals for decades. There's also a graveyard further along the path that allows for resurrection of the dead, as he later learns. When the Creed family cat, Church, is killed on the road, Louis decides to test the resurrecting power of the site and brings him back to life. Something's wrong with Church, however. The choice of the name, like that of Creed, contains a conscious critique of the easy acceptance of life after death as a consummate good. (The film makes clear that the name's short for Winston Churchill, but what the viewer hears is "Church.") A resurrected Church is bad enough, but when the only son Gage (Miko Hughes) is also killed along the highway the desire to bring him back overpowers his father.

From the beginning of the movie the theme of death and its inevitability haunts Gage's sister Ellie (Blaze Berdahl). It also haunts the mother of both children, Rachel (Denise Crosby). Louis, a doctor, believes life should be pro-longed at any cost.

It's during a traditional burial scene that the Bible visually appears. In a cameo as the minister at the graveside, Stephen King stands with a Bible open in his hand. This is for the burial of Missy Dandridge (Susan Blommaert) the woman who did the Creeds' washing. Having experienced chronic pain, she hanged herself, leading the minister to offer spare words of comfort. Indeed, as he enters the scene he's just closing a small, powerless Bible. The only place for Scripture is among the dead.

The comfort of the iconic book nevertheless rings hollow with the tragic loss of a child. Gage inevitably gets run down by a speeding truck. During his funeral, where a Bible might be expected—indeed demanded—none appears. The funeral's clearly in a Christian church, but not even a pew Bible pops up. Instead a fistfight breaks out.

The visual Bible in this movie is an impotent iconic book. It lacks any salvific power or magic. In fact, *Pet Sematary* is in many ways a critique of traditional religious views. In the introduction to the 2001 novel printing, King notes that the story was so bleak even to him that he put it in a drawer for quite some time before sending it to his publisher. Resurrection is a frightening thing, and the Bible—whence the idea originates—is virtually invisible. An iconic Bible speaks by its absence where it would be expected, as well as by its presence.

Stephen King novels gained credibility as horror movie fare since the release of *Carrie* (1976) in cinematic format. Boosted to stratospheric stature with the release of Stanley Kubrick's *The Shining* (1980) an adaptation that King famously dislikes, his novels have nevertheless became the emperors of on-screen horror. Exceptional production values and trademark Kubrick touches ensured that *The Shining* would remain near the top of horror film rankings for many years. (A Rotten Tomatoes list of the top 50 horror movies, posted October 28, 2010, but now no longer available, was soundly castigated in the comments for not including *The Shining*.) When a Stephen King film like *Pet Sematary* challenges biblical convention, it speaks for horror. Among other things, this indicates that convention is fairly firmly established. Otherwise, why challenge it?

This is illustrated in the thematic use of the Bible in the movie. Resurrection is a religious concept long predating Christianity. In American popular thought, however, the dying and rising god is Jesus Christ. (Bill Maher goes a bit overboard with his list of other dying and rising gods in *Religulous*, but his point is taken. Probably the most directly related "dying and rising" god is Baal, and we'll have occasion to meet him a couple of places further on.) Resurrection is considered an essentially Christian, and therefore biblical, idea. It appears frequently in horror, for example, in *Re-animator* and *The Lazarus Effect*, among other films, but the Bible is missing from these two examples beyond the title of the latter.

As with the concept of prophecy predicting the future, experts would disagree with popular assumptions of life after death. Since biblical scholars no longer hold (if they ever held) public sway when it comes to interpreting the Bible, acceptance of resurrection as biblical truth is highlighted in a movie like this. *Pet Sematary* complicates this positive aspect of eternal life. Coming back from the dead changes a person, distorts their souls. (This will also be seen in *The Evil Dead*, addressed below in Chapter 4.)

The Bible offers no comfort. Indeed, its expectations create the very horror that drives this movie. A film like *Pet Sematary* blends a visual use of Scripture with a thematic one. We'll see this several times again in the coming chapters.

It might be best to write that down.

Memento (2000)

Christopher Nolan's *Memento* is more of a thriller than horror, but it does show a couple of murders and has some graphic imagery. To a significant number people, forgetting who they are is a source of horror. *Memento*'s use of the Bible, though, crunches enough like popcorn to consider it in this chapter.

Memento is a movie that's difficult to follow fully. The final scene—actually, the first scene of the story—introduces some aspects that seem to complicate the whole thing and since you never know who's telling the truth, it's a little difficult to say anything definitive. Nevertheless, the use of the Bible in the movie fits with what we've seen above.

Leonard Shelby (Guy Pearce), the protagonist, suffers from short-term memory loss. Unable to form new memories, he has to write everything down, or photograph it, to recall who he's seen or what's happened. Despite this deficiency he's seeking his wife's killer. The last thing he can remember is her murder, and the story unfolds from the end to the beginning, from Leonard shooting Teddy (Joe Pantoliano) to the events that led up to that point.

For much of the movie Leonard is staying in a hotel. Since he can't form new memories reading a book is somewhat superfluous. If you can't remember what you've just read a few pages ago, making any progress in a book is tenuous indeed. Nevertheless, as Leonard narrates in a voice-over, "There's nothing in the drawers. But you look anyway. Nothing except the Gideon Bible, which I, of course, read religiously." The scene shows him paging through a book that he can't remember reading. The Bible here is an utterly helpless book. Like Homer Simpson, Leonard's looking for answers, but this book doesn't have any. To remember things he gets (or gives himself, in a kind of horror lite) tattoos. None of Leonard's tattoos (like those of Max Cady that we'll see in *Cape Fear*) are biblical.

In a subsequent scene, Leonard pulls open the nightstand drawer again, but a handgun sits on top of the Bible. He can't remember how the gun got there, or even whose it might be. He slams the drawer shut on text and tool.

This scene, however brief, speaks to popular perceptions of the Bible, based on two contexts: its presence in a hotel room, and as a book that saves. Let's go back to the hotel room.

Memento isn't the only film to make use of hotels as repositories of Gideon Bibles (remember the remake of *Psycho*). The Gideons (official name Gideons International), as noted above, have been placing Bibles in hotel rooms for decades. The Gideon Bible's a fixture at mid-to-budget priced hotels. They're free to take although, based on experience, most seem to stay put. Viewed objectively, this is a strange practice. The Bible as a key to salvation generally requires a bit of interpretation. In other words, hotel rooms have the reputation as locations of what some consider immoral behavior. Placing a prophylactic Bible there makes some sense, however ineffective it might be in practice.

Americans expect to find a Bible in hotel rooms. That expectation is met in *Memento*. The climax of *The Seventh Sign* will depend upon it.

The second perception of the Bible, however, involves salvation. This naturally requires remembering what you read. The other book that features in *Memento* is a novel with the cover torn off. Leonard remembers his wife reading it, but he subsequently burns her, well, mementos. As he watches his wife rereading the book in his long-term memory he says, "I always thought the joy of reading a book is not knowing what happens next." The point of reading is remembering, and the point of reading the Bible is being saved from whatever threatens the reader.

Leonard's threatened by the loss of memory. He can't remember what he reads in the Bible and can't be saved. When he next opens the drawer, a lethal weapon rests atop the sacred text. Leonard, it becomes clear, is being used by others. He can't be reached by its promised salvation. The Bible here is ineffectual, if not deceptive. It offers something it can't, in his case, deliver.

Memento is a strange movie. Its use of the Good Book is also unusual. Since the Bible can't save, it's at least effective for manipulating someone who can't remember what he reads. And reading Scripture might just make a monster a man, at least according to our next film.

Van Helsing (2004)

At first glance, this is an unusual celluloid chimera to call horror. Stephen Sommer's *Van Helsing* is an action-adventure film with a horror theme rather than straightforward genre horror. Re-envisioned from Bram Stoker's *Dracula*, the movie casts Van Helsing (Hugh Jackman) as a swashbuckling monster hunter. Mr. Hyde, Frankenstein's monster, werewolves, and vampires populate this blockbuster, but the atmosphere doesn't feel like horror. Yes, a vampire being killed by a werewolf should count, but the concerns of being a big movie take precedence over the mood that dominated the Universal monsters to which the film pays homage. There are few startles, for example, and the camera is objective giving distance from the violence. Several characters act as comic foils. Nevertheless, since it's a "monster movie" it can be found here in our bucket of popcorn.

Although the Bible occurs in only a single, brief scene in this film, its function there is highly unusual in horror cinema. The Bible's entirely good and actually humanizes a monster. That in itself is worthy of chewing over.

In this universe Van Helsing is a mercenary monster hunter who can't remember his past. It turns out that he's himself somewhat supernatural, having been at the battle of Masada (in the first century of the Common Era) and still alive nearly two millennia later. He's made aware of the plight of the Valerious family that's being picked off by Dracula (Richard Roxburgh). This family's in danger of being locked out of Heaven unless Van Helsing intervenes by destroying the vampire. In his quest he's attended by Carl (David Wenham), a friar with an ancient order of monster-fighting monks. Carl serves as comic relief, but he solves the puzzle of how to kill a vampire.

Dracula has been busy mating with his three wives for centuries, but their spawn can't be hatched without the life-force of a man artificially animated—thus Frankenstein's monster (Shuler Hensley) is necessary to complete his scheme. Van Helsing rescues Anna (Kate Beckinsale), the scion of the Valerious family, from a vampire attack. The couple teams up to try to save her werewolf brother. As they search for a means of destroying Dracula, they fall into the basement of the windmill destroyed in the film's opening sequence of the mob violence against Frankenstein's monster. The villagers burned the windmill, and, presumably, destroyed the monster. When Van Helsing and Anna land in an underground lair they discover something has been living there, as a massive pile of bones demonstrates. Exploring the dark grotto, Van Helsing finds a Bible. Holding it up he declares that, whatever's living there, it's apparently human. Of course, the monster immediately shows up.

The iconic Bible is used in this one brief instance of an over-full movie, to be the monster's hope of salvation. Indeed, Frankenstein's monster is presented as the most moral and thoughtful of the film's characters. Dracula's vampire children can only be vitalized (saved) by a Bible-reading monster. Nobody questions the Good Book's efficacy. Indeed, the order behind Van

Helsing's mission is a Christian one. The Bible's carefully laid back down in its place before Van Helsing is thrown into a pool of fetid water.

Gabriel Van Helsing is "the left hand of God." His remit is to kill evil monsters, not all monsters. The Bible proves Frankenstein's creation isn't evil. The Bible, in other words, saves this monster from his slayer. More than that, it makes a monster a human.

One element is obviously missing here, and ironically so in a movie universe (or "diegesis") crammed with mythical monsters. There's no magic associated with the Bible. *Van Helsing* is set in a world full of supernatural creatures. The namesake protagonist fights them with scientific discoveries made in a religious laboratory. The Bible, however, is an entirely naturalistic element. It's a *Ding*. It simply is. Its iconic status is unquestioned, and it functions effectively in one brief scene. No other book is so powerful yet so easily left behind.

Pirates of the Caribbean (2003–2011)

Before finishing out this bucket of popcorn, let's chew a handful of horror-tinged fun—the kettle corn of scary movies. The *Pirates of the Caribbean* franchise can't really be considered horror, but it does have monsters in every installment. Consider the plot in very broad strokes....

Captain Jack Sparrow saves Elizabeth Swann from a literal shipload of living dead pirates. These undead pirates fire cannons upon a human city, pillage, plunder, and randomly murder the citizens. They can't be killed. The curse of a bloodthirsty pagan god is eventually lifted and they become mortal again. Sparrow, however, had made a deal with Davy Jones, a submarine monster responsible for ferrying the dead to the other world. The deal was that for a specified period Sparrow would be captain of his own ship. His time is up and he's devoured by the kraken. The once again undead Captain Barbossa sails a shipload of pirates into the realm of the dead—a kind of Purgatory—to bring back the now dead Sparrow. An epic battle takes place between mortals and bouillabaissed monsters that ends in the disembodied, still-beating heart of Davy Jones being stabbed to death. Will Turner has his chest cut open and his still beating heart placed in a box. Elements of Poe and Lovecraft abound.

Viewed from this angle, several standard horror elements are clear. Living dead? Check. Violence? Check. Dead who don't know they're dead? Check. Deal with the Devil? Check. Monsters? Check. You get the picture. Besides, the Good Book's here too. The franchise also contains a few instances where the iconic Bible builds on the themes we'll see repeatedly below. For those who like to hang out to see what comes after the credits, here's a brief glimpse of pirates and their sacred books.

Curse of the Black Pearl—the first film—opens with talk of murder and an ominous ship ablaze. As subsequent scenes make clear, about half of the characters are the living dead. "You best start believing in ghost stories, Miss Turner"—Captain Barbossa (Geoffrey Rush) bellows at Elizabeth Swann (Keira Knightley)—"you're in one!" Startle moments and walking skeletons climbing aboard ship and killing everyone would've been considered horror fare not too many years ago.

In the second and third installments (*Dead Man's Chest* and *At World's End*), the makeup of Davy Jones (Bill Nighy), captain of the *Flying Dutchman*, is based on Cthulhu, the monster invented by horror writer H.P. Lovecraft. His face is an octopus with far too many tentacles, suggesting the scene in *Alien* where the title monster wraps itself around Kane's face. Davy Jones' crew consists of man-sea creature hybrids—monsters in anyone's book. They're vicious and merciless. Their job, as revealed in the third film, is to ferry the dead to the land beyond. Ghosts are seen swimming under water and floating on jolly boats in what is a very creepy movie scene in its own right. The kraken appears as a sea monster in these two movies. It destroys ships and eats people. Even the outlier episode four, *On Stranger Tides*, has man-eating mermaids with shark teeth. These supernatural creatures are the denizens of the horror realm, here presented in a fantasy-adventure film series with scary elements, not unlike *Van Helsing*. The monsters are thematic to the series and the story would be impossible without them.

The initial movie, *Curse of the Black Pearl*, contains no obvious iconic Bible moments. It's the only movie in the original four that doesn't.

The second installment, *Dead Man's Chest*, features the Bible in a scene reintroducing the comic relief pair Pintel (Lee Arenberg) and Ragetti (Mackenzie Crook). The two abandoned, now mortal, pirates are shown rowing toward an island where the beached *Black Pearl* stands. Ragetti is leafing through a Bible, prompting Pintel to ask him why. Regatti replies that since they are no longer immortal, they have to be concerned for their souls. Pintel reminds Regatti that he can't read. Ragetti, in his defense, exclaims, "It's the Bible. You get credit for trying."

In this scene, the Bible, at first glance, functions much as it does in American society—an insurance policy against eternal damnation. As in school, credit's available for effort. It's also clearly an iconic book. Regatti can't read. A book that can't be read might be thought to have no function, but clearly here the Bible's used as many Americans commonly understand it. It's a book that magically brings salvation. Compared with *Memento*, the expectation's very much the opposite.

Upon closer inspection, however, there's a further element of magic in it as well. The *Pirates of the Caribbean* films all feature supernatural elements, but this scene is naturalistic. For scoundrels who've lived their lives in sin, counting on the Bible for safeguarding souls functions very much like a magic book. Especially if the reader is illiterate. The knowledge contained in the Bible doesn't save, but the act of trying to read it does. "Pretending to read the Bible," Pintel insists, "is a lie. It's a mark against..." (pointing emphatically to the sky). Immediately after this exchange a large wave capsizes the boat, sending the two pirates into the sea. A healthy dose of magic attends the outlook of both pirates regarding the Bible and it's played out in nature.

The third feature, *At World's End*, brings Captain Jack Sparrow (Johnny Depp) back to life after being eaten like popcorn by the kraken. The crew of the *Flying Dutchman* reappears in all their scaly gruesomeness. Throughout the series reference has been made to the Code of the Pirate Brethren, written by actual pirate Henry Morgan and an unidentified Bartholomew (possibly Bartholomew Roberts?). This code has the force of law not unlike the Bible. In actual history, ship's crews who turned pirate sometimes had to sign a code of conduct and swear on an actual Bible to keep it. This particular film in the series takes many aspects to outlandish extremes, as in the scene of the fortress of Shipwreck Cove where this "Bible" is kept. The canonical text, the Pirate Codex, is no exception.

Among the meeting of the nine pirate lords, dispute breaks out concerning procedure. This is to be resolved by reading the code. A massive book (so large that it takes two men to carry it), bound in leather and with a gold-stamped title is brought to the table to be consulted. The blackletter script of the huge tome is clearly reminiscent of Scripture. This iconic law book serves as a stand-in for the Bible. Like Holy Writ among pirates, its authority is undisputed. (A brief diversion on this point: the decidedly non-horror *Muppet Treasure Island* features a scene where Long John Silver [Tim Curry] is sentenced to death by his fellow pirates. They hand him the black spot. Silver, sensing his opportunity, rails at them in a faux sermon about tearing a page from the Bible to give him his death sentence. The pirates, superstitious by the standards of the *Hispaniola* crew, quickly bow to the authority of Holy Writ.) Once again an iconic book appears, offering salvation. There's no magic in this instance, but the book saves the pirate court from devolving into a complete melee where they would easily become the victims of the awaiting British fleet.

On Stranger Tides, unlike the three previous films, is based on a novel. It has a more literate feel to it. New characters are brought into Captain Jack Sparrow's orbit, including a young missionary, Philip (Sam Claflin). In this installment Blackbeard (Ian McShane), Barbossa and Sparrow are locked in a race to find the fountain of youth. In order to access the mythical font they require a mermaid tear. Mermaids, however, are man-eating monsters that devour any human caught in their swarms. One has to be captured and made to cry.

A special glass coffin is brought along for the operation, and when filled with water it's the means of carrying a dangerous mermaid. Philip, ever sensitive, notices that the mermaid can't breathe when the coffin is sealed shut. In order to save her life, he slides open the lid and slips his Bible in as a spacer to allow her air. There could hardly be a more obvious salvific use of an iconic book. Without magic, the Bible saves the mermaid's life.

The final three *Pirates* tetralogy features employ the Bible in a salvific role as an iconic book. It also has magical expectations in its first appearance. Although this may appear as a scurvy digression, it anticipates much of what we'll observe in straightforward horror films.

Sweeping Up

Popcorn comes in many varieties. We've seen how horror, in bite-sized pieces, introduces the Bible, often iconically, into the story. These examples provide the background to the comparatively extensive usage of Scripture we'll see in the movies that follow. This precedent will also prepare us for further functions of the Bible in the movies that will appear in following chapters. We will come back to a bit of popcorn left in the bottom of the bucket at the very end just before the lights come up.

In the movies cited in this chapter we've seen the Bible as a sign of respectability and convention. Importantly, it's also become clear that horror remakes tend to treat Scripture differently than the original films. Changing social outlooks may account for this, but we saw an expanded use of the Bible in *Psycho* and a reduced appearance in *The Wicker Man*. Holy Writ marks a character as "a good guy." Neil Howie, Sam Loomis, and Leonard Shelby are after the same thing: justice. The Bible affirms that. The Good Book is also sometimes used thematically, as in *Pet Sematary*. Its trope of resurrection carries over into *Van Helsing* where it also amplifies the respectability of *Psycho* and *The Wicker Man*, making a monster into a human being. "It's not evil," Van Helsing explains of Frankenstein's monster.

Memento has a Gideon Bible that reflects the salvation of memory. There's a hint of abusive intent when a gun appears on top of it. Instead of saving, a gun kills. The situation, however, is one where the Bible can't save because reading can't take hold.

Pirates of the Caribbean continue the respectability theme. Reading the Bible is good. Obeying the Code is good. The Bible can save a life, literally. We'll see all of these thematic uses of the Bible throughout this book.

Now we turn to yet another movie featuring Johnny Depp in an early collaboration with director Tim Burton. From Captain Jack Sparrow to Detective Ichabod Crane, the move from undead pirates to undead Hessians seems a natural enough one. To find the headless horseman, however, we need to make a trip up the haunted Hudson Valley.

2

The Iconic Bible

Lord Crane, wearing full clerical garb, bursts into the room and throws a black Bible into the hearth ashes. He's furious enough to commit murder. Grabbing his young wife's hair, he violently forces her face down to read a passage, presumably one from the Old Testament prohibiting witchcraft. Mercilessly he drags his spouse through a spotless white chapel to his personal torture chamber beyond. There death by iron maiden greets her. Her bloody corpse falls out, eyes still open, onto her young son, Ichabod.

* * *

Horror-themed movies go back to the earliest days of film. One of Thomas Edison's first moving pictures was based on *Frankenstein*. Scary ideas translate well to celluloid. Flickering lights, darkened room, and strange images—a perfect witch's brew for fear. Consider F.W. Murnau's 1922 classic *Nosferatu: eine Symphonie des Grauens*. This silent—if copyright-infringing—adaptation of Bram Stoker's *Dracula* shows that as soon as filmmakers got behind cameras they started thinking of how to scare people. The category of "horror film" didn't formally exist then—most film critics give the earliest credit for that to *Dracula* (1931). Since then directors have been searching for new ways to frighten us. One way they do it is by throwing in the Bible.

Horror movies are made irrespective of the Bible, of course. There are hundreds, at least, in which the Bible plays no role at all. When the Bible shows up, however, it's as an iconic book. In this chapter we'll be considering the iconic Bible in horror.

Although movies of this genre aren't generally viewed for serious study of the Bible, they do nevertheless reveal popular outlooks on the Good Book. Here we'll pay attention to horror movies where, in a somewhat more expanded way than in those in Chapter 1, the Bible is shown functioning in the plot. Looking at these cases leads to some basic conclusions as to how Americans understand the Bible.

In some horror films the Bible has more of a thematic role than an explicit visual or vocal role, as noted above. This leads to different ways of interpreting the Bible. Movie makers don't create their films with Bible interpretation foremost in their minds; that's fairly certain. As a commodity, movies are made primarily to be sold to consumers. "Bible believers" aren't a strong horror film-consumer demographic. In fact, a debate continues to rage among evangelicals as to whether it's appropriate for "Christians" to watch such movies as these or not. The films are made without the attempt to win this type of viewer. Writers, directors, and producers generally have little to gain in being considered expert biblical interpreters. (In some cases, however, there may be an attempt to send an evangelical message. We'll explore this in the case of *The Omen* in Chapter 5.)

What makes the movies of this chapter so fascinating is their reflection of everyday perceptions of the Bible. In a country where university courses on the Bible are declining, and many people gather their information from popular media, movies such as *Noah* (2014) or *Exodus: Gods and Kings* (2015) may function as "scripture" for those who don't study the Bible formally. This chapter surveys four movies that use the Good Book iconically, and in the next chapter, five that "abuse" it. In this context "abuse" means that at least part of the plot involves a use of the Bible to oppress or subdue others. While some might argue that the Bible does this anyway, that's not the standard Christian (or Jewish) take on it at all. Whether used or abused an iconic book remains iconic.

The films covered in this chapter, indeed, for the rest of the book, with one exception, are American products. That stands to reason as the Bible is an icon closely associated with American outlooks on life. Most of the films discussed here date from the 1970s and later. The original *Blob* comes a bit earlier, but the remake, which falls in the '80s, will be the focus for its discussion.

Since the last chapter ended with Johnny Depp as the leading man, this chapter will begin with director Tim Burton's early collaboration with the same actor. Obviously some of this will connect back to the previous chapter, but the Bible is used in more extended ways here. From *Sleepy Hollow* we'll move on to consider how other films use the Bible and then we'll move on to those that obviously abuse it in the next chapter. Most of the movies in this chapter show some subtle hints of biblical abuse, but that only becomes central in Chapter 3.

Uses of the Iconic Bible

Cinema makes use of the iconic Bible in many ways. It can be a prop (as it mostly was in the popcorn pieces *Psycho*, *Wicker Man*, *Pet Sematary*, *Memento*, and *Van Helsing*). It was used as a thematic cue for one movie (*Pet Sematary* again). The four movies explored here—*Sleepy Hollow*, *The Blob*, *The Seventh Sign*, and *The X-Files: I Want to Believe*—with varying shades of horror, all make use of the iconic Bible in their plots. In *The Blob* it may appear peripheral at first but the ominous ending of the film depends on it. *The Seventh Sign*, by comparison, is both thematically based on the Bible and Scripture plays a distinct role in the movie. *The X-Files: I Want to Believe* features the Bible as a supernatural element in the world of a skeptic who also happens to be Catholic.

This mix of celluloid is, in some sense, random. These are all, however, films that use Scripture intentionally and in generally positive ways. The mix shows the wide range of Holy Writ in horror-themed movies. Nobody is especially abused by it, although that potential is occasionally there (*The Blob*, and implicitly in *The X-Files*). In all cases the Good Book is iconic. Its usages will compare favorably with those we saw as we munched on our popcorn.

Sleepy Hollow (1999)

Sleepy Hollow was the former name of a small village (now called Tarrytown) in the Hudson Valley of New York state. It was the final home of one of America's first home-grown fiction writers, Washington Irving. While Irving wrote longer pieces, both fiction and non-, he's best remembered today for being the author of "The Legend of Sleepy Hollow." This short story was originally published in 1820 as one story in a set of brief pieces called *The Sketch Book of Geoffrey Crayon, Gent.* Numerous retellings and re-envisionings of the story have appeared over the decades, in a variety of media. For the most part, religion plays no part in the original or subsequent versions.

Known as a religious skeptic, Irving didn't feature religious themes in this work. In fact, "The Legend of Sleepy Hollow" seems to make fun of Yankee credulousness. The story isn't explicit, but the Headless Horseman is strongly implied to be Brom Bones, a ruffian from Sleepy Hollow who has a prior claim on Katrina van Tassel. The Bible plays no role in the story beyond the accurate depiction of the life of a schoolmaster in Irving's day. Crane uses a Psalm book to teach singing—historically accurate for this period. The ending, as with ghost short stories, is intentionally ambiguous.

Early in the development of cinema the story appealed to movie makers.

Edward Venturini directed the silent film, *The Headless Horseman* as early as 1922. Disney's 1949 *The Adventures of Ichabod and Mr. Toad* (directed by James Algar, Clyde Geronimi and Jack Kinney) followed Irving's story fairly closely. Indeed, the original depiction of Ichabod Crane by his creator is cartoonish: "He was tall, but exceedingly lank, with narrow shoulders, long arms and legs, hands that dangled a mile out of his sleeves, feet that might have served for shovels and his whole frame most loosely hung together. His head was small, and flat at top, with huge ears, large green glassy eyes, and a long snipe nose, so that it looked like a weathercock perched upon his spindle neck, to tell which way the wind blew."

This didn't prevent later treatments of the story from taking a more serious tone. Henning Schellerup's 1980 television movie *The Legend of Sleepy Hollow* introduced elements that seem to have inspired Tim Burton's more famous retelling. Although Ichabod remains a school teacher, he's a skeptic in Schellerup's version but, perhaps more tellingly, the Headless Horseman really is a ghost. With 104 minutes' running time, Schellerup had to pad the short story with several new elements to fill up the time. One element he didn't add, though, was the Bible. Obviously, it could be that the Bible as a plot element simply didn't occur to the writers. It isn't obvious that it fits.

The enduring popularity of Irving's narrative also shows itself in the Fox network television series *Sleepy Hollow*, which ran from 2013 to 2017. This program built on Tim Burton's influential re-imagining of who Ichabod Crane might be. It also focused on Scripture in the story.

The question of how the Bible functions in such a story as Washington Irving's "Legend of Sleepy Hollow" is key to understanding how popular American thought views the Good Book. Tim Burton's willingness to challenge convention perhaps made placing a revered book into a questionable role more likely here than in some other horror venues. The Bible is obviously iconic in *Sleepy Hollow*, as an overview shows.

It all begins with a conspiracy.

The Van Garrett family, the wealthiest land-owners in Sleepy Hollow, have a falling out over inheritance. The Van Garrett patriarch, Peter (Martin Landau, uncredited), has had an affair with widow Emily Winship (shown only as a headless corpse and therefore also uncredited). This affair has led to a secret pregnancy and a secret new will. The Van Garrett family is related by marriage to the Van Tassel family. The Van Tassels are part of Irving's original story, of course, represented by the love interest of Ichabod Crane, Katrina. In the film Katrina's father, Baltus (Michael Gambon), has become a prominent member of the community, partially for having inherited the Van Garrett estate.

Unbeknownst to Baltus, his second wife, Lady Van Tassel (Miranda Richardson), seeking revenge for the foreclosure on her family when she was a child, has summoned the Headless Horseman to kill those who've wronged her. After they've all been eliminated, she'll inherit the Van Garrett fortune. The conspiracy involves those who know of the secret will: the Reverend Steenwyck (Jeffrey Jones), Dr. Lancaster (Ian McDiarmid), Magistrate Philipse (Richard Griffiths), and Notary Hardenbrook (Michael Gough). Baltus Van Tassel, although he has prospered because of the death of Peter Van Garrett and his son Dirk—the secret will only being known of by Steenwyck, Lancaster, Philipse, Hardenbrook, and Lady Van Tassel—remains unaware of the conspiracy.

Early in the film constable Ichabod Crane (Johnny Depp)—here an avowed rationalist—is sent to Sleepy Hollow to investigate three mysterious murders. Unlike Irving's character, he's presented as an unconventional "detective" in the late eighteenth century. He arrives at the Van Tassel farm on Halloween where he meets the town elders. Not believing their story that the Van Garretts were beheaded by a ghost, he pulls his notebook—the first iconic text of the movie—from his satchel to begin his investigations. This ledger is leather-bound and has a red marker ribbon—signs commonly found with the iconic Bible and visually resonant with it. The difference, of course, is that the ledger is blank until filled with the rational—and often quite macabre—notes of Ichabod Crane. In fact, before beginning his journey he looks through and carefully packs this notebook. It is seen with him throughout the film.

"They tell me you've brought books and trappings of scientific investigation," the Reverend Steenwyck says as Crane opens his notebook before the town elders. In a move that's full of double meanings, the minister informs Crane, "This is the only book I recommend you read," as he drops a heavy Bible on the table. Ichabod obligingly opens the cover—there's a family tree of the Van Garretts and Van Tassels inside—before dropping the cover and stating that nothing supernatural is going on. He lays his rational "Bible" (his notebook) on top of the iconic Bible.

What of Steenwyck's meaning? Since the Headless Horseman is indeed real, on one level his words to Ichabod clearly mean that he should get his soul in order. The minister isn't completely cynical. On another level, since the conspiracy's meant to frame Baltus Van Tassel, the family tree glimpsed inside the Bible is a not-so-subtle hint that Baltus is behind the crime. Steenwyck, as will be revealed, is slaking his lust on the scheming Lady Van Tassel and is thus motivated to set Baltus up for a fall.

The Bible appears in this early scene as both a book of spiritual consolation for one presumed to die soon and as an iconic book that has the power to reveal (falsely) a murderer. This is accomplished through extra material added to a sacred book, a theme also later utilized by the Fox television series. The added material, in the movie, is the incriminating family tree.

That very night Jonathan Masbath (Mark Spalding) is murdered by the Horseman. On the gray dawn that follows, Ichabod has his first opportunity to examine a corpse scientifically. As he arrives on the scene a tableau is already in place. The town elders are standing around the body while on a rise above them the Reverend Steenwyck looks down, wearing a black cape, Bible open in his hands. He says nothing and the Bible is shown here in its role as a potential comfort, but also as a book that's helpless to save. Masbath is already dead. At the same time the Bible, not being read aloud, is bringing no consolation to anybody. It's challenged by science as Crane tries to deduce what has happened with chemicals and reason.

At Jonathan Masbath's burial the Reverend Steenwyck once again holds the Bible open in public. He reads from the first letter of Peter about the Devil seeking whom he may devour—an odd passage for a funeral. The reading here seems to underscore the diabolical nature of the Horseman. His black steed is named "Daredevil" and the Horseman is a "seed of evil." The Bible here serves to console, which may be one of its standard functions in conventional movies. The consolation, however, is limited in that the choice of readings is frightening and says nothing about Heaven. Very fitting for horror. We'll speak of the Devil in Chapter 5.

Tipped off by Magistrate Philipse that there has been a fifth victim, Crane exhumes the dead and performs an autopsy on widow Winship. Clearly unfamiliar with female anatomy his notebook is brought out and lies open on the operating table as he tries to figure out where to make an incision. His "bible" leaves him coated with blood, but ultimately wiser—the widow was pregnant when she died. The iconic book gains on the conspirators.

Ichabod, falling in love with Baltus' daughter Katrina (Christina Ricci), comes to believe she's a witch. Finding her alone one sleepless night, Ichabod discovers her reading. The book she hides from him is a book of spells, a grimoire, and as we'll see, a very important sacred text. Crane notes this unusual secrecy, and Katrina confesses her mother was a witch. This realization sparks his memories of his own mother, who was also a witch. (The witchcraft theme, absent from Washington Irving's story, is likewise borrowed by the television series.) What is a grimoire?

Primarily, a grimoire is a magic book. Grimoires may be more than simply spell-books, although they are presumed to be effective in working magic. Any book that has a magic function might be labeled a grimoire. A number

of cultural usages of the Bible demonstrate that it's sometimes clearly intended
as a healing device (think of people being "slain in the spirit" while being
thumped with the Bible). Such folk usages show that, in the experience of
many people the Bible obviously has a physically salvific role, when combined
with the proper accessories. The Bible saves magically. Salvation means, as
its name implies, being saved from something. In evangelical Christianity it's
believed that people are fallen creatures that have to be saved from sin. This
is one of the clear deliverables expected of biblical magic. The Bible saves
from Hell.

Grimoires, in common parlance, are spell books. Some would classify
ancient Egyptian magic scrolls, such as the Egyptian Book of the Dead, as
grimoires. The genre of grimoire is named for medieval European books that
were produced for magical purposes. A primary association of grimoires,
since at least the late Middle Ages, was witchcraft. Grimoires themselves were
considered sources of power—they were frequently handwritten and were
thought to hold the essence of the person who wrote them. Grimoires don't
appear in a single form or style. As eclectic books they're often idiosyncratic.
In the case of horror focusing on books, it's good to keep in mind that grimoires can be something other than spell books. Remember, any magical
book can be a grimoire. Noting how the Bible functions in horror films brings
this point to the foreground. Like standard grimoires, the Bible can be manipulated and has secret powers.

Katrina offers Ichabod a grimoire entitled *A Compendium of Spells,
Charms, and Devices of the Spirit World*. He protests having no interest in
such things, but Katrina presses it on him, insisting that he wear it next to
his heart. Like most iconic books, this one holds hidden meaning. Iconic
books are never simply incidental. This one, however, is thin and clothbound,
not immediately iconic. It's shown to be effective only as the story unfolds.

Ichabod, always the skeptic, is nevertheless tolerant of witches. In flashback scenes young Ichabod (Sam Fior) is shown witnessing his mother's powers, including levitation. Then things turn wrong. Ichabod's father (Peter
Guinness), shown wearing a black robe with preaching tabs, points out the
evidence of his mother's witchery. This is the scene that opened this chapter.
The Bible is an uncompromising *Ding*.

In this instance the Bible appears to function as a book of rules. There's
more than a hint of abuse here, but Scripture remains a symbol of respectability. Clergymen, despite their foibles, are respected members of society. This
is a typical interpretation that appears in horror movies—the Bible is the law.
Theoretically all people—and supernatural creatures—will necessarily obey
it. As we'll see repeatedly, this view of Scripture is in line with American

expectations of the Good Book. Films reinforce this view, as is clearly demonstrated in *Sleepy Hollow*. The passage in the Bible most appropriate to the scene comes from Exodus where we read "Thou shalt not suffer a witch to live." We can't say, however, if that's the passage in this scene even by freezing the frame. It goes by too swiftly.

Interestingly, the Bible remains in the ashes as Lord Crane drags his wife off to her death. The tacit statement of the value of the text is left for the viewers to consider. In some Christian traditions the Bible is never to be laid on the floor, and other books are never supposed to be placed atop it. We've now seen both in this movie. Scared yet?

As the plot progresses, the Bible reappears as Ichabod pieces together the trap the conspirators have set for him to find. Using the family tree in the Bible, he writes in his own black-bound notebook, "5 to 4," "conspiracy," "the secret," "points to," and "Baltus." The Bible in this scene functions in its iconic role of revealing the truth, but in a perverted way. It's actually giving Ichabod false information; information that he copies into the notebook that has guided him, Bible-like, throughout his investigation. This notebook contains scientific observations and functions as a secular bible. It is also, however, wrong. It's worth noting that Ichabod never intended for his string of observations to be read as an accusation. Bibles leave themselves open to misinterpretation.

Katrina, upset by the evidence of the new will that Ichabod has uncovered, burns it so that nothing stands to implicate her father. That night the Headless Horseman attacks, leading Dr. Lancaster to confess the conspiracy, only to be bludgeoned to death with a cross, as the scene takes place in a church. Baltus, aghast at the violence, shoots the Reverend Steenwyck for the murder and the Horseman impales and beheads Baltus, thus, for Ichabod, closing the case. (If we were talking about religion and not just the Bible, this scene would be a very rich vein to mine. "Why should I die for you?" Baltus asks Lancaster and Steenwyck before all three are murdered.) As he prepares to leave Sleepy Hollow, Ichabod burns his black notebook, recanting his secular bible. He has seen the Horseman with his own eyes and his own handwritten scripture has, in the words of Lancaster, "played him false." The Bible has triumphed over science.

At this point in the movie it might seem that the iconic texts have run their course. Ichabod leaves town, but Lady Van Tassel reveals to Katrina that she hadn't been murdered by the Horseman, as everyone had assumed. She would inherit all the wealth but for Katrina's presence, so she once again summons the Horseman, this time to behead her stepdaughter. Ichabod, meanwhile, realizes that the facts don't add up. He pulls the grimoire from his pocket and understands that Katrina has been trying to protect him, not hex him. The spell book is salvific. He hurries back to the Van Tassel farm to rescue Katrina and as they end up at the Horseman's lair in the haunted western wood, Lady Van Tassel shoots Ichabod. The Headless Horseman, learning who it is that had actually stolen his head, gallops off with Lady Van Tassel, back into the underworld, sparing Katrina. Ichabod, meanwhile, arises. He was shot in the heart, but not shot dead. The grimoire given to him by Katrina had stopped the ball from killing him. The book of spells therefore, while apparently not sacred text, has proven effective.

The trinity of iconic books in the movie, then, may be summed up as: the Bible, Ichabod Crane's ledger, and a grimoire. The Bible is shown to be a book of secrets, a text with information apart from the contents of the Bible itself. The Bible, through the family tree, shows both false and true information about who the murderer is. The information in the Bible provides a red herring in order to conceal a crime. It was also the excuse for murdering Ichabod's mother, "an innocent," he calls her in a flashback, "a child of nature." He declares his father "a Bible-black tyrant." Definitely a mixed set of perceptions for this odd couple. Ichabod Crane's scientific notebook and ersatz bible, leather-bound and beribboned, has been burned. It was false scripture. (For more on this see Chapter 4.) *A Compendium of Spells, Charms, and Devices of the Spirit World*, the grimoire, has proven to be a true text after all. Katrina's spells have protected Ichabod and the innocuous book has saved his life.

The Bible, instantly recognized as an authoritative book, proves to be a misleading one. The information is true—the Van Garretts and Van Tassels are intermarried—but its function is to divert a non-believer toward an incorrect conclusion. In no sense is it magical here.

When magic does appear, in the form of Ichabod's mother, the Bible justifies her cruel death. This supernaturally-themed movie has no room for a magical Bible. The Bible suppresses magic. It is entirely within the natural world. *Sleepy Hollow* thus presents ultimately a negative view of the iconic Bible's ability to save.

Ichabod's notebook, curiously, shares some of the Bible's traits but ultimately also misleads. Ichabod uses it for maps, sketches of body parts and medical instruments, and for solving crimes. When it also leads him astray, although he believes it to have been correct, he burns it. A rationalistic book fares no better than the Bible here. The truths (scientific and deductive) in the book are destroyed along with the falsehood.

The grimoire is also damaged, but not destroyed intentionally. Of all the performative texts in the movie, the grimoire is the most effective. It actually saves a life. Those who used, or whose names appeared in, the actual Bible ended up dead (except Katrina). The grimoire, while not outwardly resembling scripture, functions as a Bible should. It offers salvation and it delivers on that promise.

Unlike the later television series, the iconic Bible in the movie should be classified as a book intended to save, but powerless to do so. It remains an iconic text, but ultimately a powerless one. The Headless Horseman, diabolical though he may be, gets his way in the end.

The next film we'll watch, *The Blob*, also shows an iconic Bible that can be understood as potentially misleading. First we need to ooze over to the theater and see what we can see.

The Blob (1988)

Like most remakes, Chuck Russell's *The Blob* takes significant liberties with the original version (Irvin S. Yeaworth Jr., and Russell S. Doughten Jr., 1958). It's because of these liberties that this film is included here. The use of the Bible is also somewhat unusual in this instance, as we shall see. The basic plot—a monstrous Blob from space terrorizing a small town—remains the same as in 1958. The Chuck Russell version, however, ups the ante on the horror with many of the main characters being consumed, including a child.

The Blob in the remake is actually a government experiment in chemical warfare. Once unleashed it's impervious to destruction, except from cold. Brian Flagg (Kevin Dillon) and Meg Penny (Shawnee Smith), the teen leads, discover the monster's weakness and save Arborville, California (the original was set in Downingtown, Pennsylvania) from gooey doom. Early in the film, the Reverend Meeker (Del Close) is introduced, for comic effect. He's shown in a drug store, wearing a clerical collar, and overhears as one of his teen parishioners is buying condoms. Prior to that he's shown at the high school football game which has left the town otherwise deserted. Notably including, according to the opening montage, the churches. What's the real religion in Arborville?

As in the original, the Blob attacks a diner. Brian and Meg escape after hiding in a freezer and fending off the Blob's attacks until the cold forces it away. The Reverend Meeker arrives just in time to see the monster slithering off. "Oh my God!" he significantly says before running to the devastated cafe to see if he can help. Throughout this scene he's shown with a large black Bible under his arm. He hears a voice inside. Once he comes to the broken glass of the front door, he puts his Bible on the floor and enters the diner, only to find that the "voice" he heard belongs to a disturbed cat. He notices, however, the frozen Blob pieces at the freezer door and saves them in a jar. He has dropped his Bible and discovered a new god.

Placing the Bible on the floor, or more dramatically dropping it, will become quite familiar by the end of this book. As an iconic text, laying the Bible on the floor serves as a kind of foreshadowing of unpleasantness to come, for two reasons. One is that it's considered inappropriate by a number of Christians to ever put a Bible on the floor. The second reason is that Scripture acts as totemic protection, like a talisman. When you don't have it on your person, like a crucifix before a vampire, you're vulnerable. Movies tend to bear this out, often, but not always, immediately after the deed.

Meanwhile, Meg and Brian flee only to be captured by Dr. Meddows (Joe Seneca), the government scientist behind the organism. Brian escapes to overhear Meddows discussing the truth behind the attack, and admitting that people will die. "It's my cross to bear," he tells his staff. The phrase is a biblical one, but not a direct quote.

Back in town, the Blob has famously attacked the movie theater and has chased Meg into the sewer. As it bursts out into view the Reverend Meeker wanders onto the street saying, "This has all been prophesied!" He's accidentally ignited in an unfortunate flame-thrower accident, and is horribly burned. Meg, finding a fire extinguisher, puts out the flames and the minister is pulled into the town hall while the Blob continues its attack until stopped cold by a snow-gun truck. Life, it seems, can get back to normal in Arborville.

The final scene of the movie opens on a tent revival. The Reverend Meeker has abandoned his clerical collar and has grown his hair long. A Bible stands open to Revelation as he preaches about the coming end of days. Strangely, we think, since the threat is gone. Right? Worried, one of his congregation wanders back after the service to ask him when the end will be. "Soon," he assures her. "The Lord will give me a sign." He lifts the jar with the now thawed Blob pieces alive and ready to take over the world.

As in *Sleepy Hollow* and *Psycho*, this is another instance of the Bible being added to a story where it formerly had not appeared. There's neither Bible nor minister in the 1958 original. Interestingly, the Bible here represents the spiritual health of the minister, and possibly Arborville. It's treated as an iconic book, but instead of saving the bearer from the monster, it actually follows the believer into a new religion. Since the Blob has no Bible, it's fit into the religion the minister already knows.

Moss Woodley (Beau Billingslea), the mechanic who works on the snow-gun trucks early in the movie, tells Brian there will be snow that year to bring in the skiers that keep the town alive. Immediately before the final scene, in the context of the Blob being frozen by the artificial snow, Moss exclaims to

Brian "you've got to have faith!" The very next scene is the final one of the movie where the Reverend Meeker tells his congregation that they too must have faith. His faith, however, is in the Blob.

The Bible serves to signal a few things here. Along with clerical garb, it helps to identify the Reverend Meeker as a religious leader. He puts the Bible down just before he discovers frozen Blob bits. His abandoning of the Bible and its protection end up in his being scorched by a flame-thrower. Once he's converted to the religion of the Blob, Scripture serves to predict the future. Like the original, the remake ends with a questionable future because what the Bible predicts, as an iconic book, comes true. And what it predicts is the end.

The original movie contained the Blob in the Arctic, but no religion began based on the creature. No Bible was needed. No preacher appears among the straight-laced citizens of the town in 1958. The 1988 version has added the Bible and subverted it. The Bible serves whatever god the worshipper chooses. Iconic, certainly. Salvific? It depends on whose version of the faith you believe.

It could be argued that this is a subtle form of abusing the Bible as well. In the next film, from the same year as this, another end-time scenario is played out. This time, however, it's based on an entire world derived from the Bible.

The Seventh Sign (1988)

Abby Quinn (Demi Moore) is worried about her unborn baby. She's unaware that in Haiti, the Negev of Israel, and in Nicaragua, that three of the four horsemen of the apocalypse are out for a joy ride. David Bannon (no relation to Steve; played by Jürgen Prochnow), aka Jesus Christ, has been breaking old-fashioned wax seals that contain prophecies in these countries and has now moved into the apartment over Abby's garage in Venice, California. What could go wrong? It should be pretty obvious already how biblical *The Seventh Sign* is. Indeed, the title (*The Seventh Seal* had already been famously taken) indicates that this is horror that draws on the Bible. But it doesn't stop there.

This diegesis, or movie universe, is biblical. The premise of the entire story is that the "biblical" end of days has come. This setting, which we'll encounter from time to time in horror, is a fiction constructed by cobbling together verses and parts of verses from the Bible. The fact is, Scripture contains no single account of what the "end of the world"—a rare phrase in the Bible—will be like. The whole idea of the end of the world as we know it wouldn't have made any sense to people in biblical times. Their world was a three-tiered layer cake with the realm of the dead (Sheol) below a flattish earth layer that was in turn under a dome that kept back the endless waters of chaos and doubled as the residence of God. The Bible describes how this kind of world can be flooded. It might also be fried, if you listened to the Zoroastrians. The Bible doesn't have an overarching end-time narrative. A vague sense of an end is there, but since it comes from many different sources, there's no single view of it.

Certain Christian sects, beginning in the 1800s, started scouring the Bible for specific signs of the end of the world. These groups stitched together verses from different parts of the Good Book into a patchwork quilt of the end times that they took for a roadmap. This artificially fabricated account sounds very biblical because the pieces come from the Bible. Certainly some people in ancient times—even Jesus—thought "the end" might be near. Film-makers find it an irresistible storyline. Cinema that dramatizes a catastrophic end of the world and that brings in overt Christian elements (such as apoc-alyptic features like seals, plagues, horsemen, etc.) is, in other words, based on this biblically-inspired universe. *The Seventh Sign* is a textbook example of this, and includes the iconic Bible as well. Back to the story....

Jimmy Szaragosa (John Taylor), a young man with Down Syndrome, is on death row for killing his parents. They were brother and sister and he's being touted as "the word of God killer" by the press. In an interview with his lawyer, Abby's husband Russell (Michael Biehn), he cites the book of Leviticus as his motivation for the murder and refuses to go through testing that might declare him incompetent. He knew what he was doing, and "it was not wrong." Leviticus lists punishments for several forbidden sexual liaisons for the people of ancient Israel, including that between brother and sister. Jimmy reads it literally, that his parents deserved to die. His lack of repentance will sentence him to the gas chamber. But wait, there's more Bible to come. Sprinkled with some Talmud.

A sparrow flies inside the Quinn's house during dinner, but Bannon insists it be left alone. Sparrows sing when a soul comes down from the *guf*, the repository of souls, he says. Before going any further it's worth noting that there's no "*guf*" in the Bible (or in a standard computer spellcheck). In fact the concept of "soul" is somewhat undeveloped in the Hebraic world of biblical times. For example, the Pharisees of the New Testament era believed in an afterlife while the Sadducees were somewhat skeptical of the concept. The idea of a "soul" is generally considered to be a Greek one. The Hebrew word sometimes translated as "soul" in the Bible has a literal connotation of "breath." In Greek the cloud of concepts around "soul" includes mind, per-sonality, and will.

Abby, who tragically lost her last fetus, becomes convinced that this stranger renting their spare room knows something about her unborn son. She follows him into a synagogue where Kaddish is being sung. As she's asked to leave, Bannon breaks another seal leading to spasms that seem to threaten her baby. She's rushed to the hospital. Meanwhile, Father Lucci (Peter Friedman), who has been investigating these signs, assures the college of cardinals that they all may be explained scientifically. This is not, he lies, the apocalypse.

There's so much biblical mythology going on here that we'd better take stock at this point. The premise of the end times, as we've already seen, is biblical in this context, even if somewhat artificially contrived. "The course has been set," David Bannon tells Abby. Once the apocalypse has begun, there's no turning back. At this point the four horsemen—the first four seals according to Revelation 6—have come on the earth. In the movie this is shown in terms of natural disasters and war, which are close to the biblical outlook for generalized future troubles.

The Bible as motivation for a murder (as in Jimmy's case) is an old trope in crime dramas, but is here tied in with the end times. Jimmy will be "the final martyr," in a departure from the actual book of Revelation. The idea of a final martyr is a completely non-biblical fiction. In the movie, the literal seven seals on are parchments written in a mysterious form of Hebrew, making the Bible a kind of book of magic once again. The word "prophecy" is repeatedly used to describe predictions of the future. The Bible considers prophecy more generally as speaking for God. Back to the screen…

Abby snoops around Bannon's apartment and finds a copy of the prophecy with her child's due date on the top. Convinced that David is after her baby, she takes the copy to a rabbi, accidentally stepping on the fifth seal on her way out the door. Rabbi Ornstein (Rabbi William Kramer), a Hasidic Jew, refuses to see her after she touches him, which leads Abby to his next-door neighbor, Avi (Manny Jacobs). Abby begs Avi to help her with this strange prophecy she's found. He tells her that the numbers aren't her baby's delivery date (not even Jesus' birthday is listed in the Bible), but are a reference to Joel 2:29, a prophecy of the end times. Interestingly, unlike most books of the Hebrew Bible the book of Joel is actually numbered differently in Hebrew than it is in English. The ancient prophecy proves the English correct, apparently, since this is the numeration used. Avi learned the secret form of Hebrew on the parchment from the rabbi across the hall and agrees to translate it for Abby.

Meanwhile Abby begins to research the *guf.* She learns that when it's empty a soulless child will be born and the world will end. The prophecy about a soulless person is non-biblical. That stands to reason since "souls" are kind of up in the air in the Bible as well. This *Seventh Sign* world is based on the Bible, but it isn't a Bible film. Determining that the *guf* is empty, Abby telephones her husband, interrupting his call to the governor to get a stay of execution for Jimmy. This is "some kind of Bible sign," she insists. Frantic, Abby confronts David, who reveals that he is Jesus' second coming. Before he came as the lamb, but this time he's the lion. She stabs him but sees that he literally cannot die again.

Avi goes to church. He wants to learn what all this means, but the minister (John Heard) assures him that none of Revelation is to be taken literally. Eschatology (the fancy word for the study of end times) is symbolic. Avi, he suggests, is too young to worry about such things. Horror often involves clergy who don't take the Bible literally when they should. In a sense, horror condemns those who don't "believe the Bible." It's conservative in that way.

Father Lucci rescues Abby from an apocalyptic hail storm. Taking her to the religious house where he's staying, he reads to her from Revelation. "You are the seventh seal," he tells her. God's grace is now empty. This really is the end. There is a profoundly sexual meaning to Abby as "the seal." Her "breaking," which is giving birth, will be the final act. The soulless child will initiate the end of time. After Abby leaves Father Lucci reveals himself to another priest as Cartaphilus, the "wandering Jew." This idea requires a bit of unpacking.

An anti–Semitic figure of medieval Christianity, the "wandering Jew" is based on a mix of Cain's curse in Genesis 3 and the phrase "a wandering Aramaean," in reference to Abraham (notice the name Avi, short for Abraham), from Deuteronomy 26. In the Middle Ages a legend developed that a Jew taunted Jesus on his way to his crucifixion and was condemned to wander the earth until the second coming. In some versions of the story the character is associated with Pontius Pilate, as he is in *The Seventh Sign*. Father Lucci is Cartaphilus, and he's here to ensure that the world does indeed end because he's tired of wandering.

Avi finds Abby as she's fleeing and she explains that they need to figure out how to stop the next sign, before the eclipses—a standard biblical warning. Here it's based on Joel 2:31, "The sun shall be turned into darkness, and the moon into blood, before the great and terrible day of the Lord come." Abby urges Avi to figure out the sign quickly, but he says, "It's not my book. It's the New Testament." He tells Abby to pull into a motel. Once again we meet the recurring motif of the Gideon Bible. Here it's a book of answers. A Jewish boy can work out the Christian apocalypse and he's the one who knows that the motel's a place to go for a Bible late at night. The Gideon Bible, as in *Psycho* (1998) and *Memento*, is a cinematic standard for finding references before the invention of the internet.

While Avi reads the Bible Abby watches television. Jimmy, she realizes as he comes on the news, is the final martyr. At this point Revelation is left behind—remember, there is no such figure. If Abby is the seventh seal, Jimmy is the sixth. She calls Russell telling him to stop the execution. She races to the prison with Avi.

Father Lucci is Jimmy's chaplain. The boy is praying in his prison cell, the Bible, closed, on the bed in front of him. Although he relies on the Good Book, it's the end of the story for him. He's led to the gas chamber, but Abby and Avi burst in demanding that this be stopped. Lucci grabs a guard's gun and a firefight ensues leaving Jimmy dead (and the sign fulfilled) and Abby shot as well. Nature begins to show all the signs of breaking down, but Abby is rushed to the hospital and her baby is delivered stillborn. She declares she would die for him at which point all of the hurricane winds and earthquakes stop. The baby is alive. Abby is dead. Her self-sacrifice, like that of Jesus, was for the salvation of the world. David Bannon is in the delivery room and tells Russell the *guf* is full again. On the way out he tells Avi to write it all down so that people will believe. A not-so-subtle reference to the Gospel of John. Roll credits.

If the end times agenda isn't from the Bible, how did it become so widely accepted? The work of the self-taught preacher Cyrus I. Scofield was disproportionately influential in this regard. Scofield, whose annotated Bible still sells remarkably well, was a dispensationalist. That's a two-dollar word for an evangelical Christian who divides history into predetermined periods, or "dispensations." Those periods of history include the end of the world and the events leading up to it. Through clever, if forced, cross-referencing the Bible can be made to predict a somewhat unified, if completely artificial, view of the last days. Verses from many different books have to be lifted from their context and made into a kind of "Bible code" for this method to work.

This idea, deceptive in its simplicity, has a strong grip on the imagination of Americans. Almost everyone has heard of the Rapture, for example, although the phrase doesn't even occur in the Good Book. This way of looking at things completely distorts the Bible itself, but this is horror we're talking about!

The Seventh Sign is not, despite what some commentators claim, a Bible movie. It may be considered a movie about biblical mythology—David/Jesus tells Avi to write it all down, just as John is instructed in Revelation. The end times, however, aren't described in any kind of coherent way in the Bible. As popular as this kind of apocalyptic imagery is, the end of the world is a picture puzzle of forced-together references from different biblical books like pieces from several different puzzles. Joel is one, and Revelation is another. Isaiah, Daniel, Matthew, and 1 Thessalonians must be thrown in at a bare minimum, with bits and pieces from many other books as well. The end result is anything but coherent since the Bible was never written to be a single book with a single ending.

The Bible may be a *Ding*, but it wasn't the intention of any of the writers that it would all be gathered together as it is today. The books were collected together long after being written over a period of hundreds of years by different people. They weren't written as an account from creation to the end of the world. You can't turn to Revelation and get a roadmap to the end times. Even Cyrus Scofield had to back and fill to make it work.

The Seventh Sign, like many other movies, uses a composite script to frame its story. It's largely based on the "dispensationalism" of Scofield which is based, in turn, on the beliefs of an obscure sect called the Plymouth Brethren. The Bible isn't exactly screenwritten, as even *The Ten Commandments* shows. The end times became a fascination in the late nineteenth century. Ministers, feeling the pressure from the rapid growth of science—especially Darwin's theory of evolution by natural selection—convinced themselves that the Bible could be pressed to reveal what Jesus said even he didn't know: when would all this happen? Some clergy began to devise end times scenarios.

Even today the conflicting and contradictory accounts of the final days have led literalists to divide into Premillennialists, Postmillennialists, and Amillennialists. The "Rapture" was artificially constructed from a single verse in Paul's first letter to the Thessalonians. Those who turn to Revelation to find the Rapture generally experience great disappointment. It's not there.

The Seventh Sign isn't the only movie to utilize this magical view of the Bible. We'll see it again in *The Omen*, and to a lesser extent in *The Prince of Darkness* and *Rosemary's Baby*. There are many horror movies that won't be treated here that build on it as well. The Bible is a *Ding* that has a tenacious grip on the popular imagination. So much so that many people think the signs are still evident, even if they aren't part of the biblical worldview.

The Bible here is both iconic and thematic. We might want to call in Mulder and Scully about now.

The X-Files: I Want to Believe (2008)

The last regular example of the iconic Bible for this chapter will be the second *X-Files* theatrical release. Although this book doesn't delve into the world of television, it has to be noted that this movie follows on as a kind of hybrid from the popular television series. In this case, *The X-Files* had been a long-running series before the two (to date) feature movies appeared. The first theatrical movie was interlaced with the TV series. The second film stands mostly independently. Since the cancellation of the series an abbreviated tenth season was filmed, but with no tie-ins to the story played out in *I Want to Believe*.

Unlike the other supernatural-themed Fox television series *Sleepy Hollow*, the Bible played no regular role in *The X-Files*. Two FBI investigators, Dana Scully (Gillian Anderson), the skeptic set against Fox Mulder (David Duchovny) and his more open-minded approach, were the protagonists. Scully was written as a believing Roman Catholic. The monsters the pair faced across the original nine seasons often had religious origins; the Bible had no key connecting role in the plot in any season. It showed up from time to time, but not in a consistent way. There was a "mythology" still widely popular among hopeful fans, but this revolved around the ultimate conspiracy theory and human-alien hybrids. Not exactly the stuff of Holy Writ. (Some would argue that the Bible does describe such hybrids in Genesis 6; suggested, for example in, *The Fourth Kind* and much of "ancient astronaut" lore. See Chapter 7 for more on this topic.)

The first feature film of the *X-Files* franchise, *Fight the Future*, continued the series' mythology story arc and was sandwiched between seasons 5 and 6. The second movie, *I Want to Believe*, took a different turn and represents the common theme of the films in this chapter—the Bible as part of the story itself.

The X-Files: I Want to Believe begins with a typical horror story. An Eastern European scientist, Franz Tomczeszyn (Fagin Woodcock), dying of cancer, is being kept alive by transplanted organs from kidnapped human victims with the ultimate goal of transplanting his head onto a healthy, female body. Why female? Well, it's complicated. He's married to Janke Dacyshyn (Callum Keith Rennie), his able-bodied partner who delivers organs for a living and moonlights as a trafficker for his lover. Their medical team has successfully transplanted dogs' heads, and now they're ready to try on a human.

This Frankenstein-themed plot intersects with that of Father Joseph Fitzpatrick Crissman (Billy Connolly), a psychic, pedophile priest who helps Mulder and Scully with the investigation. Father Crissman has repented of his crimes and is guided by his powers to find victims of the illegal transplanting operation. Tomczeszyn was one of Crissman's childhood altar-boy victims, and that psychic connection provides the priest visions of the women being targeted by the traffickers.

Scully, conflicted by her disgust at the priest and her own battle to save a young boy with an incurable disease, openly mocks and taunts Crissman. During the initial interview, Mulder and Scully, along with FBI agents Whitney (Amanda Peet) and Drummy (Xzibit), find Father Crissman kneeling in prayer in his apartment. A large Bible lies open on a stand in the background. It functions merely as a prop here. Scully, who can't accept the threat to her faith represented by a pedophile priest, is asked to leave. During the subsequent investigation Crissman tells her, "Don't give up."

This brief message works at Scully until she visits him alone one night at his apartment as he's reading his Bible. She confronts him regarding what he meant by "don't give up," as well as regarding his sinful past. Crissman is sitting on his bed with a smaller Bible open on his lap, the large open Bible still in the background. He and Scully end up arguing. "Proverbs 25:2," he yells, "It is the glory of God to conceal a thing: but the honour of kings is to search out a matter!"

"Don't you quote scripture to me!" Scully shouts back. Crissman lapses into a fit. He convulses, Bible open on his lap, but Scully's not buying it—she takes it as an attempt at drama on his part. The Bible falls to the floor. This is never a good thing. The priest is dying.

When the FBI backup arrives Scully learns that Dacyshyn and Tomczeszyn are married, and that the latter was one of Crissman's victims. The case appears to be closed. The priest, the Bureau presumes, was working with the criminals because of his attachment to Tomczeszyn. Mulder, isolated from Scully and knowing none of this, wants to prove Crissman is really psychic, and innocent. Mulder is captured by Tomczeszyn's people after being run off the road, and has to be rescued by Scully and FBI assistant director Walter Skinner (Mitch Pileggi). But first they have to find him. Mulder's no longer with the FBI and the only clue is his totaled Ford Fusion.

Driving along the road where Mulder's (actually Scully's) car was found, Scully tells Skinner to stop. She approaches a line of mailboxes, stopping at 25:2 (the chapter and verse Father Crissman quoted from Proverbs). Flipping through the mail she finds bills for medical equipment and the address. The biblical reference was prophetic, or psychic. Maybe both. Scully and Skinner rescue Mulder and arrest the illicit medical ring.

Up until season 10, *The X-Files* took the supernatural seriously. In *I Want to Believe*, the supernatural element centers on Father Crissman. He's genuinely psychic, or perhaps divinely inspired. His seizure before Scully reveals the actual address that will lead her to her fallen partner. The Bible here is iconic and salvific. It leads Scully and Skinner to Mulder, and he's saved from certain death by Scripture.

Scully and Mulder try to reconcile their differences. They have been lovers, but they have conflicting outlooks. Scully tells Mulder that she wants to believe. "I acted on that belief," she says, noting that it saved Mulder's life. Clearly she's referring to her finding the address through Crissman's citation of Proverbs.

Not only is the Bible iconic here, but it also participates in magic. In the popular imagination "prophecy" is prediction. This idea has a very long pedigree, beginning in the Hebrew Bible itself where the measure of a true prophet was, by late standards, whether his (or somewhat rarely, her) predictions came to pass. In the past several decades biblical scholars have come to understand prophecy somewhat differently—it's either political or an outgrowth of social justice concerns. Telling the future plays little, if any, role in it. The general population, however, has the predictive element constantly reinforced in popular culture as well as in some churches. Conservative Christian groups especially continue to teach that prophecy is prediction. Even well-informed adults who pay little attention to religion can identify prediction as prophecy. Scholars tend to keep the discussion of what prophecy really is among themselves while members of the public continue to accept the magical, predictive outlook.

Prophecy predicting exactly where Mulder may be found is a magical understanding of the phenomenon. While *The X-Files* can be playful at times ("Signs and Wonders," episode 9 of season 7, stands out as a religiously-themed installment with the Bible that can't be taken at face value), this use of the Good Book is cast in a completely earnest script. There's nothing inherently improbable about doing organ transplants and extrapolating that a head might be transplanted (again we find ourselves in *Re-animator* territory). *I Want to Believe* projects a naturalistic story line where the only supernatural factor is Father Crissman's psychic ability and the Bible plays a central, magical role in it.

As in the other movies considered in this chapter, the Bible is iconic, salvific, and magical in this *X-Files* movie. Since the fan base for the movie was generally viewers of the television show, it's worth noting that supernatural-themed television programs also tend to view the Bible this way.

Iconic Reflections

This chapter has considered horror's use of the Bible as an iconic book. As an iconic book, it saves either physically or spiritually. Scripture tends to have a magical tinge to it. Sometimes it's entirely natural, but the very concept of salvation implies supernatural agency—saving some poor mortal from a threat that's anything but natural. Even if the Good Book's a prop, it's never just a prop. It has magical power. That power is hidden knowledge or the ability to predict the future.

Sleepy Hollow, The Blob, The Seventh Sign, and *The X-Files: I Want to Believe* all present the Bible as a potentially useful, powerful book. Those uses can be quite diverse, although they all involve salvation at some level. Notice that the Bible itself is treated with respect. It's unquestioned. When it falls to the floor, trouble follows.

The conspiracy against Baltus Van Tassel is implicated by extra material in Holy Writ, according to *Sleepy Hollow*. It was a book somewhat abused as well since it's the excuse for murdering Ichabod Crane's mother. Its salvific function is transferred to a grimoire that saves Ichabod's life. Any actual saving comes from magic books—even in the confines of a church.

The Blob takes it in a different direction. The Bible becomes mercenary to the cause of a minister who changes religions. Early on in the movie a sign of respectability, once it fails to save the Reverend Meeker from the flames, it shifts to a book foretelling end times. Its misuse here also bears a tinge of abuse, but it's generally more positive. The congregation unfailingly believes it, making it dangerous, but also safe.

The entire universe of *The Seventh Sign* is biblical. This is "the apocalypse" predicted by Scripture. The iconic Bible appears as a book that has to be read and the interpretation of which takes esoteric knowledge. The Gideon Bible is found in a motel room drawer and it's the only book that can prevent the unfolding end of times. Here there are no obvious abusive elements about the Good Book. It simply is. It's a *Ding*. A *Ding* that knows how it's all going to end. That ending, however, is hardly positive for the human race. Scripture inspires fear.

In *The X-Files: I Want to Believe* the magical, salvific element involves a psychic priest. The Bible is cast positively and saves Mulder's life. It, however, appears in the hands of a pedophile cleric. Abuse is implicit if not obvious. Two lives (those of Mulder and the current intended surgical victim) are physically saved. Perhaps Scully experiences a spiritual renewal in her medical life. The Good Book, however, consoles a sexual predator.

What about the Bible as a *Ding*? Notice that it's a sacred book taken literally, as evangelicals understand it. The evangelicals set the terms. In other words, it's a magical book when it comes to predicting the future. Scholars in the movies, such as priests and clerics, are portrayed as ambivalent about it. Even Reverend Meeker, once he comes to believe in the Blob—which has an established scientific explanation—understands the Bible as predicting it. He himself, of course, will open the jar on the apocalypse.

The study of this *Ding*, if undertaken by scholars like Avi, ultimately uncovers its literal meaning. It's a magical book because it knows the future. Horror respects the Bible—it's conservative in that way. Scripture's a performative text, if not always effective at saving, and it matches the Protestant Bible we saw in the Director's Commentary. Even when Catholics and Jews read the Bible it tends to be the Protestant one that prevents the end of the world. If Father Crissman's Bible is Catholic it's not apparent from the way it's used. The book he cites, Proverbs, is a Protestant favorite and the Good Book saves lives.

The Bible, as a *Ding*, in these four films, is good. There are subtle hints that the Good Book can be misused, but overall it's a positive element. Horror movies, however, don't treat the Bible as positively as, say, *The Apostle* does. There's always a hint that something's wrong. Although this isn't a scientific survey, it appears that the normal iconic Bible is somewhat rare in horror. Its positive functions were foreshadowed in various popcorn pieces, but it's far more common for the iconic Bible to be a means of abuse. It's this special kind of Bible abuse that will occupy the next chapter.

3

Good Book Gone Bad

Jarod, Travis, and Billy Ray have a night of kinky, three-way sex on their minds. The high schoolers drive to the trailer where Sara Cooper lives. She's been phishing and these boys have taken the bait. Subdued by men hidden in her bedroom, Jarod wakes up in a cage covered with a cloth, his hands bound. He can hear a sermon using Leviticus 20 to condemn homosexuals. The cover slips off the cage. He watches in horror as another young man, entombed in plastic packing wrap at the foot of a large cross, is unveiled. The boy resembles an insect in a cocoon. Reverend Abin Cooper continues his sermon calmly. Lyrically. The desperate boy, gagged so he can't call out or even beg for forgiveness, is growing increasingly frantic. Cooper make the comparison with an insect explicit, but notes the young man is bound for Hell because of his homosexual activity. Jared watches, unbelieving, as the men of the congregation use more plastic wrap to strap the boy's head to the cross, leaving mouth and nose uncovered. The victim struggles in vain. "Send him to Hell," the sinister minister calmly instructs. A pistol is produced and the boy is shot straight down through the top of the head. The pistol had been hidden in a hollowed out Bible.

* * *

Now that we've witnessed some standard uses of the iconic Bible in horror, the movies in this chapter will be those in which Scripture is used for nefarious ends. Sometimes innocently and sometimes intentionally. Holy Writ becomes awful when used for evil, instead of being used for good. The Bible as a *Ding* remains iconic, but its many negative usages vary widely.

The Bible can be abused pretty openly in horror. The previous chapter had hints of this abuse already, but here the bad side of the Good Book will be plainly in view. We'll look at five movies where the Bible is iconic and abused: *Carrie, Children of the Corn, The Shawshank Redemption, Red State,* and *An American Haunting*. As we saw in the last chapter an iconic book as a *Ding* is instantly recognizable. It's a good *Ding*; in fact Americans sometimes call it the Good Book. That doesn't mean that it always plays nicely.

A certain skepticism toward the Bible has been evident in American culture for many years. It may not often show up in cinema in general, but horror will often go where other genres don't dare. An early television episode of *Dragnet* emphasized this point. Sergeant Friday had to arrest an elderly woman because she'd shot a man. Throughout the half-hour drama it became clear that she'd shot him because he'd abused one of her books. Only at the end did *The Holy Bible* get held up, with a bullet hole through it. You felt sorry for the lady. Her Bible had been abused and she was acting in its defense.

This was back in the 1960s (sometime during the 1967–1970 series). At this time the idea that the Bible could be blamed for anything felt quite foreign. Sympathies were on the side of the elderly woman who, although technically wrong for killing someone, had a righteous cause for doing so. The early horror of *Psycho* had passed with only a Bible tucked under an arm. Who thought that horror was about to pressgang the Good Book as a bad guy?

Most of the samples in this chapter treat Scripture as the source of abuse. One, *An American Haunting*, has the Bible as a victim. In either scenario what was considered an iconic good has become a source of horror. Of these five (or six, depending on how remakes are counted) silver screen screams three of them derive mainly from one source—Stephen King.

Stephen King continues to be, as of this moment, a very prolific author. Although many of his novels have been cinematically adapted, the movies don't always follow his storylines closely. We can't really speak of a Stephen King genre, but there are commonalities that run through his plots. Religion and horror are two of those common elements, often combined. This chapter will consider three movies (four, including *Carrie*'s remake) based on his work. Each features the Bible in a way that could be considered both iconic and abused. We'll also watch the non–King *Red State* and the above-mentioned *An American Haunting*.

Even in horror iconic Bibles are generally shown positively. These are some cases, however, where Scripture's lost its shine.

Carrie (1976, 2013)

Stephen King's first published novel was *Carrie*. It has been adapted into two major feature films sharing that title—the original Brian De Palma movie of 1976, and the Kimberly Pierce effort of 2013. (The television movie won't

be examined here.) In the gap of nearly 40 years between them public acceptance of the Bible in horror films seems to have increased in tolerance. The
same may be said of Christian imagery, as *Carrie* also indicates. Once again
remakes reveal different doses of Holy Writ. Scripture's use in 1976, the viewer
senses, is just a bit tentative. There's a line that mustn't be crossed in American
sensibilities. That will become clear as we consider how the Good Book
appears in this narrative.

Brian De Palma's treatment of the story is considered a cinematic classic.
Carrie (Sissy Spacek) is the naive child of a religious—fanatical—mother ever
watchful for sin. Zealously, Margaret White (Piper Laurie) witnesses for her
faith, and abuses Carrie for the onset of menstruation as a sign of sin. Early
on in the movie Margaret visits Mrs. Snell (Priscilla Pointer) on a mission
call. She has a black, leather Bible tucked under her arm, which she searches
through for a passage to present to her host. She begins to read from Exodus
but Mrs. Snell interrupts, offering her money for her cause. The Bible is ineffectual here. Margaret isn't even able to begin reading it before the money
comes out and the Bible is clapped shut. We get the sense that Scripture makes
people uncomfortable—they'll even pay not to have to hear it.

When Carrie arrives home from school, we're shown the religious paraphernalia all over the interior of her house. Her mother, aware of what has
happened at school through a telephone call, summons Carrie and begins to
read to her from a religious book. This isn't the Bible, perhaps because the
Bible doesn't actually say what the story demands from it. This book is paperback and clearly not iconic. Margaret forces her daughter to repeat after her
as she reads from the book: women are sinful and the sign of that sinfulness
is blood. Carrie objects and each time her mother hits her face with the book.
Was America ready to accept a child being hit by an open Bible in the mid–
1970s?

Following this abusive episode, Margaret White shuts Carrie into a
prayer closet dominated by an unconventional crucifix. Jesus is represented
as being pierced with arrows in the characteristic iconography of Saint Sebas-
tian. This foreshadows Margaret's death scene, but it also protects Christian
sensibilities by not making Jesus' standard iconic crucifixion an element of
horror. (Please note, Mr. Gibson!) An open Bible stands at Jesus' feet in the
prayer closet. At least it can be assumed to be a Bible—the camera never gets
close enough to verify its identity. Its position and appearance suggests so.
If it is a Bible, the intent is salvation, but the text here is inert. Carrie doesn't
even look at it.

Carrie soon discovers her telekinetic powers. When her mother sends
her to bed, Carrie, crying before her mirror, causes it to shatter. The broken

pieces of glass rain down on the closed Bible on her dresser. As in the prayer closet, the Bible in the bedroom is more than simply a prop. At the very least it's a significant prop. Despite its promises, it can do nothing.

When Carrie and her mother are eating supper by candlelight, Margaret is shown as reading an open Bible as they dine. It's at this point that Carrie informs her that Tommy Ross (William Katt) has invited her to the prom. The Bible, open and actively read, remains powerless. When Margaret forbids the date, Carrie reveals her powers. The Bible is forgotten. As Carrie sews her dress for the prom, her mother bows and prays before the open Bible to no avail. Carrie will go to the dance. After she leaves to meet Tommy her mother quotes from Exodus, "Thou shalt not suffer a witch to live." Here at last the Bible has an effect. Carrie, a witch in her mother's eyes, will not survive the night—this is a Bible "prophecy" come true.

At home following the famous blood-drenched carnage scene at the high school, Margaret stabs her daughter in the back after narrating the story of her own descent into sin. Telekinetically killing her mother, Carrie pulls her corpse into the prayer closet as the house begins to collapse. The Bible remains open on the prayer desk as again detritus falls upon it. After Carrie dies, the "crucifix" is shown with the face of Margaret and we see that the Bible still stands open at the savior's feet.

The Bible here is clearly iconic. At the same time it's also, as in *Sleepy Hollow* and *The Wicker Man*, unable to save. More than that, it's abusive. Carrie—technically the monster in the movie—is oppressed by it. Depending on the viewers' sympathies, this could be a good thing or a bad thing. The Bible is used to abuse, but its value remains ambivalent. Only in its predictive ability (not permitting a witch to live) does Scripture have any power, and that power is through Margaret's mistaken identity of her daughter as a witch. The Bible is bleakly presented here as the iconic book with no actual authority. At the same time, the Bible itself is treated visually with respect. "The witch" dies in the end. Or does she?

In Kimberly Pierce's retelling, the perception is somewhat different. Criticism of the 2013 film focused on the fact that not much had changed since the original to justify a new flick. The remake, critics remonstrated, was somewhat slavish. The role of the Bible, however, is one point of difference.

Initially, notice that Margaret White (Julianne Moore) doesn't go around trying to convert people. In fact, she stays at home and uses self-destructive behaviors to punish herself for her sins. There's no call on Sue Snell's mother to convert her, therefore no Bible.

The day of Carrie's first period, her mother berates her, as in the 1976 version, for being sinful. Instead of using a book, Margaret has Carrie (Chloë

Grace Moretz) repeat sentences she says about sin. "That's not even in the Bible," Carrie protests. She's correct about that. The things her mother says are not biblical. When Carrie flat out refuses to say one of the statements her mother hits her head with a Bible, knocking her down. The 36 years between the movies has shown a development here. *Carrie* in 1976 was challenging enough with the theme of menarche and the crazy, religious mother. The Bible is never used to physically assault anyone. All that's changed this time around. The use of Scripture is purely abusive here. Striking someone with the Bible surely qualifies.

When Carrie is forced into the prayer closet, the crucifix is noticeably more conventional than in De Palma's version. Scenes of torture of the saints accompany the traditional crucifix in Pierce's vision, and there's an open Bible at its foot. Blood drips from the crucifix but we're not shown if it lands on the open Bible or not. There may still be limits to how far film-makers will go for fear of defying Holy Writ.

As the movie progresses it stands out that the Good Book appears less frequently here, at least visually, than it did in the earlier version. It's present in spirit, though. The poem Carrie recites in class was originally about Samson—something that Tommy Ross (Ansel Elgort) reveals. The actual poem is "Samson Agonistes (Samson the Wrestler)" by John Milton. Milton, an Elizabethan poet, is quite often associated with the King James Bible. Both are examples of well-known Elizabethan English classic pieces and both deal with spiritual issues. While this doesn't really count as the Bible, Tommy cites it as referring to a biblical character. Then he insists that Carrie attend the prom with him.

Also new to the Pierce version is Carrie's intentional practice of her telekinesis. This involves several library books that are levitated in her room. It's difficult to tell if the Bible is among them, but the scene would suggest not. These aren't iconic books but their function is to unlock the power within the girl. In fact, they appear more powerful than the Bible in the film. They save Carrie from her mother's aggression that's intended for salvation.

As Carrie sews her prom dress, Margaret is shown with her in the room, reading the Bible that sits open on her lap. The intended function of the Bible here is to control Carrie; it's an attempt to prevent her from going to the prom. Carrie has already revealed her telekinetic powers to her mother, so Margaret can only feebly protest. The Bible has no power here. While Carrie is awaiting Tommy her mother says "Jezebel fell from the tower," a reference to 2 Kings 9 where King Ahab's widow Jezebel is thrown down from an upper window to be trampled to death by horses and devoured by dogs. Being eaten by dogs, in the biblical world, was a sign of the ultimate disgrace. In that sense Margaret White's words are, as in the original, prophetic. The text has shifted from Exodus to 2 Kings between the movies, but Scripture's uttered with the same intent. Here the coercive use is an abusive threat.

After the carnage scene at the school gym, and the final destruction of Chris Hargensen (Portia Doubleday), Carrie returns home but can't find Margaret. The Bible lies closed on her mother's bedside table when Carrie searches her room. When Carrie finds her, and Margaret is about to sacrifice her, her mother quotes the Lord's Prayer before stabbing Carrie. Although this prayer has its origins in the Gospels, it could be known simply by rote learning or attending church. Still it counts as at least an extension of a Bible quote. The crucifixion scene of Margaret White—impaled with knives and other bladed objects—doesn't require the bizarre crucifix of the 1976 film to make its reference clear. Ultimately, however, Carrie winds up dead in a *Pietà*-like scene of the girl holding her dead mother on her lap. As the house collapses, the Bible doesn't appear, as it does in the De Palma version.

What, then, does *Carrie* say about the Bible? It's a book abused in both renditions, but exactly how depends on the version. Brian De Palma's 1976 treatment uses the Bible more, at least visually, but in less challenging ways. It may have been too much to show child abuse with a Bible then but it can still be used to repress Carrie. In Kimberly Pierce's version some three-and-a-half decades later, the Bible is visually less obvious, but at the same time is used more offensively and is spoken of more often. In the intervening years, we have seen televangelists "slaying in spirit" by striking people with the Bible. Nones have been on the rise and the Bible, although iconic, is somewhat of an unknown to this demographic. In any case, it becomes a powerless *Ding* unless physically used as a blunt instrument of faith.

The parent slaying child with a sharp object theme we already glimpsed briefly in *The Shining*. This trope draws from the Abraham and Isaac story. Here the genders have been altered, but the motivation is the same—the parent believes God is telling her (him) to offer up her only child.

This outlook on the Bible is negative, no matter how it's presented in this cinematic treatment. If the viewer sees Carrie as a monster the Good Book fails to control her. If the viewer sees Carrie as an abused girl, her mother intends Scripture to prevent her successfully becoming a developed, fulfilled individual. Either way it's an abusive book. And this carries over into the next Stephen King story.

Children of the Corn (1984)

The dangers of unsupervised religion and an abused iconic Bible also appear in the movie version of this Stephen King short story. *Children of the*

Corn (directed by Fritz Kiersch), like *Carrie*, is a film that foregrounds religion. Finding the Bible requires a little sleuthing, but it appears both visually and by implication. Implied Bibles are common in horror.

The corn children of the title are what used to be called a cult. They've formed a new religious movement and slaughtered all the adults of Gatlin, Nebraska. Their home-grown religion is based on the teaching of a child prophet named Isaac (John Franklin). There is, in fact, a monster that lives in the corn fields, "He Who Walks Behind the Rows." Burt (Peter Horton), a medical intern, and his girlfriend Vicky (Linda Hamilton), end up in Gatlin and have to figure out what has gone awry. Or die.

As the film opens, Grace Baptist Church of Gatlin fills the screen with the sermon title "Corn Drought and the Lord" on the church announcement board. When the congregation comes out, the first man has a Bible tucked under his arm. Just like *Psycho*. Gatlin is obviously a very religious community. The Bible is iconic here, but inert. If it weren't for further developments in the story, it might be thought simply a prop. Gatlin appears wholesome and pious. But something's not quite right. That very Sunday the children, excluding the narrator Job (Robby Kiger) and his sister Sarah (AnneMarie McEvoy), murder all the adults.

When the opening credits begin a child's drawings (later revealed to be those of Sarah) are shown in the montage. One of them quotes "And a child shall lead them" from Isaiah 11:6. The child is presumably Isaac. The Bible isn't shown here, but its quote authorizes the religious hostile takeover that has occurred. Scripture has authority in Gatlin, but the religion revealed to Isaac makes no direct use of the sacred text. Slogans that sound biblical are painted in blood around the town, and when Isaac preaches it's with biblical cadences and form. Crosses are used, but made of corn. It's as if the Bible is slightly blurred in this new religion.

In the church the children celebrate of the birthday of a boy named Amos (John Philbin). Vicky has been kidnapped and crucified on a corn cross. Burt, unaware of this, stumbles into the service taking place to prepare Amos for his death—he's being given to He Who Walks Behind the Rows. Burt bursts into the church profanely demanding "What the Hell's going on here?" Amos assures him that it is as it has been written. Burt says, "What do you mean, 'It is written'?" He holds up a Bible. "What, in this? You rewriting the whole thing or just the parts that don't suit your needs?" He flips through and throws the Bible onto the floor. Uh-oh.

Despite the larger issues the film has, this is a complex scene. Burt simultaneously affirms and disavows the iconic Bible. His statement implies that the Good Book is potentially, well, good, and can offer salvation. His action of throwing it on the floor implies that the Bible is just a book. Worse than that, a Bible on the floor almost always leads to disaster in horror. Here the disaster is Malachai (whose name is curiously misspelled for the movie, played by Courtney Gains). Burt's motivation is unclear. He's clearly disturbed by Amos cutting himself, and as a medical man this would be natural enough. He doesn't believe in "He Who Walks Behind the Rows" and is thus a kind of horror atheist. The Bible offers no actual salvation, but is this because Burt has disrespected it, by throwing it down, or is it because Scripture simply can't save?

How Burt responds to the Bible relates to the way he and Vicky made fun of the radio preachers they heard as they drove into Gatlin. The suggestion seems to be that the kids took all this religious rhetoric seriously. They still recognize the Bible and, to some extent, use it. Burt, as a man of science, sees this as unenlightened belief. Dangerous belief.

The Bible is being rewritten, or at least not quoted precisely, by the children, Burt implies. Grabbing the list of names of children who've died young (those who have been offered up) Burt sees that most, but not all, have been renamed with biblical names. Job, whose escape opened the mystery, Isaac, the religion's leader, and Malachai, the right-hand strong arm of the movement, all have biblical names. This list, written in blood, has the force of an iconic document. Pacts with the Devil, in folklore, are signed in blood. Indeed, Amos' blood is to be drunk by the children gathered in the church. The slogans in blood and the list in blood have taken the place of the Bible in some sense.

The popular understanding of prophecy as foresight plays a strong role in this film. Isaac is revered as a prophet, and Sarah is revealed to have the "sight"—in other words she's a traditional "prophet." She can predict the future accurately.

The brewing power struggle between Isaac and Malachai leads to a schism with Isaac crucified and Malachai taking charge. Throughout, in the cornfield, there has been the crucified, desiccated corpse of "the blue man," revealed to be Officer Hodgkins. Symbolizing traditional authority, and therefore traditional religion, he was murdered (off screen) early in the movie diegesis. Crucifixion, in modern thought, is a biblical phenomenon, although the ancient Romans used it widely for many offenders apart from the founders of new religions.

As the film builds to a climax, He Who Walks Behind the Rows raises a demonic storm. Job reveals that Officer Hodgkins was attempting to set the corn on fire when he was caught. He was reading "a page torn out of the Bible." Job, it turns out, has been carrying this single page of the Good Book with him for the past three years. As he pulls out the folded leaf, a verse can be seen outlined in red. The verse is Revelation 20:10. Ultimately, it turns out to lead to salvation. Although Burt doesn't really understand it, Vicky (now rescued) does and Burt manages to set the field aflame and send the Devil back to Hell. The function of the Bible remains complex—has Job saved the Bible, or has the Bible saved Job? Maybe both. It functions quite a bit like the Good Book in *Sleepy Hollow*, bearing cryptic messages to ward off evil.

Children of the Corn isn't a profound film. Its use of the Bible, however, is more intricate than it might seem at first. Burt disregards it, but once he realizes that the monster is real, he relies on a single page from very near the end of the last book of the Bible to save the two worthy children (Job and Sarah) from destruction. The Bible is abused here in the sense that it's the basis for a death cult. Children kill those about to pass into adulthood, based on their reading of the Bible. This is Bible abuse.

At various points Isaac proclaims that this is "the end." This apocalyptic idea is itself biblical (as noted in the last chapter, and will be discussed further in Chapter 5) and even when secular "end of the world" scares periodically circulate, otherwise disinterested eyes turn to the Bible for guidance. In this movie, however, the prophecy is correct since the arrival of Burt and Vicky spells the end to He Who Walks Behind The Rows and the religion that's sprung up to worship him. The world is safe again. Until the sequels.

No matter how convoluted, the instructions to salvation are ultimately included in the iconic Bible. There's no magic in it. It's used to oppress victims, no matter how willing. The use of Scripture to support a cult of death still relies on Scripture to save those deemed worthy. The result? Bible abuse.

The Shawshank Redemption (1994)

The third Stephen King cinematic adaptation in this chapter, *The Shawshank Redemption*, isn't generally classified as horror. Still, it's Stephen King and it has elements of horror, even if not a precise fit for the genre. Also, for the purposes of this book, it features the Bible in a way that enlightens other films. Scripture's iconic function here is both abusive and salvific. The Good Book is seldom an unremitting positive in King-based films, and this is a prime example of where it is, even amid abuse.

Andy Dufresne (Tim Robbins) didn't kill his wife. The prosecuting attorney, however, convinces the jury that the skillful banker did. And it's off to notorious Shawshank Prison. Although Warden Norton (Bob Gunton) at first appears to be an upstanding Christian man, he turns out to be one of the classic villains of film. "I believe in two things: discipline and the Bible. Here you'll receive both. Put your trust in the Lord; your ass belongs to me. Welcome to Shawshank." His opening greeting to Dufresne's incoming class sets the tone. The Bible isn't shown in this scene, and the only prisoner shown handling a Bible in this flick is Dufresne. The function of Scripture in this early scene is intended as a threat. Indeed, it's intentionally abusive. An inmate is beaten nearly to death that very night.

Think about it this way—these hardened criminals in Shawshank aren't readers. They can't be expected to know the Bible. Here it represents the law. All the "thou shalt nots" that everyone's heard of. Warden Norton begins his speech after stating, "Rule Number One: No blasphemy. I'll not have the Lord's name taken in vain in my prison." This is one upstanding public servant! The command is actually one of the Ten Commandments. Hanging on his wall is a framed cross-stitch sampler that reads "His judgment cometh and that right soon." It's easy to think it too comes from the Bible, although it doesn't. It sounds so biblical—it also sounds very much like Stephen King, for those who are attuned to his novelistic style.

Although the Bible isn't shown in this scene, it hangs over the entire movie by the mood it casts. That mood is, appropriately for a prison drama, one of unrelenting judgment. Abusive judgment. Then comes the turning point in the film. Word has come to the warden that Andy Dufresne is good with numbers. Very good.

A surprise inspection is ordered. Dufresne's cell is called. He's sitting on his bunk, Bible in hand. He closes the cover and stands as the warden approaches. As his cell is being ransacked, the warden takes the Bible from him. "Pleased to see you reading this," the warden says. "Any favorite passages?"

Dufresne, knowing how to flatter Norton's love of power, replies, "Watch ye therefore: for ye know not when the master of the house cometh." Clearly a reference to the warden.

Warden Norton counters, "Mark 13:35, I've always liked that one, but I prefer 'I am the light of the world: he that followeth me shall not walk in darkness, but shall have the light of life.'"

Dufresne correctly identifies the source as John 8:12. In classic Stephen King style, there is more going on here than meets the eye. Double meanings are rife. Throughout the inspection, Warden Norton handles the Bible but doesn't actually open it. Maybe having memorized it he doesn't have to. He walks out of the cell with it.

Turning around he slips it through the bars to Dufresne, telling him, "Salvation lies within." The joke's on the warden, of course, since we'll learn that the Bible is actually Andy Dufresne's book safe for hiding his rock hammer. And here the meaning regarding Holy Writ becomes literal. The salva-

tion from wrongful imprisonment, Dufresne's ticket out of Shawshank, physically lies within that Bible. Not from the spiritual truths, but from the extra
material made of wood and steel. As in *Sleepy Hollow*, something extra is
added to the Good Book.

But not so fast—the story can't be complete without Andy earning the
trust of righteous Warden Norton. This is done by quoting the text of the
Bible. This is as good an example of the performative aspect of an iconic
book as any. Quoting the Bible leads Dufresne to the realm of power—the
very warden's office—from which he will secure his financial salvation after
his twenty-year escape plan. He's hired as Norton's personal accountant.

Meanwhile Tommy Williams (Gil Bellows) arrives at Shawshank. It turns
out that he shared a cell with Elmo Blatch (Bill Bolender), the real murderer
of Andy Dufresne's wife. The warden finds out that Dufresne has a credible
case for retrial and knows, since Andy's been cooking his books for years,
that he can't let the banker go. Warden Norton needs Andy Dufresne to keep
squirreling away illegal moneys for him, so he can't have him killed. He also
can't let him get free—he's too dangerous. In a nighttime interview the warden
gives Williams his symbolic last cigarette as he asks him if "hand on the Bible
and all that," he truly heard Blatch's confession. When Tommy affirms this,
the warden has him shot dead.

This is only an incidental mention of Scripture, but it's more significant
than it seems. Witnesses in court place their hands on the Bible to signal that
anything they say will be true. In this case, a declaration of the truth leads
to instant death. The Good Book is complicit in the murder of Tommy
Williams. Another instance of abuse.

Dufresne now knows his framing is complete. He can't get out of Shawshank
by legitimate means. Of course, he's been digging his way out for the better part
of two decades. On the night of his escape, Dufresne switches the Bible for the
warden's cooked books that Norton locks in his safe behind "His judgment
cometh and that right soon." The next morning the newspaper breaks the story
of his corruption, and slapping the paper on his desk, Norton goes to the wall
safe. Within one safe is another. He pulls out Andy Dufresne's Bible. "Dear Warden," the ex-prisoner has written on the fly-leaf, "You were right. Salvation lay
within." The warden, for the first time in the film, actually opens the Bible.

There, beginning in Exodus, as in *Carrie*, he finds the cutout of the rock
hammer that led to salvation for Dufresne. He drops the Bible in horror. It
remains on the floor for the remainder, short though it may be, of his life.
Dropped Bibles lead to trouble.

There's so much going on here that it might be good to hit "pause" a
moment and excavate it.

The Bible is salvation and damnation simultaneously. Andy Dufresne, through material extraneous to Scripture—namely, a rock hammer embedded into the text—has found literal salvation. Such is the power of an iconic book.

At the very same instant, that Bible signals to Warden Norton that his accounts book is missing. Holy Writ has been substituted for money. And the headline in the newspaper reveals that the contents of his own real, if hypocritical, Bible have been made public. The Bible in his hand is his condemnation.

The book of Exodus is the story of the Israelites' liberation from slavery in Egypt. It's also the story of Andy Dufresne. He has been freed, apparently by the mighty hand of God. Actually, by his own hand. The rock hammer cutout proves that.

A dropped Bible in movies is a visual sign of judgment. The warden has no hope. Like the cross-stitched saying on his wall, he's been framed. Unlike Dufresne, however, his framing is righteous and necessary. He's been a criminal, complicit in murder, from the beginning. Like a dropped mic, a dropped Bible signals the end.

We just saw a Bible not dropped, but thrown down in *Children of the Corn* (remember, also a Stephen King story) just above. There's a difference here. Warden Norton, for all his faults, respects Scripture as a *Ding*. At least as a means to an end. Burt, in *Children of the Corn*, does so only obliquely as he's a man of science. Once that Bible falls from the warden's hands, he's a dead man. No swearing on this hollowed out hallowed text. His respect is shown to be as hollow as the book safe. He blows his own brains out.

Perhaps this makes clear the motive for including *The Shawshank Redemption* in this book. It may not be classic horror, but its treatment of the Bible is a shining example of an iconic book and the way that horror movies interpret that book for the public. It's sacred. At the same time, it can fool the gullible. In the end it leads to some kind of redemption regardless. Along the way, it can be abused. It's America's ambivalent sacred book.

Red State (2011)

Stephen King movies show various ways Scripture can be abused—and certainly there are others besides those discussed here. The view of the Bible as a vehicle for abuse, however, doesn't come much clearer than in *Red State*. Here, as in some of the previous films, material is added to the book. Here it'll take the form of sermons (which add to the Bible by definition) and another piece of hardware. Both will be abusive.

Kevin Smith, some suggested, was an unlikely writer/director for a horror film. Those familiar with *Dogma*, however, know that the groundwork had been laid early in his career. A "shit demon," angels ripping the heads off people, and a trio of scary, demonic teenage street hockey players all fit the bill. That movie is clearly a comedy. Satire, it might be supposed, could be horror, but it's, well, satire. *Red State*, however, is completely different.

Red State is an example of a film where religion itself is the basis of the horror. Inevitably the Bible would also be portrayed here—probably negatively, but not negative as a *Ding*. Even the intertitles for *Dogma*, after all, suggested Smith didn't wish to offend anyone's beliefs.

The story of a minister gone bad is nothing new, either in real life or in horror. It's hard to miss a couple of cultural referents from the start here, though. The Fred Phelps–like presentation of Abin Cooper (Michael Parks) and the Waco, Branch-Davidian-style shootout at the end are two notable examples. Since the horror is based on a religious cult—technically the name for such groups is "New Religious Movements," but "cult" works fine here— it's perhaps not surprising that the Bible appears in an abusive role. Since the movie is based on a biblical cult, we'll briefly summarize the action first, then consider the Bible's function.

The movie's essentially a play in three parts with an epilogue: three teenage boys looking for sex, their ordeal in Five Points Trinity Church, and a firefight with federal agents that leaves them all dead. Travis (Michael Angarano), Jarod (Kyle Gallner), and Billy-Ray (Nicholas Braun) are three high school boys desperate for sex. Living in a rural area of a red state, it's not as easy to find as it would be in a big blue city. Jarod has located a website where a woman offers to have sex with all three boys at once. She's an older woman, but she's willing. At her trailer Sara Cooper (Melissa Leo) has them chug a couple of beers each before having hidden members of her church subdue them. They're taken to Five Points Church where they are to be ritually murdered for their crimes of sexual intent.

Perhaps the most uncanny aspect of the movie is Reverend Cooper's sermon. Calm, low-key, and full of hatred, he quotes Psalm 127 and Hebrews 11, telling the congregation—mostly his children and their families—that knowledge of the Scriptures is essential. Throughout this whole scene Jarod is in a cage, tasered when he shouts too much, and a human form draped in a sheet stands eerily beneath a large cross. Abin Cooper cites Psalm 138 where the psalmist hates his enemies with a perfect hatred. The sin that bothers the reverend most is homosexuality. He quotes the passage in Leviticus that condemns the practice. At several points in the sermon Sara—the woman who lured the boys in—unfolds and folds her hands over an unopened Bible in her lap. The minister doesn't preach from an open Bible. He wanders about the chancel, speaking extemporaneously.

Then the scene described at the beginning of the chapter takes place. A gun concealed in a book safe made from a Bible is the murder weapon. The dead boy is dropped into a cell beneath the floor where Travis and Billy-Ray are tied together, saved as future victims. Jarod is taken from his cage and strapped to the cross with plastic wrap, obviously Cooper's next intended victim. He yells out that he's not even gay, but the Reverend Cooper notes he was preparing to have sex with a married woman at the same time as his friends, which might be even worse. He's gagged so that he can't interrupt the service.

Just then an outdoor monitor shows an approaching police car. Travis has cut himself and Billy-Ray free on a broken bone extruding from the dead boy dropped into their underground cell. They discover a bunker under the church where the Five Points congregation has been store-housing automatic weapons. Billy-Ray is killed in a standoff and the shots fired alert the police officer outside that something is amiss. Sara's husband is also killed in the gunfight and Abin soothes her by quoting 2 Timothy 4.

Special Agent Keenan (John Goodman) is called in. He mentions that Cooper is like Fred Phelps, but worse. His church is weaponized. Meanwhile Travis, rifle in hand, tries to free Jarod but ends up running outside where he is shot by an inept local sheriff (Stephen Root). The shot gives away the AFT blockade of the church. Once the Five Points congregation realize they're surrounded, they start shooting. In the midst of the firefight Cooper quotes Matthew 24 to his daughter to encourage her, bullets zipping past them.

Cheyenne (Kerry Bishé), Sara's daughter, frees Jarod from the cross, hoping that together they might save the younger children. He staunchly refuses. His friends have been shot dead, and he no longer cares. Cheyenne tells him the AFT agents have been instructed to kill everyone. Jarod's not moved by this.

Meanwhile the church members quote Psalm 23, "The Lord is my shepherd," as they unpack more guns. Jarod, finally convinced by Cheyenne, goes outside to surrender, but the two youths are shot dead by an agent following orders.

A loud trumpet sounding from the sky stops both federal agents and Five Pointers. Abin Cooper proclaims that the Rapture has started and the fighting is over. The cult members lay down their guns and approach the agents, taunting them that the end of times has begun. Agent Keenan arrests the remaining members of the church instead of killing them, as ordered.

In the epilogue Keenan explains what happened to two other agents, in a hearing. The trumpet sound came from some stoner hippies living in a commune at the edge of church land. They were playing a prank, not knowing that people were being killed just out of earshot.

The closing scene shows Abin Cooper singing a hymn to himself as he paces in his prison cell. His Bible sits on his desk, unopened.

So, what can we say about the Bible in this unusual horror film? One of the most obvious features of the Good Book is that the only time it's shown open, it reveals a handgun. In the book safe, the words of the Lord have been cut out in order to make a convenient hiding place for a lethal weapon. The idea of a biblical book safe also occurs in *The Shawshank Redemption* (just discussed) and the same trope of a gun-safe had been used in *V for Vendetta*. Such a use speaks loudly, if not eloquently, about the role of the Bible. As we saw in *Sleepy Hollow* and *The Shawshank Redemption*, extra material is needed.

Scripture is never an open book in this movie. In every instance where the Bible is shown, except as a book safe, it's closed. This is a Good Book gone bad. It has become a weapon. It doesn't lead to salvation since nearly everyone who uses it is either killed or locked in prison—about as opposite of saved as you can get. It's abuse personified.

More than that, once again extra "text" is added to the Bible. A gun in the Good Book requires the actual "word of God" to be removed to make room for a weapon of lethal force. This pistol becomes part of the sacred text. That extra text is used to kill a boy not guilty of any crime, except by one small cult's definition of sin.

The Bible as a *Ding*, however, is also treated respectfully by the film. Never is it intimated that the Bible supports the Five Pointers—it's always shown closed to them. Their evil interpretation of it is just that—an evil interpretation. An abuse of what might otherwise be good.

In a movie like *Red State*, the Bible is actually inherent in the entire premise of the movie. Fundamentalist cults, like those of Cooper, or even a real-life Phelps, grow out of a particular form of biblical interpretation that began to hit the mainstream in the 1920s. The idea—illogical and impossible—that one can obey all of the Bible's contradictory rules has become the basis for many sects that insist their "literal" interpretation is the only true one. The Five Points Trinity Church, although fictional, could not have existed without the Bible. In a word, the film is a prolonged screed against biblical literalism, and not against the Bible itself.

In the end Agent Keenan is shown to be the one with what might be called a Christian consciousness. He doesn't want to start the raid, as ordered, nor does he wish to kill all the cult members. He disobeys a direct order by arresting instead of shooting the pastor and his remaining followers. He's promoted for not following orders.

Yet Abin Cooper remains unrepentant. Pacing back and forth in his prison cell, singing the praises of his God, he leaves his Bible firmly shut. On the visual level, the Bible isn't blamed. On the macro-level it's left up to the viewer to decide. Is this abuse biblical?

For our last cinematic Bible lesson in this chapter, we turn to a traditional ghost story. Or is it a ghost? No matter the entity, it's an enemy of the Bible. And this time the abuse attacks Holy Writ.

An American Haunting (2005)

Throughout this film fest we've seen some common elements in the way the Bible appears as an iconic book in horror. Not all movies present the Bible the same way, but for the most part the premise—whether upheld or not—is that the Bible saves. That's its expected role. *An American Haunting* features a Bible too weak to save anyone. In fact, it can't even save itself. Here it will itself be the victim of abuse.

In the initial development of this book, this movie was among the first to come to mind. Brent Monahan, the author of the novel upon which the movie is based, mixes fact and fiction, in his treatment of the time-honored Bell Witch story. This film is a rarity where a non-human entity physically dismembers a Bible.

This ghost/witch tale is based on a fictionalized account of the traditional Bell Witch of Tennessee (said to be a true story). The movie, directed by Courtney Solomon, begins with a church drama. John Bell (Donald Sutherland), a well-to-do farmer in the late 1810s, has been accused of usury by the church council of Red River Baptist Church. Despite his sin, he believes his neighbor Kathe Batts (Gaye Brown)—the wronged party—is a witch. He helplessly watches as a poltergeist-like demonic entity assaults his daughter Betsy (Rachel Hurd-Wood) following the hearing. The story is somewhat confusing since at the end of the day, or night, it's John Bell who's been sexually assaulting his teenage daughter. The haunting, it appears, is to remind her of the repressed memory.

The Bell family is presented as religious. They attend church and generally abide by its rules. After the night attacks begin John seeks the help of James Johnston (Matthew Marsh). It's not made clear if Johnston is a clergyman or simply a religious neighbor. As a Baptist at the turn of the nineteenth century, he knows his Good Book. He sits watch with the Bell family after the attacks on Betsy begin. He gathers the family around the table and pulls out a large, leather-bound Bible. "A few chapters from the Bible will take care of the troubles of this house," he confidently drawls. He begins reading from the song of Hannah in 1 Samuel and continues reading into the New Testament as the candle burns down. He has the family repeat an exorcism prayer three times. Is this a ghost, or a demon?

Like most students, Betsy has trouble staying awake at school. This is compounded by her sleepless nights due to the entity attacks. In the movie this draws her to the attention of her teacher Professor Richard Powell (James D'Arcy). The Professor is secretly in love with Betsy, but professionalism prevents him from declaring so. When he learns of the disturbances, like most characters called "Professor," he declares that a rational explanation must exist. He's also invited to sit watch with the Bells, which invitation he accepts that weekend.

While he's present, a mild form of attack occurs. He tries to explain it away as a nightmare when the adults are gathered downstairs. A crucifix—an odd accoutrement for a Baptist house—flies off the wall and across the room. Johnston, who's also present, again turns to the Bible. As the entity blows through the room, knocking things over and extinguishing candles, Johnston begins reading from Scripture. Amidst the mayhem the Bible falls to the floor and slides away from him. The pages then begin to fountain up into the air as Johnston curses the entity. Clearly the Bible can't stop it. The Good Book is a victim of abuse. Professor Powell, now a believer, asks the entity whether the reading was from one of the Gospels, or the Psalms of David. He takes its answer as a sign of its intelligence. The next morning as clean-up begins, one of the slaves is gathering up scattered pages of Holy Writ. Is this a commentary on the hypocrisy of a churchman molesting his daughter? The Bible is rescued by a slave woman.

The Good Book functions as a kind of ouija board in the nighttime scene—although it's destroyed, it provides the means of communication. Whatever this entity may be, it's a religious one. Later, as the adults are again gathered at night and the entity attacks, Johnston is shown intensely searching the Scriptures—clearly a new Bible—helplessly as the attacks continue.

The Bible in *An American Haunting* is an iconic text that has very limited power. At times it seems almost to stop the entity as it might a demon (but see Chapter 6). But the entity is at times more of a poltergeist and doesn't always respond to the Bible. In fact, it unbinds and defaces the very Bible being read to halt its actions.

Among the sexual stipulations of Holy Writ is that forbidding a man to violate his daughter. John Bell, in addition to usury, is committing incest. Kathe Batts is no witch. The wicked one, in the eyes of the Good Book, is John Bell.

A kind of nihilism accompanies this portrayal of Holy Writ. The Bible can be read but it can't stop the horror. It can't even stop its own abuse. Nor is it entirely clear what the entity is. Modern paranormal experts might explain such a poltergeist as the emotional disturbance emanating from a biologically maturing girl who experiences sexual violence from her own father. The solution, in as far as the movie provides one, is for the girl to kill her father and marry her teacher. The Bible simply can't help. Sometimes the Bible humanizes monsters—at other times it becomes their prey. It can both abuse and be abused.

Final Bible Thumping

The iconic Bible stands for salvation. It's a magical book. That doesn't mean that it can't be abused. This is horror cinema after all. In all these movies the Good Book is intended to save. Whether it has the power to do so is seriously in question. In other words, horror seems to be afraid of the Bible. It respects it as a *Ding* with fear and trembling. Holy Writ can inflict harm.

Margaret White, the children who live in the corn, Warden Norton, and Abin Cooper all abuse the power of the Bible. They use it to beat children and adults. It is used to threaten, contain, and control. And in *An American Haunting* Scripture itself is the victim of abuse.

It might be expected in a horror context that something's presumed to be wrong in the divine world. After all, if the Bible could just step in and save the day there'd be no movie. All characters would have to do is find a motel with a Gideon Bible to save the world—remember *The Seventh Sign*. While Scripture ultimately stands for good, it lends itself to subtle or overt abuse in horror. It seldom saves, although that's its expected function. Even when it does, lots of people have to suffer. What's going on with this *Ding*?

America, for all its secularism, is a nation rooted in religion. The Bible, as a *Ding*, is highly symbolic. One of the possibilities here is that it has come to stand in for God. There've been hints of this already, but this chapter raises the bar a bit. Horror movies really can't show God as a character, and yet religion can be frightening—it can abuse. One way to handle this is to let the Good Book stand in for a deity that can't be shown. Perhaps the biggest issue religion deals with ties directly into the world of horror—the explanation of evil. We all experience evil in our lives, and we've been taught that the Bible (read "God") will help. What happens when Scripture doesn't save? You recite those verses you were taught to memorize and harm comes nevertheless. What about when the Good Book itself is causing the evil?

This kind of issue is one that horror is especially well qualified to address. Each of the silver scream examples in this chapter shows that even what is good and powerful can become evil and even more powerful. In the end does the Bible abuser get her or his comeuppance? Not always. There will be some doubt left. If Carrie has survived, what about her mother? The *Children of the Corn* will spawn sequel after sequel. Abin Cooper may be in prison, but Fred Phelps and his acolytes are out there still. Even more bleakly, in rural Tennessee the Bible can't even protect itself, yet it influences government decisions. Hope, as in Pandora's box, appears among the movies here only in *The Shawshank Redemption*. There alone does the Bible abuse lead directly to, well, redemption. Warden Norton is dead. Andy Dufresne and Red (Morgan Freeman) are free men. Free to live happy lives without the Bible. Across the border.

If the Good Book does stand in for God, horror may show just how deep the trouble is. If that's the case with the Bible we know, what about the Bible we don't know?

4

Deceptive Scripture

Ringo has Jules' Star Model B aimed straight at his face. Point blank. The robbery Ringo's been attempting is on pause. Jules is explaining why he hasn't killed Ringo and Yolanda yet. Gun still cocked, in Ringo's face, Jules asks if he reads the Bible. "Not regularly," he confesses. Jules replies:

> There's a passage I got memorized. Ezekiel 25:17. "The path of the righteous man is beset on all sides by the inequities of the selfish and the tyranny of evil men. Blessed is he who, in the name of charity and good will, shepherds the weak through the valley of the darkness, for he is truly his brother's keeper and the finder of lost children. And I will strike down upon thee with great vengeance and furious anger those who attempt to poison and destroy My brothers. And you will know I am the Lord when I lay My vengeance upon you." Now … I been sayin' that shit for years. And if you ever heard it, that meant your ass. You'd be dead right now. I never gave much thought to what it meant. I just thought it was a cold-blooded thing to say to a motherfucker before I popped a cap in his ass. But I saw some shit this mornin' made me think twice. See, now I'm thinking: maybe it means you're the evil man. And I'm the righteous man. And Mr. 9mm here … he's the shepherd protecting my righteous ass in the valley of darkness. Or it could mean you're the righteous man and I'm the shepherd and it's the world that's evil and selfish. And I'd like that. But that shit ain't the truth. The truth is you're the weak. And I'm the tyranny of evil men. But I'm tryin', Ringo. I'm tryin' real hard to be the shepherd.

He uncocks his pistol and tells Ringo to fish his wallet from the garbage bag.

*   *   *

The Bible isn't always what it seems. As we've seen already, an iconic book like the Bible can easily transfer its identity to other books. This may seem like something insidious at first, but we need to recall that the Bible as a *Ding* didn't really exist for those who wrote it. The earliest texts were those among a body of books, some of which eventually became authoritative and "scriptural." In other words, other books had to be considered alongside Holy Writ. As we'll see later on, in Roman Catholicism the Bible was to be read in community, and it exists alongside books like *The Breviary* and *The Roman Ritual.* The idea of a stand-alone sacred book that could solve all your spiritual problems was a distinctly Protestant idea.

Long before Martin Luther and the Reformation other books shared the stage with the Bible. In America especially the Bible became iconic, driving political and social agendas. The other books, however, obviously didn't disappear. As the Bible became all-powerful, other books began to draw on that power. Some are books that don't actually exist.

Consider how many times one might hear the phrase, "the Bible says" when, in fact, the statement that follows is non-biblical. "God helps those who help themselves." Sayings like that. Even entire books that aren't the Bible, if they are powerful, become the same *Ding* in popular imagination. This can happen through different channels.

This chapter looks at three specific ways deceptive Scripture can be mistaken or substituted for the *Ding* itself—as false Bibles, Anti-Bibles, and "living Bibles." False Bibles are either quotations from the Bible that aren't authentic or other books that speak as if they're the Bible. In horror cinema these books are taken seriously without question. We'll consider *Pulp Fiction* more because of its fame than its horror, *The Fog* (both versions), and *Stigmata.* The Bible, remember, doesn't always say what a director or writer wants it too. Anti-Bibles are a step further along—these are books that work the opposite way from how the Bible is supposed to operate. Instead of salvation they bring damnation. They may be literal or figurative alternate Scripture. We'll see them in *The Evil Dead, The Ninth Gate,* and *Constantine.* Finally, "living" Bibles appear in films where a character becomes the Bible. That character may be bad (*Cape Fear*) or good (*The Book of Eli*). This kind of Bible may be false or true. Or a combination of both.

Not all of these movies are classic horror, but they all fall into either the thriller or horror realm and they all feature the Bible, in some form or other. No matter whether it's authentic or not, it's true. Having said that, let's read some False Bibles.

False Bibles

As a *Ding* the Bible, often closed, is a fixed object. One of the dangers of being shut, however, is that nearly anything religious-sounding can be said to be biblical. This isn't restricted to horror. Many movies offer fabricated Bible verses. When a viewership is biblically illiterate it's as simple as a parlor trick to have a straight-laced, straight-faced character claim the Good Book says what the writer/director wants it to say. It's a big book and few viewers will bother to check things out in it once the curtain's fallen. Compared to the films of the last three chapters there's a real difference here. Carrie (in the 2013 version of her story) protests that "it's not in the Bible." Even most of *The Seventh Sign's* quotes come from Scripture. In this section false Bibles won't hold themselves to such a standard of, shall we say, verisimilitude?

False Bible come in a variety of forms. We'll see four in this section, divided over three movies, one with a remake. Due to its formative role in cinema in general, and its promotion of the overlooked prophet Ezekiel, there's no better place to start than *Pulp Fiction*.

Pulp Fiction (1994)

The Italian horror cinema genre called *giallo* (yellow) takes its name from the standard cover color of pulp fiction productions in that country. Many horror movies have originated in pulp fiction, so it's only appropriate to give this important film its due.

Of all the movies in this book *Pulp Fiction* is perhaps the most difficult to classify. What is this thing? Drama? Crime drama? Thriller? Comedy? The scene where Marsellus (Ving Rhames) tells Zed (Peter Greene) that they're going to "get medieval on your ass" is rife with horror. Marsellus has just been raped. The leather-clad gimp (Stephen Hibbert) is tied up in a creepy basement watching Butch (Bruce Willis) struggle against his ropes just outside the door. Butch and Marsellus are covered in blood, having been through a car accident and being hit by a car, respectively. They are ball-gagged and can't cry for help. That's pretty horror-show.

Pulp Fiction is famous for its biblical awareness. Although false biblical verses are common in cinema, Ezekiel 25:17 will never be quite the same after Jules' rendition. *Pulp Fiction* is an excellent opportunity to introduce a successful example of a false Bible.

The story, presented in non-linear form, concerns the redemption of a hitman. (Redemption is thematically biblical as well.) Jules Winnfield (Samuel L. Jackson) and Vincent Vega (John Travolta) are out to retrieve a valuable briefcase that belongs to Marsellus Wallace, a rich crime boss in Los Angeles. To open the case, the combination 666 has to be entered. Here's the first explicit Bible reference. The whole 666 meme begins with Revelation 13:18. Although Revelation will be discussed quite a bit in Chapter 5, the basic premise of Revelation 13 is that an enemy, the Beast (later associated with "the Antichrist"), is afflicting Christians. Historically this is most likely a reference to Nero, the Roman emperor at the time. This Beast is cryptically given the number 666.

Since it would've been dangerous to write "Nero" outright in a document for public circulation while he was still in power, Revelation presents this as a mystery. This unnamed man's number is 666. It is quite possible that the original read 616, but culturally that's of no significance. Like the Bible being a *Ding*, 666 is already a *Ding* too. Everyone knows what it is—the number of, and subsequently the mark of, the Beast. This will be explicitly explained in *The Omen*, in the next chapter.

Now Nero did use some truly horror-show tactics to suppress Christians. For example, he had a reputation for putting them in cages and burning them alive (as in *The Wicker Man*) to provide torchlight in his gardens at nighttime. He certainly earned his reputation as the Beast. Ever since the late first century, or early second, it has become a cottage industry to try to work out who "the Antichrist" (often conflated with the Beast) might be by adding up names to 666. (Many believe Revelation is predicting a future ruler since the book is seen as "prophecy.") The thing about numbers is they're readily manipulated. You can convert letters of names into numbers, in various combinations—use the middle initial or not, title or not—and fudge them around until you come up with 666 for just about anyone. It's such a well-known *Ding* that road signs for various routes 666 around the country are routinely stolen by those with Apocalypse memorabilia fixations.

In *Pulp Fiction* 666 is the first obvious biblical reference. On some editions of the DVD, once you click "Play Movie" the tumblers on the case spin to 666. The case opens and the movie begins. Now back to our story.

Jules and Vincent have entered the apartment of the young men who've kept the briefcase that should've been delivered to Marsellus. Jules shoots one of the men (Roger, played by Burr Steers) on the couch. Brett (Frank Whaley), visibly shaken, tries to avoid being the next victim. Jules asks him if he reads the Bible. He then quotes the famous fictional verse, Ezekiel 25:17, spelled out in full at the start of this chapter. Fake Bible verses are very common in movies. The verse actually reads "And I will execute great vengeance upon them with furious rebukes; and they shall know that I am the Lord, when I shall lay my vengeance upon them" (King James Version). It is worth considering this a moment. In a culture that has high biblical awareness and low biblical literacy, it's fairly easy to convince people that something is in the Bible somewhere. Well, it's a big book. Lots of obscure stuff could be, and is, hidden in there. Surely there's room for a quote like this. Jules' verse must be in there somewhere, mustn't it? Talk about verisimilitude.

In what role does the Bible appear here? It's the ultimate unquestioned authority. Although the verse is largely made up, it justifies Jules executing his hits. We'll come back to his explanation of the verse, quoted above, momentarily. Back to the action.

Brett is eliminated in a flurry of bullets, and a fourth man comes out of the bathroom, firing multiple rounds at Jules and Vincent at close range. Unharmed, they blow him away. The one surviving man in the apartment, Marvin (Phil LaMarr), is accidentally shot in the head on the drive across town. Jules and Vincent get cleaned up at a friend's house and head to a diner for breakfast. At the diner Ringo (Tim Roth) and Yolanda (Amanda Plummer) attempt a robbery. This leads to the scene quoted above, which is the final scene in the movie.

So we come back to Ezekiel 25:17. Jules has Ringo at gunpoint. The professional hitman is lecturing the petty thief about the meaning of his favorite Bible verse. Prior to the robbery Jules and Vincent had been discussing whether their survival of the fourth man's close-range shooting had been a miracle or not. Jules takes it as a sign, and he is quitting—retiring—from his hitman career. He could've killed Ringo and Yolanda easily. He's decided to show mercy.

As he explains Ezekiel 25:17 to Ringo, he uses what is known as the allegorical method. That is to say, the figures in the verse don't refer to their referents literally. The shepherd is not a literal shepherd. Jules is trying to figure out, through what is technically called "exegesis" what this verse actually means. He comes to the conclusion that he is the "tyranny of evil men" but he wants to be the shepherd. Showing the petty thugs mercy, he even gives them all his cash and sends them away unharmed.

To finish the story: Vincent and Jules leave the restaurant and turn the case over to Marsellus. Vincent runs into Butch Coolidge, a washed-up boxer who's been instructed to throw his next fight in the fifth round. Jules presumably retires to the life of Caine and Vincent takes Marsellus' wife Mia (Uma Thurman) out for a night on the town. Butch doesn't throw the fight. He kills his opponent and gets ready to flee the country. He shoots Vincent. He accidentally, then purposefully, runs into Marsellus and the two of them are tied up for a homosexual gang rape in the basement of a pawn shop. Butch breaks free, saves Marsellus, and leaves the city forever.

Pulp Fiction, in many ways, embodies what's at the heart of this exploration. Even hardened criminals know the Bible is a powerful tool. What it actually says is less important than what we want it to say. If you make your living snuffing others, the Bible can justify that. The initial execution scene presents Jules very much like a preacher or a prophet. God's wrath is called down. And although "motherfucker" appears to be his favorite word—his wallet has "Bad Motherfucker" burned into it—he tells Vincent not to blaspheme. This contradiction digs at the very roots of the dilemma of people who respect and fear the Bible but also find it largely irrelevant. *Pulp Fiction* may not be classified as horror, but its insight into how the Bible is understood clarifies the issue in a way that is otherwise difficult to explain.

Our next false Bible movie is classic horror. A double-feature no less. *The Fog* is a John Carpenter movie, later remade, that has both a real Bible and a false Bible. Remember, iconic books can change identity. Especially if nobody's keeping track of the details.

The Fog (1980, 2005)

Following up his freshman success with *Halloween*, John Carpenter got lost in *The Fog*. A classic story of ghostly revenge, its use of the Bible is unusual in that it loses its potency to another iconic book, a different kind of false Bible. *The Fog* is another example of a movie with a remake, like *Psycho*, where the Bible appears while virtually absent from the original. With a priest as a significant character, you might expect some Scripture. The remake delivers some, but the original has the false Bible variety. Let's start with 1980.

The people of Antonio Bay, California, aren't aware as they approach their centennial that the town's founders built the city on blood. A century earlier, a wealthy leper named Blake (Rob Bottin) wanted to establish a colony on land a mile from what would become Antonio Bay. Six early town conspirators, including the priest—Father James Malone—instead followed the tradition of mooncussing and built a deceptive fire on shore to guide the leper's sick ship, the *Elizabeth Dane*, onto the rocks of Spivey Point. They then collected the gold from Blake's fortune once the sea had claimed the contagious unfortunates.

A hundred years later a mysterious fog covers part of the town for two nights. Ghostly figures emerge, killing anyone they can reach. The current minister, Father Malone's grandson (Hal Holbrook), drinking alone in his study, is startled when a stone falls from the wall. Behind the stone is a leatherbound book. If you've been reading since the beginning, you'll know that this is an iconic book. The priest opens it to read, "Journal of Father James Malone 1880." The current Father Malone can't put it down. The original town fathers' plan is laid out as a confession. It's the "Bible" of the movie. False scripture.

The next day Kathy Williams (Janet Leigh), the organizer of the centenary celebration, calls on the priest. It's in this scene that the Bible first appears. In Father Malone's study, a Bible stands open, ignored, on a book stand. The priest reads from the journal as Mrs. Williams and her associate Sandy Fadel (Nancy Loomis/Kyes) listen with increasing disbelief. The journal is treated like a sacred book while actual Holy Writ is completely ignored. Distraught by his family guilt, Father Malone says he can't offer the benediction after the ceremony. The town is descended from murderers.

That night the fog reappears, along with its ghoulish seamen. The only safe place in town is the old church on Beacon Hill. Mrs. Williams and Sandy, as well as local fisherman Nick Castle (Tom Atkins), Andy Wayne (Ty Mitchell)—the minor son of the local radio announcer—and Elizabeth Solley (a hitchhiker vehicle to get Jamie Lee Curtis into the movie), all converge on the church. Father Malone is resigned to their fate, and he refuses to help. Nick grabs the wine bottle from the priest's hand and smashes it against the church wall, where its fragments fall on the journal of the original Father Malone. Realizing that they need that journal as the fog closes in, Nick brings it back into the study and they figure that six must die for the original six conspirators. The ghosts begin to break in through the windows. The gold, they learn from the journal, was stolen by the priest and Father Malone and Nick struggle to pull a large cross, cast from the stolen booty, out from the wall. Perhaps the cross will placate the ghosts.

Amidst the mayhem, the Bible is shown, open on its stand, between two lighted candles and beneath an icon. It's completely ignored. Father Malone struggles out with the cross, which is taken by the ghosts. He, of course, does get his after we think the ghosts are gone.

Here's an example of a false Bible—the journal—eclipsing the real thing. The actual Bible shows up in the background, never read or even referred to. The journal, on the other hand, is read religiously. The role of this false Bible is to condemn the guilty, a task normally reserved for the Good Book.

The Fog was remade in 2005, directed by Rupert Wainwright. Interestingly, it's been noted that the remake focuses less on "religion" than the original, where the climactic scene took place in the church. The 2005 version places its climax in the town hall of Antonio Bay (now set on an island in Oregon). Ironically the Bible is more obvious in the remake although the church is less evident. In fact, the church is shown only in one scene in the Wainwright version, and it's locked. Father Malone (Adrian Hough), however, does quote the Bible when he shows up, something he didn't do in the original.

The trope of the drunken priest is perhaps too good to pass up even for a remake, but Father Malone in 2005 isn't explicitly the grandson of a priest. His grandfather Patrick (Christian Bocher) was one of the conspirators who burned the *Elizabeth Dane* after stealing all the money from the lepers on board. The cause of the fog shifts from the anniversary of the incident to the accidental dredging up of the wreckage by Nick Castle's fishing boat (which also appears in the original version). The anchor snags some remains from the *Elizabeth Dane* and the fog rolls in.

The character of Father Malone shows up relatively late in the movie, drunk and in the cemetery where he's found by Elizabeth Williams (Maggie Grace). Written in red on the side of his family mausoleum are the words "Mene, mene, tekel, eupharin," from Daniel 5:25. The last word is, interestingly, misspelled. Elizabeth, unaware of what this might be asks the priest. "It's from the Bible," he says. "It's the writing on the wall." He's correct—the origin of that phrase comes from this Bible story in Daniel. It's false in the sense that it's misquoted, but what does it mean?

In the biblical context Belshazzer, king of Babylon, has thrown a feast. In his exuberance, he has the sacred vessels plundered from the Jerusalem temple brought out as secular drinking cups. A mysterious hand writes "mene mene tekel upharsin" on the wall. The words, written not in any known language according to the Bible, mean "God hath numbered thy kingdom, and finished it…. Thou art weighed in the balances, and art found wanting…. Thy kingdom is divided, and given to the Medes and Persians." Not exactly what you want to hear at the height of a party. Belshazzer gives half his kingdom to Daniel, then loses the whole thing that very night. The movie is trying to convey this sense of dread by using this mysterious biblical quotation. The drunken Father Malone, for those aware of the biblical story, reflects the drunken Belshazzer. He's also the prophet Daniel because he can read the writing.

Elizabeth finds the diary of Patrick Malone, but it doesn't have the same visual command that it had in 1980. It's almost a false false Bible. Once again it explains the plot against the lepers. "The answers are in here somehow," Elizabeth insists. That's an expression typically used of the Bible (remember Homer Simpson). The diary is nevertheless a stand-in for Scripture.

The next meeting with Father Malone includes him quoting the Daniel words correctly, "Mene, mene, tekel, upharsin." He then gives his translation, "We've been weighed in the scales and found wanting." This ties in to the scales on the hallmark of the metal items taken from the *Elizabeth Dane* which have been washing up on shore. It ignores the other two parts of the writing that provide the context for being weighed in the scales. Quoted out of context, this Bible is false.

The fatal fog closes in and the principals gather in the town hall. Before being sliced to death by the broken glass of shattered artifact cases, Father Malone has his last say: "The sins of the fathers are visited on the heads of the children." This biblical-sounding quote doesn't occur in this exact form in the Bible. It's a loose rendition of Numbers 14:18, or the Ten Commandments—there are several passages that address the passing of guilt for sins from generation to generation. The idea's biblical although the conclusion isn't made explicit in Holy Writ. Some places in the Bible each generation is responsible for its own sins. In others, most notably Exodus, Numbers, and Deuteronomy, the sinful activities of parents can doom their children for generations. In that sense, *The Fog* reads the Bible correctly.

Comparing these two films shows that even a false Bible can change. In 1980 the Bible sits there, respectfully in the background. The journal, a false Bible, is consulted instead. In 2005 religion is almost absent, but the Bible is more active, being not seen but quoted. Like many Bible quotations in the movies, it's a precursor of doom. Because Elizabeth is willing to sacrifice herself (itself a biblical trope), Nick Castle (Tom Welling) becomes the "final boy," the only surviving scion of that sinful original generation. The function of the Bible here is prophetic—it correctly predicts the doom to come. Even a false Bible can't get that wrong.

Stigmata (1999)

In *Stigmata* we encounter yet another type of false Bible. Without going into all kinds of unnecessary details here, it's enough to know that the Bible Christians recognize doesn't include all the books from early Christian times. Other documents just as old as the Bible exist. Some even older. These books were known by many early Christians but were never included in the standard list of books that became official Scripture. That process was long and complicated and involved some horror movie elements itself. Bishops behaving badly.

What you need to know before we start our next flick is that one of those ancient books was the *Gospel of Thomas*. It's a real book and some scholars argue it should be included in the Bible. Problem is, the Bible's entrance exam's been closed for quite a few centuries now and getting all, or even most, Christians who use it to consider adding another book, well, let's just say it's not likely to happen. The Bible's already a *Ding*. So dim the lights and get ready for horror that features this false Bible of a lost gospel.

In Belo Quinto, Brazil, an old priest, Father Alameida (Jack Donner), hunches over an ancient manuscript. Upon his death a statue of Mary sheds tears of blood. Hundreds of faithful flock to the church. Father Andrew Kiernan (Gabriel Byrne) makes his way through the crowd. On a side trip from his assigned investigation at Sao Paulo he stops to test the statue. Father

Alameida's coffin stands open in the sanctuary. A supernatural wind blows
through, setting doves to flight. A small boy takes the rosary from the dead
priest's hands and sells it to a tourist. The woman mails it as a gift to Frankie
Paige (Patricia Arquette), her daughter in Pittsburgh.

So begins *Stigmata*, an underrated horror film that gets the incessant rain
in Pittsburgh just about right. The false Bible in *Stigmata* is a fictional *Gospel
of Jesus Christ*, said to be written by Jesus himself. The end cards will reveal
this is actually the *Gospel of Thomas*, just mentioned. Although quite biblical
the movie is based on a false Bible. (By the way, this is simply a category to
view the film and makes no judgment on the actual *Gospel of Thomas*.)

In Vatican City Cardinal Daniel Houseman (Jonathan Pryce) accepts
Father Kiernan's report from South America and removes him from the case.
A scientist turned priest, Andrew Kiernan investigates claims of miracles for
the Congregation for the Causes of Saints. The Cardinal clearly doesn't want
him looking into this mysterious dead priest. Meanwhile in Pittsburgh
Frankie is taking a bath, wondering if she's pregnant. Suddenly she's dragged
under the water and receives stage one stigmata—her wrists are punctured.
She's rushed to the emergency room.

At the Vatican library Andrew Kiernan visits Father Gianni Delmonico
(Dick Latessa), a priest who's been secretly translating the *Gospel of Jesus
Christ* for the church. Father Delmonico reveals that three translators are
given every third page and that only someone with great power ever sees the
full document. The church is afraid, he implies, of anyone getting ahold of
an alternative gospel. He notes that there are 35 ancient gospels, some of
them suppressed. Unlike those in power the translators are like blind men in
a cave, groping for light.

Before we go on here—while this may be news to some people, biblical
scholars work on obscure ancient documents that aren't in the Bible all the
time. New documents are occasionally recovered and most never make the
news like the *Gospel of Judas* did a few years back. The church (Roman
Catholic, in this instance) doesn't suppress this scholarship, but actually
encourages it. That openness doesn't make for gripping horror, though. How
many gospels are there? The answer's complicated by the incomplete status
of ancient manuscripts and the fact that authors of the period mention gospels
that haven't survived. According to experts about three dozen non-biblical
gospels are known, showing Father Delmonico to be about right with 35.
Someone did their homework. Back to the flick.

Frankie has a vision of a woman throwing her baby into traffic. Her
friend Donna (Nia Long) takes her home on the subway. Frankie, acting possessed, confronts Father Durning (Thomas Kopache). The subway car rockets

out of control. Grasping the handholds, Frankie is scourged with invisible whips as Father Durning watches. She's sent to the hospital for more tests, and the doctors suggest she might have epilepsy. Father Durning acquires the surveillance tapes of the subway incident and sends them to the Vatican. Cardinal Houseman, seeing a way of getting Father Kiernan onto what he mistakenly thinks is an unrelated case, sends him to Pittsburgh.

A word about stigmata. Stigmata are actual phenomena that occur, but the current explanation is generally that they are self-inflicted. Most commonly stigmata appear as bleeding wounds on the hands and feet. Stigmata don't happen in the Bible, but the idea is based on the wounds of Jesus according to the gospels, so it's "biblical" in that sense. Let's just say stigmata have a biblical context. Historically Francis of Assisi ("Saint Francis") was the first stigmatic. The word "stigmata" can be translated as "signs."

Father Kiernan finds Frankie at work and interviews her but stops when he learns she's an atheist. As he explains what stigmata are, he tells her only the holiest of people ever receive the wounds of Christ. Frankie reveals that she has been writing in a language she doesn't know. She gives Kiernan an Italian quote from the ancient gospel. She's developing feelings for this priest, but it's all business with him. She researches epilepsy and stigmata. At the club that night she finds Donna and is about to leave when she receives the wounds from the crown of thorns, the third stage of stigmata. Andrew Kiernan meets her outside her apartment building and chases her as she flees. More supernatural signs occur. She scratches Aramaic onto the hood of a car with a broken bottle. She shouts at Kiernan in the same language. Andrew and Donna take her to Father Durning's church. Back in her own mind, she notices the crucifix. Since crucifixion involves nails through the hands, not the wrists, this can't be stigmata, she states. But Father Kiernan informs her that scientifically her wounds are more accurate. He's actually correct on this point.

When Father Delmonico hears, over the telephone, the tape of Frankie's unknown language he warns Father Kiernan that this is a Galilean dialect of Aramaic that hasn't been spoken for 1900 years. He should cease investigating.

A word about Aramaic. Aramaic is an ancient language closely related to Hebrew. Most Jews during the New Testament—or Early Rabbinic—period spoke Aramaic, including Jesus. The Bible itself was originally written in Hebrew and Greek, but there are small sections of Aramaic in it. The familiar "Hebrew" script is actually an Aramaic script. The letters shown in the inscriptions in the movie are closer to actual ancient Hebrew letters but they add to the effect by being unfamiliar to most viewers.

Andrew visits Frankie again. She's apparently possessed. She's writing Aramaic all over her apartment wall. Andrew photographs it and sends it to Father Delmonico. The older priest begs him to leave the investigation, to put away the evidence forever. The Vatican, getting a glimpse of the photographs emailed to Delmonico, insists that Andrew cease his work on Frankie's case. The two, however, are clearly falling in love.

While at an outdoor cafe, Frankie receives the fourth set of wounds as her feet are supernaturally pierced. Andrew nurses her in her apartment but refuses to sleep with her. Frankie, again possessed, assaults the priest and levitates into a cruciform pose. Andrew assures Frankie that no one has ever received the fifth and final stigmatic wound of a spear thrust to the side. It would be fatal.

Cardinal Houseman, along with his deacon and Father Durning, find the two in her apartment and take them to the Archdiocesan offices. Houseman dismisses Father Kiernan back to Father Durning's church. There he meets Marion Petrocelli (Rade Sherbedgia), an excommunicated priest who, along with Delmonico and Alameida, had been translating the *Gospel of Jesus Christ*. It was a gospel written by Jesus himself. Petrocelli and Alameida were excommunicated, but the latter kept up his work of translating the forbidden gospel. It's now lost forever. The church has suppressed it. Meanwhile at the Archdiocese, Cardinal Houseman attempts an exorcism on Frankie, followed by attempted murder. The girl cannot live if she threatens the church.

Andrew realizes that Frankie has been possessed by Alameida and he arrives at the Archdiocesan office just in time to save her. The room bursts into flames and Andrew asks Alameida to take him instead, *a la The Exorcist*. The fire extinguishes itself and Frankie, now resembling Saint Francis (who she's named after—the original stigmatic) recovers from her wounds.

Father Kiernan returns to Belo Quinto and recovers the lost gospel from under the floor of the church. The end intertitles reveal that the *Gospel of Thomas*, found at Nag Hammadi, Egypt, is the closest gospel to Jesus' actual words. The Catholic Church, it says, does not want to include it in the Bible.

There is a touch of heavy-handedness in this. The Catholic Church, indeed, any church, can't add anything to the Bible. It's a *Ding*. As such it can't really be altered in any substantial way. Catholics and Protestants alike acknowledge that the *Gospel of Thomas* is a remarkable book. It was found at Nag Hammadi in the 1940s, but it was also known from fragments found elsewhere in Egypt. Many scholars do suggest that it may be the closest we might come to the actual words of Jesus, but there's no consensus on that point. Catholics aren't forbidden from reading it, and it's mostly of interest to biblical scholars.

The suppression of gospels hasn't really been a problem since the first few centuries of Christianity. The way the Bible came together was through a gradual process of accumulation. Prior to Christianity, Jews had gathered the first five books of the Bible—the Torah, or Pentateuch—into a "canon" or collection. To these were added a collection of prophetic books. This was probably the "Bible" of Jesus. Before any New Testament pieces were added, a third section of the Hebrew Bible, or Old Testament, came to be circulated with the Torah and Prophets. This section was called "the Writings." Paul's letters began to be gathered and several gospels were written. An early consensus settled on four Gospels: Matthew, Mark, Luke, and John, as representing Jesus and his teachings. These, and Paul's letters, were used in churches along with the "Bible" of the "Old Testament." The book of Acts and other letters were included eventually, and also Revelation, or The Apocalypse. The process took centuries.

Various books were disputed along the way (Song of Songs, Ecclesiastes, Revelation), and some were never part of the "official" collection (many gospels, *The Didache*, *The Shepherd of Hermas*, and other texts). Books like the *Gospel of Thomas* were known in the early church, but they were not included in the Bible. They weren't exactly suppressed either.

Having said that, *Stigmata* makes good use of both horror themes and a book that never made it into the Bible—in that sense it's a false Bible. There would have been no story here had the fiction of the gospel's suppression not been added: girl gets stigmata. Not an especially gripping tale. As it is, *Stigmata* revolves around the translation and significance of a gospel that until recently was little known outside the rarified realms of biblical scholarship. The *Gospel of Thomas* is a "sayings gospel"—it doesn't narrate the life of Jesus but contains his teachings. The acting out of the wounds of the crucifixion is somewhat ironic in that setting, but together with a "mystery gospel" it makes appropriate use of an iconic book.

The *Gospel of Thomas* is a "Gnostic" gospel. The Gnostics, while perhaps not an organized group under that name, were early Christians who had different beliefs about the nature of Jesus—and of reality—than the form of Christianity that "won" by becoming the official religion of the Roman Empire under Constantine (also the title of another film to be considered presently). Scholars now are accustomed to speaking of Christianities rather than suggesting that there was one, correct form of the religion. Many competing views existed side-by-side and what eventually became Roman Catholicism wasn't "the original," but rather the most enduring form. The Orthodox would dispute even that. While it isn't unusual for a horror movie to play the "based on a true story" card, here the true story is more complicated than a Dan Brown movie.

The film is about the Roman Catholic Church refusing to accept the Bible (here a fictional gospel or false Bible). Lest there be any doubt on the point, the end cards make it explicit. The problem is that both the history of the church and the Bible are much more complex than they might seem at first. And things get even worse with Anti-Bibles.

Anti-Bibles

Take a step beyond false Bibles and we'll reach Anti-Bibles, the second kind of deceptive scripture we find in horror. Anti-Bibles may or may not include the actual Bible. These are sinister scriptures that are clearly based on the iconic Bible. Anti-Bibles are evil books, or books of evil religion. Instead of an iconic Bible's salvation, they lead to damnation. Sometimes the victims wander into this territory accidentally (as in *The Evil Dead*) and other times it's intentional (*The Ninth Gate*). What these books have in common is their iconic status, but they function as Bible opposites. It makes sense that we find one among the wicked departed.

The Evil Dead (1981)

If you've come this far along this spooky journey you'll know that the iconic Bible comes in a number of different physical forms. In many horror movies the Bible is the familiar, leather-bound book, Genesis through Revelation. In other instances the Bible is actually not the Bible but another ancient, or old, book that looks like the Bible and which inevitably, in psychological guise, suggests the Bible. Sometimes the Bible itself comes with such psychological freight that to interject the actual sacred text into a movie would destroy the mood. Who knows? The Bible might really be regarded as a magical text and writers or directors don't want to risk offending the powers that be.

The Evil Dead is amazing for its longevity and continuing popularity. Sequels are still being made. The first installment of the franchise offers an excellent example of an Anti-Bible. The plot is quickly summarized: five young people go to a cabin in the woods for the weekend. They find a book of curses that brings demons against them. One by one, they're possessed and dispatched. In the dawn's early light, only one survives.

Iconic books, we've noted from the beginning, are in some ways interchangeable. They don't swap places completely, but by their nature they suggest one another. Ancient sacred books, especially in an American context, point toward the Bible. We have seen this in some of the movies already discussed, and we'll see it again. Bible and non–Bible easily morph into one another. Books that clearly aren't iconic are easily distinguished from the Bible.

This reminder helps for *The Evil Dead* since the book in question is most decidedly not the "Holy Bible." It's a fictional grimoire written in Sumerian. The Sumerians were rediscovered in the nineteenth century by "biblical archaeologists" traveling and digging in what is currently Iraq (also the nation of *The Exorcist's* nemesis). The Sumerians had been long forgotten by the time of the Bible (where they're not even mentioned). They are, however, the most ancient civilization known and they seem to have invented writing itself. In the popular imagination they're more often associated with "ancient astronauts" than horror. (*The Fourth Kind*, for example, is based on that premise and crosses over between alien abduction films and horror and includes Sumerians. See Chapter 7.) The Sumerians wrote on clay tablets, not in books.

Sam Raimi's *The Evil Dead* is a cult classic. Known for it's over-the-top gore and establishing the motif of five college kids in a cabin in the woods (revisited in *Cabin Fever* and parodied in *Cabin in the Woods*) the movie has the group discover a creepy old book. The book's in the basement of the cabin, along with a tape recording that reads the incantations written inside. The tome is identified as the *Book of the Dead* in a Sumerian version called the *Naturom Demonto*. All of this requires a bit of explanation.

The *Book of the Dead* is a name given to ancient Egyptian scrolls intended to prevent the deceased from getting hijacked on the way to the afterlife. The Egyptians and Sumerians didn't exchange literature. Some scholars suggest writing might have developed independently in Egypt, but the Sumerians had largely disappeared by the time trade relationships flowered between Egypt and Mesopotamia (the Sumerians lived in southern Mesopotamia). If there had been literary borrowing it would've likely gone the other way since the Sumerians developed writing first. In any case, the Egyptian *Book of the Dead* is an actual grimoire—a book of spells. Its magic was intended to help the reader navigate the hazards on the way to the afterlife. Spells and instructions are provided to help the dead overcome obstacles along the way.

To make matters more interesting, there is another, completely unrelated ancient text called *The Tibetan Book of the Dead*. This is the *Bardo Thodol*, written in the fourteenth century (CE) and therefore very far removed from the Sumerians. In the popular imagination, though, it sounds a lot like the Egyptian grimoire because of its English title. Neither the Egyptian nor Tibetan books have anything to do with *Naturom Demonto*.

The Sumerians had no known "Book of the Dead" and *Naturom Demonto* is a book invented for the movie. The script shown in the film's book is cuneiform (wedge writing), something that was never done on paper—whether made of human flesh or not.

Grimoires, as explored in Chapter 2, share conceptual territory with the Bible in the popular imagination. Indeed, Ancient Near Eastern texts were originally discovered by scholars looking for further information on the Bible. Today, in many university settings, Ancient Near Eastern courses are still taught by Bible faculty (and vice versa). What makes *Naturom Demonto* an Anti-Bible, then? For a society with only vague ideas of such things, an ancient iconic book is an iconic Bible. In this case, it's essentially an evil twin of Holy Writ. An Anti-Bible.

This book's role is the exact opposite of salvation. It's clearly an effective ("performative") book. Reading its contents brings damnation to the readers. Consider that the Bible is informally called "the Book of Life." This is the *Book of the Dead*. In the popular imagination the Bible is about Heaven and its minions. The *Book of the Dead* is here presented as a book of demons, the denizens of Hell. As we might expect by now, this doesn't end well for the college kids. Splatter films seldom do. Ash (Bruce Campbell), the protagonist, is a sole survivor of the five—another "final boy." The iconic book has shifted from "white magic" to "black magic." From salvation to damnation.

Interestingly, *Naturom Demento* is occasionally misidentified as H. P. Lovecraft's fictional *Necronomicon*. One source defines it as "a bible of black magic and witchcraft." Others have noticed the biblical comparison here as well.

Horror films are so much fun in part because they're countercultural. They break taboos and outrage viewers. *The Evil Dead* was intended to do just that. The scene of the tree rape is still decried as misogynistic and unnecessary to the film. The use of *Naturom Demonto* was, perhaps, not a conscious choice of a book to function as an Anti-Bible. That's a category this book is assigning to it. Other films have neutral or zero-sum power Bibles. An evil Bible, however? That's more problematic. We'll see a couple more below.

The Bible is so deeply engrained in our culture as a magical book that it informs the perspective of any other magical book in horror. For a modern viewing public an ancient book of immense power triggers associations with the Bible. This was true in the early 1980s as well. A writer or director may choose to redirect the Good Book in a transgressive way, but that doesn't change the fact of its origin in Holy Writ. This idea is carried on directly, and even more obviously, in *The Ninth Gate*.

The Ninth Gate (1999)

Roman Polanski returned to the Devil theme after *Rosemary's Baby* (see Chapter 5) with *The Ninth Gate*. While many people are under the impression that the Devil shows up frequently in the Bible, that's simply not true. A handful of passages refer to him and arguably the only episode where he takes a leading role is the story of Jesus' temptations (he tempts Jesus to turn stone into bread, throw himself from the temple tower, and fall down and worship him). Beyond that references to the Devil occur here and there, but he's certainly not what you'd consider a main antagonist in line with current beliefs. The idea of an "Anti-God" appears to go back to the Zoroastrian (Persian) religion where a universal dualism reigned. This flick could be considered with the diabolical world in the next chapter as well. Instead, let's focus on its use of an Anti-Bible.

The Ninth Gate presumes a corporeal Devil—the movie is about a book he (or more properly, she) wrote. The story revolves around Dean Corso (Johnny Depp), an unscrupulous antique book investigator. Notorious for his ruthlessness, he's hired by Boris Balkan (Frank Langella), an exceptionally wealthy owner of the world's largest collection of books on Satan. Balkan's passcode to his private collection, both on his elevator and the actual door is the rather guessable 666. Balkan has been trying to raise the Devil. Literally. The book necessary to do so is *The Nine Gates of the Kingdom of Shadows*. It's a book—made up for this movie—that exists in only three copies, said to have been written by Satan himself. Or by Aristide Torchia, in 1666 (note the year). Balkan, who is so bad that not even other Devil aficionados want to have anything to do with him, purchased the book from an Andrew Telfer (Willy Holt), whose suicide opens the movie. Balkan hires Corso to find out if the book is authentic, since rumor has it that only one of the three copies is.

Clearly a book written by the Devil can be classified as an Anti-Bible. It's an iconic book and the damnation it offers is considered salvation by Balkan. Corso is merely mercenary about it—he's in it for the money. His experience of "damnation" will, however, be his salvation.

Since the other two copies of *The Nine Gates* are in Europe, Corso will need to travel there to compare the copies, says Balkan. Then strange things start to happen. Corso notices people following him. His apartment is ransacked in his absence. Liana Telfer (Lena Olin), Andrew's widow, comes to his apartment and has sex with him and then attacks him when she doesn't find the book. His friend Bernie Rothstein (James Russo), a used bookseller who assists him, is murdered in a bizarre way. Although Corso wants out, Balkan insists he press on to Europe.

In Toledo, Spain, Corso locates the Ceniza brothers, who sold the book to Telfer. They vouch for its authenticity. On the train to Sintra, Portugal, he meets a girl (Emmanuelle Seigner) he's seen before, in Balkan's class and in a library. He supposes she's following him. He visits the lonely, elderly Victor Fargas (Jack Taylor), owner of the second copy of *The Nine Gates of the Kingdom of Shadows*. Discovering that the engravings differ from those in Balkan's copy, he notes that in each three of the nine were engraved by LCF, or Lucifer. The remaining six in each are by AT, Aristide Torchia. After being chased down by a murderous driver, Corso returns to his hotel to find the girl yet again. She awakens him the next morning to take him to Fargas' manor to show him the old man has been murdered. The second copy of *The Nine Gates* has been burned, but not before the engravings had been torn out.

The girl flies with Corso to Paris where the last copy of the book resides. Baroness Kessler (Barbara Jefford), an expert on the Devil, refuses to let him examine the book when she discerns Balkan is involved. Hiding Balkan's copy in his hotel room, Corso convinces the Baroness that the engravings differ in each of the copies, but he's attacked and she's murdered before he can solve the mystery. The book is burned in a fire that destroys her library.

The villainous driver again tries to run Corso down. As he gets out of the car and beats up Corso, he's fended off by the girl, who floats to Corso's rescue. At the hotel, his book is missing—Liana Telfer has posed as his wife while he was out and had stolen the only remaining copy. At this point it's worth noting that the name Telfer has a more than passing resemblance to "Teufel," the German word for "Devil." Indeed, when the girl and Corso follow Liana to her ancestral estate, a Satanic ritual is underway in which she tries to raise the Devil. Balkan intervenes, killing Telfer and taking the book back himself. What of Balkan's name? If we turn to *The Late, Great Planet Earth* (see more in Chapter 5) we learn that the Antichrist is likely to arise from the Balkan Peninsula. The villain's first name, after all, is Boris. The girl, flying down from the upper story, prevents Corso from attacking Balkan. Corso surmises that she's been working for Balkan all along.

Balkan now has all nine original engravings by Lucifer. Three had been removed from Kessler's book before the fire. In the lower rooms of a ruined castle, Balkan prepares to summon Satan. His mission goes awry and he ends up immolating himself. Corso saves the engravings and flees. The girl, waiting in Corso's stolen car, rewards him with sex and it's pretty clear that she is, against the backdrop of fire, the Devil. He asks why the ritual didn't work. She reveals that one of the engravings is a forgery. In the now closed Ceniza bookstore, Corso finds the true page with the original engraving and returns to the castle which accepts him in a blaze of unnatural light.

The Nine Gates of the Kingdom of Shadows is another Anti-Bible. In opposition to the Bible which is "written by God," *The Nine Gates* is a book written by the Devil. As with the Bible there were human scribes. Only three engravings in each copy are from Lucifer's own hand. The books, however, are leather-bound and sacred. They're also performative—using the book in the correct, diabolical, way will raise Satan. This, considering *Rosemary's Baby*, is rather a recurring theme among these Polanski films.

Like the iconic Bible, the iconic Anti-Bible needn't always be read to be effective. In *The Evil Dead* the book was inert without reading, but here that's immaterial. In fact, the ritual raising of the Devil is done irrespective of the text—only the captions of the engravings matter. When Corso enters the castle at the end, he isn't even shown reading the Latin captions. An iconic book works without even having to be read at all.

So is there such a book? As we saw in *Sleepy Hollow*, actual grimoires are often referenced as iconic books. In this case the title and look of the book are intended to resemble *The Book of Shadows*, a grimoire associated with witchcraft (and featured in *The Blair Witch Project 2: Book of Shadows*). "Books of Shadows," however, are intended to be handwritten by the witch. They do not necessarily invoke the Devil. They do occasionally have a pentagram embossed on the cover, such as shown on *The Nine Gates of the Kingdom of Shadows*, but this particular book is an entirely fictional grimoire. Like much else in the movie, it's a chimera.

The Ninth Gate is a movie rich in leather-bound, ancient books. The entire story revolves around them. One's an Anti-Bible apparently more powerful than the Bible itself. The only reference to the Bible in the film comes when Balkan jokes with Corso early in the story that he would bet a Gutenberg Bible that he (Corso) spends half the night with his eyes open. Of course, for Balkan a Gutenberg Bible, or any Bible, would mean nothing.

Films like this are important since many people don't find information on the Devil from the Bible. The conception of Satan largely comes from popular media. Horror movies are one of the major sources for general perceptions of the Devil in the absence of actual biblical references. We'll explore this further in the next chapter. Here we have an entire universe fabricated around an Anti-Bible.

Our last movie of this category could also be placed in the diabolical world of the next chapter, but it's included here because it too has an Anti-Bible. Since Anti-Bible is a category that's used in this study to understand these iconic books, it stands to reason that they are all very different from each other. To find this final example, we'll need to take a side trip into Hell.

Constantine (2005)

Based on graphic novel characters, *Constantine* is a labyrinthine story based on fictionally developed Christian mythology not unlike that of *Dogma*. The storyline, which cites the Bible, goes far beyond its source in developing a Christianesque universe. In addition to the Bible (which is a false Bible) there's also an Anti-Bible. As in *The Ninth Gate*, Lucifer is treated literally, but the divine universe and our world are kept apart on separate planes. Only half-breeds can cross over, so the demons Constantine generally encounters are only half-demon. We'll look more closely at demons in Chapter 6.

John Constantine (Keanu Reeves), our truculent protagonist, is an exorcist. This role falls to him because he could see entities as a child. When nobody believed him, he committed suicide, thus earning a place in Hell. Since coming back from death he's tried to earn his way back into God's graces by dispatching demons. As long as the proper balance of good and evil is maintained, he may send half-breeds back to Hell.

The movie opens with a biblical-sounding quote, but with no source cited: "He who possesses the Spear of Destiny holds the fate of the world in his hands." This is followed by an intertitle that explains the spear has been missing since World War II. The Spear of Destiny isn't a biblical concept, but it's based on a biblical story. Constantine explains to Angela (Rachel Weisz) in the movie that what killed Christ wasn't crucifixion, but the spear thrust to his side. According to the Gospel of John Jesus was already dead when the soldier stabbed him—crucifixion did indeed kill him. The four Gospels never directly state the cause of death, actually. Technically crucifixion is death by suffocation. In any case, for the *Constantine* universe that means the spear, which has Jesus' blood on it, has immense power. It killed God. In some exorcism rites, historically the spear was actually invoked to drive out demons.

As the movie opens Manuel (Jesse Ramirez), a Mexican living in poverty, discovers the artifact under the floor of a ruined building. He then becomes invincible. Constantine, meanwhile, is called to an exorcism. This is no half-breed demon, however. A soldier demon has crossed over and inhabited a girl. The Bible, again, knows no half-breed or soldier demons. The closest it comes are the children born to the women visited by the sons of the gods in Genesis 6. They aren't demons, however, but "men of renown." They may or may not be the same as the giants mentioned later in the same chapter. (This makes up the backstory of *The Fourth Kind*, discussed in Chapter 7.) The Bible is coy with information on the early days of the earth. The origin of demons will be discussed more fully in Chapter 6. In this movie world, or diegesis, Constantine declares that full demons can't cross over onto this plane so that's the fact with which he works.

Angela Dodson (whose name is a clue to her disposition) is a detective. Her twin sister Isabel (also Rachel Weisz) commits suicide in a psychiatric hospital. Her sister's death and John Constantine's lung cancer bring the two of them to the hospital at the same time. Angie and Constantine meet again in a church where they've come to see separate authorities. Angie wants to see a priest about her sister. She wants her to have a Christian burial, not permitted by the rules of the church for suicides. Constantine, meanwhile, speaks to the angel Gabriel (Tilda Swinton) about getting into Heaven. When Gabriel explains he can't be admitted because of his own suicide, Constantine hefts a heavy Bible from its stand and flips the pages in agitation saying, "Who goes up, who goes down, and who understands this stuff?" He throws the Bible to the floor. We've seen this before. A Bible thrown down is like a gauntlet. Shortly after, demons attack. Meanwhile, Constantine and Angie's sister Isabel are thus both doomed to Hell because of "the rules."

The Bible here has the role of a book of commandments. Its laws cannot be broken. There's no possibility of ambiguity. The Bible, however, does not actually address the fate of suicides. Since he requires more information from Hell, Constantine visits Papa Midnite (Djimon Hounsou), the owner of a supernatural club who maintains strict neutrality between sides. There he encounters Balthazar (Gavin Rossdale), a demon who reminds him his time is short.

Angela discovers that Constantine knows about the occult. He rebuffs her until demons cross over and attack her. She isn't a believer, but is forced to confront the demons that are now very real. Constantine agrees to travel to Hell to see if Angela's sister is there. Hell is presented as burning, hot, and full of demons.

The Bible doesn't present a unified vision of Hell. Opinions about life after death in the ancient world were quite diverse. Jesus declares that there is burning, and the book of Revelation adds the concept of a lake of fire. Further mythological development takes place over the years, until an elaborate vision of Hell reminiscent of something out of Dante becomes popular. The earliest origin of this concept goes back to Zoroastrianism, from which Christianity apparently borrowed it, via Judaism. The Hell in *Constantine* is a city glowing with heat and with burned-out cars filling ruined highways. A little bit like New Jersey. Finding Isabel there, Constantine confirms Angela's sister did commit suicide.

After yet another demonic death of a friend, Constantine explains his backstory to Angie. They try to find a clue from Isabel as to why she leapt to her death. Discovering an inscription on the window, Angie admits that she saw things as a child too.

Beeman (Max Baker), Constantine's associate, warns the two that a prediction from Corinthians 17 indicates that demons may cross over into this plane. Angie tells him that there is no seventeenth chapter in Corinthians. Beeman counters that Corinthians in Hell's Bible has 21 chapters. The real concern, however, comes from "Revelations." Beeman has a copy of Hell's Bible. It's written in Latin. He reads it to them over the phone. The Devil's son, Mammon, can be born into this world with a gifted psychic and help from God.

Let's ponder this Bible a moment. First, the details (wherein lies the Devil). There are two letters to the Corinthians in the New Testament. The movie doesn't specify which one has 21 chapters. The title of the Bible's final book is singular: "Revelation," not "Revelations." Here Hell's Bible is treated as the complete Bible—containing more information than earthly Scripture. The other material comes from Hell. As it's pulled from its container, the sheen on Hell's Bible possesses an infernal stickiness. Like *Naturom Demonto* in *The Evil Dead*, and Corso's *Nine Gates of the Kingdom of Shadows*, it's an Anti-Bible. It contains, however, the books of the Bible that are inherently true. What an iconic book declares need never be doubted. This applies even to Anti-Bibles. Iconic books are intrinsically true. This Anti-Bible contains the actual Bible, but with more information added—a motif we've seen elsewhere. Additional material helps the Bible to save. Or damn. Mammon, the biblical word describing the evil of money, is here given as the name of Lucifer's son.

Beeman, attacked by Balthazar, dies. Admitting that she, like her twin, used to see more than other mortals, Angela asks Constantine to bring the ability back. In a diabolical baptism of total immersion, he brings her fully to his team. Since Balthazar threw the balance off by killing Beeman, Constantine wants revenge and can justify the conversion.

Attacking Balthazar with holy water from the Jordan River, the location where John the Baptist baptized Jesus according to the Good Book, Constantine weakens Balthazar to the point of enforcing the last rites upon the halfbreed demon, to send him to Heaven. Constantine is using a coercion technique. Pinning Balthazar down, he pulls a "Holy Bible" from his pocket and begins extreme unction. Once again the Bible isn't what it seems. Here it's a false Bible. The last rites aren't contained in the Bible, but rather in either *The Roman Rite* (for Roman Catholics) or *Book of Common Prayer* (for Episcopalians). The book from which Constantine reads is the Bible. Iconic books are sometimes interchangeable. This film gives us both an Anti-Bible and a false Bible.

Unless a viewer is a devout Catholic (or less likely, Episcopalian) this mistake may be easily overlooked. The point of using the Bible is magical—to send a demon to Heaven ("Hell" for the demon). Angie is kidnapped by an unseen force and Constantine insists Midnite send him to Hell via the electric chair from Sing Sing. In Hell, he is able to discover where Manuel, who carries the spear of destiny, is. He's attacking Angela in the pool where her sister died. As Angie drowns she is sent back to Hell but returns once Constantine rescues her body. She's also pregnant with Satan's son.

Gabriel shows up to prevent Constantine from sending the Devil's son back to Hell. The angel wants to redeem the most noble of humankind by unleashing Hell on earth. Incapacitating Constantine, Gabriel prepares to release Mammon with the Spear of Destiny. Constantine slits his wrists, bringing Lucifer (Peter Stormare) up to claim his soul in person. When Constantine reveals that Gabriel is about to bring Mammon into the world, Satan stops the angel, sends his son back to Hell, and demotes Gabriel to human status.

Once again this dense mythology, based on the biblical worldview, is far beyond the Bible itself. The Devil, never a coherent character in the Bible, has no son. *Rosemary's Baby* and *The Omen* play with this idea as well, as we'll see. (*Lost Souls* will also be considered for good measure.) Angels and humans, according to Holy Writ, are entirely different beings and don't convert from one type to the other. The reason for Lucifer interrupting the birth of his son appears to be that if human nobility becomes a reality then God wins over Satan. The dying Constantine sacrifices himself for Isabel's passage to Heaven and is ultimately himself redeemed.

There can be no doubt that the Bible here is magical and that a densely layered mythology has been built upon it. Many elements from this movie resonate with both the false Bibles and Anti-Bibles we've seen. Without the Bible no world would exist for *Constantine*, but the universe in which the namesake protagonist lives is wildly divergent from that of the Bible itself. In this way the movie is similar to Kevin Smith's *Dogma*. Intentionally comedic, *Dogma* takes biblical mythologies to somewhat extreme lengths. One of the reasons this is necessary in both films is that the Bible raises intrinsically fascinating concepts but doesn't discuss them thoroughly.

The Bible was not a book planned in advance, so characters and ideas from one book don't necessarily carry over into the next. Angels, demons, Heaven, Hell, the Devil, the Antichrist—all of these ideas are introduced but not explained. This situation invites more systematic development of the mythical world. This was undertaken in all seriousness by medieval theologians such as Thomas Aquinas and has continued in a more modern idiom with movies like *Constantine*. To get us there, both a false Bible and an Anti-Bible were necessary. One type of deceptive Scripture remains.

Living Bibles

Our final category of deceptive Scripture is best represented in a couple of thrillers. The original of *Cape Fear* (1962) was a kind of horror film, but the remake—which is scarier—is generally classified as "thriller." The line between these genres is very thin. *The Book of Eli* was never billed as horror, however, it makes the same point as *Cape Fear*, but in a different way. Both movies feature a character who embodies the Bible. They are living Bibles. One is bad. The other may be good, but the reality of that goodness is constantly in question. The viewer sees characters so steeped in Scripture that they, in their minds, become the Good Book. Depending on how they interpret the Bible, things can get pretty scary.

Cape Fear (1991)

Cape Fear participates in horror by virtue of being as scary as Hell. Much of the cinematography of the original 1962 J. Lee Thompson version reflects standard horror shots of movies of the era and it's sometimes classified as horror. Martin Scorsese's 1991 remake ratchets up the fear factor. It illustrates deceptive scripture extremely well. *Cape Fear* is yet another movie in which the Bible played no role in the original but was significantly added in the remake. To show this in some relief, we'll discuss the 1991 adaptation, and note how it imports Scripture missing from the Thompson original, rather like *The Blob* (see Chapter 2).

The story involves a deranged ex-convict, Max Cady (Robert De Niro), who is determined to make his lawyer, Sam Bowden (Nick Nolte), suffer. Outwardly charming and likable, Cady is a violent sociopath with a history of raping and brutalizing women.

In 1962, when the original was released, Alfred Hitchcock's *Psycho* was still fairly new and had spawned not a little shock among viewers. *Cape Fear*, in the original, has characters that would today be called Mary Sues. They don't have any obvious faults (except for Cady). The violence takes place, for the most part, off screen. As noted, the Bible doesn't appear in the film at all.

Scorsese's version opens with Cady in prison, working out. We see a large cross that serves as a set of scales tattooed across his back. The pans of the scales are labeled truth and justice. This is the day of Cady's release. Meanwhile we meet Sam Bowden and his family—his wife Leigh (Jessica Lange) and daughter Danielle (Juliette Lewis). Immediately we notice tension in the family. Although Sam is a successful lawyer, he and his wife have issues, one of them being that they have alienated their daughter. In a further development from 1962, in Scorsese's version Sam was actually Cady's lawyer and he withheld evidence (although for a good purpose) that might've cleared his client, thus giving Cady a reason to truly hate him. The Thompson version somewhat improbably had Sam (Gregory Peck) witnessing a crime by Cady (Robert Mitchum), and although that would set up an adversarial relationship, having Sam actively obstruct the legal system adds a depth of animosity to the remake.

Scorsese's Cady finds Sam and reminds him of their past. Cady then stalks him, poisoning the family dog, and making suggestive remarks about Sam's wife and daughter. Sam tries to buy him off, but Cady has spent his time in prison reading and doesn't want money. He knows the law and literature. He quotes the Bible at Sam. "Like it says in Galatian 3, 'Have you suffered so many things in vain?'" The quote, taken out of context, is from Galatians 3:4. As will be later revealed, the criminal knows the Bible far better than the "good guys." The Bible is a sign of public respectability and the ex-convict is the only one to quote it.

In order to drive Cady out of town, Lieutenant Elgart (Robert Mitchum) has him brought in for intimidation. They give him a strip search. The camera focuses on his several tattoos, generally verses from the Bible. One of the tattoos shows the Bible itself, iconically. Among the the quotes are:

- Vengeance is mine NT: Romans, xii, 19
- I have put my trust in the Lord God, in him will I trust Ps 91:2
- The Lord is the avenger NT: 1 Thessalonians iv, 6
- To me belongeth vengeance and recompense OT: Jeremiah 50,15, 28: x, 6,11
- My time is at hand NT: Matthew, xxvi, 18.

"I don't know whether to look at him or read him," Elgart quips. The citation style of the Bible verses is idiosyncratic. Noting whether a verse is from the New Testament (NT) or Old (OT) is not standard in any biblical citation system. The Psalm verse does not come from the King James Version of the Bible, which is the version all the other verses apparently derive from. "To me belongeth vengeance and recompense" actually comes from Deuteronomy 32:35, not from Jeremiah. The citation in Jeremiah is also confused with too many numbers. The point is clear, however. This man embodies the Bible. Technically often in the wrong way.

Such strange citations could well be intended to demonstrate that Cady doesn't know Scripture as well as he claims. Of course, it could also be that nobody supposed a viewer would go through the trouble of looking them all up. (Thank you DVD pause button!) The use of the Bible, in any case, is iconic. It's performative—it brings about an effect. Instead of that effect being salvation, however, it delivers judgment on the admittedly sinful Sam. Throughout the film Max cites biblical-sounding philosophical lines as well, convincing both the other characters and the viewers of his literary aptitude.

When Cady gets Danielle alone in the school theater, he plays to her emotions with religious language. He notes that her parents punished her for their sins, not hers. "Forgive them for they know not what they do," he says, quoting Jesus from Luke 23:34. He insists that he prays for her father because he has a circle of sin around his head, suggesting an unholy halo. He asks her if she knows what paradise is. "Salvation," he tells her. Here we find a point made throughout this book about the iconic Bible. The purpose of iconic books is salvation. Here that point is made by a sociopath.

Sam's private detective (Joe Don Baker), complete with booze and Pepto-Bismol, tells him that he can have Cady roughed up. In a sudden fit of conscience, Sam approaches Cady in a restaurant to warn him. Cady's sitting alone in a booth, reading his black leather Bible. After Sam threatens Cady, the ex-convict lapses into biblical language. "You could say I'm here to save you," he drawls. "Check the Bible, Counselor. The book between Esther and Psalms," he says as Sam walks away. This is, of course, the book of Job.

The thugs attack Cady that night, but his prison-toughened body takes a lot of abuse and he fends them off before quoting, "'I am like God, and God like me. I am as large as God, He is as small as I. He cannot above me, nor I beneath Him be.' Silesius, 17th Century." While this isn't biblical, it sure sounds as if it could be. Like a good scholar Cady cites his sources, even after being thrashed.

The business beating backfires. A restraining order is placed on Sam out of "Christian charity." Cady's lawyer (Gregory Peck) praises the judge for being as wise as Solomon. This is a reference to King David's son in 1 Kings. Several instances in the story of King Solomon present him as especially wise.

Sam is reading in bed. Leigh asks about the book and he flashes her the cover, *The Holy Bible*. He says Cady told him to read the book between Esther and Psalms. Leigh asks which one it is. "Job," he replies, it's about a good man who loses everything, even his children. In a chilling moment the Bible reveals Cady's real target. A stakeout in their house with the private detective goes terribly awry when Cady gets in and murders the maid and the detective, with shades of *Psycho*. The Bowdens flee the scene of the crime, making themselves fugitives. They head to a houseboat, but Cady has strapped himself to the undercarriage of their car.

During a stormy night on Cape Fear River, Cady incapacitates Sam and bursts in to rape his wife and daughter. Danielle throws hot water on him, but he declares, "Granddaddy used to handle snakes in church, Granny drank strychnine. I guess you could say I had a leg up, genetically speaking." His embodiment of the Bible now becomes clear. He hails from a southern Fundamentalist family—snake handing is only practiced by certain Fundamentalist sects, generally in southern states. Lighting a flare, he lets the hot foam run over his hand to demonstrate how he handles pain, equating the Bible and torture. "You ready to be born again, Miss Bowden?" he asks as he prepares to rape her.

There's a lot of biblical stuff going on here. Snake handling is practiced by groups that take Mark 16:18 literally. In this disputed section of the gospel, Jesus tells his disciples that they will take up serpents or drink poison and not be harmed. Most Fundamentalists groups don't put that to the test, but everything about Cady's belief system is extreme. Snake handlers take it literally. Being born again is a reference to John 3, the only chapter in the entire Bible to raise the idea. The citation is associated primarily with evangelical sects. The reference here is used to identify clearly what kind of Bible reader Cady is—an insanely fanatical one. In fact, his use of the Bible throughout the movie is extremely literal. Emphasizing its role as a horror book, rape isn't forbidden in the Bible. Cady is the Bible.

After a struggle in the houseboat, now cut loose from its anchor, Cady puts Sam on trial. He cites the biblical-sounding Dante as he condemns the lawyer to the ninth circle of Hell, reserved for traitors. A fortuitous rock in the river provides the family's means of escape from the boat, but Cady's been chained to a railing. As the wreckage slowly sinks, he first speaks in tongues and then sings a hymn. Cady's final baptism is a very religious one.

It's difficult to suggest any redeeming features of the Good Book here. It's "the law" in the worse possible way. Revenge is only part of the story in the Good Book, but it's the only part this man represents. Cady's an "eye for an eye" Christian and takes verses out of context. He has become Scripture. His words are God's words. The Bible, as a *Ding*, can be used for both good and for evil.

Cape Fear, which added the Bible for the remake, posits a Bible-believing sociopath as perhaps the most frightening nemesis imaginable. Intelligent, well-read, charming, and ruthless, Max Cady can cite the Bible and show it to you in his tattoos. He is the Bible. He can lie as easily as he can tell the truth. And he is out to harm you.

The Book of Eli (2010)

The last use of deceptive Scripture is somewhat more benign. At least on the surface. As the viewer ponders the implications of *The Book of Eli*, however, the Good Book isn't as pristine as it may appear to be in the post-apocalyptic universe in which we see it.

The Book of Eli is a special case among non-traditional films to be considered with horror. Unlike many of the other movies discussed, to understand the Bible's role in *The Book of Eli* is absolutely central to its plot. The movie is considered here for precisely that reason. As for genre, its post-apocalyptic wasteland and muted color scheme suggest horror elements, as do the slashing and blood, but it's generally classed as action, adventure, or drama. A guy being shot through the crotch with an arrow during attempted rape seems enough like horror to be included. Besides, after Max Cady, we need a bit of Eli.

After the war, also called "the flash," civilization, at least in the United States, was largely destroyed. Eli (Denzel Washington), a survivor, has the sole Bible left in his possession. His goal? Take it west where the voice in his head instructs him to go. Along the way he has to fight off hijackers and other desperadoes who want anything of value that he's scavenged. He's essentially a wanderer, almost like Jules in the later years (check out the section on *Pulp Fiction* above and watch the final scene again, if you don't get the reference). Meanwhile, the obviously named Carnegie (after libraries, played by Gary Oldman), a small town despot, is frantic for a Bible. He sends road crews out searching for books. So far, he's been disappointed.

After the war, we're told, Bibles were burned. Some even claimed that it was the Bible that started the war in the first place. It's made it to the list of banned books in a major way. When Eli, a stranger, wanders into Carnegie's town it's like the old west. A saloon fight breaks out. Eli kills a room full of men. Carnegie insists, at gunpoint, that Eli spend the night. Under lock and key. He had confessed to Carnegie that he reads daily and his persona suggests it might just be the Bible he's packing.

In an effort to win him over, Carnegie sends the young Solara (Mila Kunis) to his room that night. Instead of sleeping with her, he has her join him in saying grace and she gets a glimpse of his Bible. The sexual implications underscore the point—the Bible is Eli's body. Under duress the next morning Solara confesses she saw a leather book with a cross on the cover in his room. Carnegie has his men line the street as Eli emerges. Carnegie says, "I need that book. I want that book. I want you to stay but if you make me have to choose I'll kill you and take that book." Eli asks why he wants it.

"I grew up with that book," Carnegie replies. "I know its power." A gunfight breaks out in which Carnegie is wounded. After the showdown on the main street, Eli walks out of town.

Let's pause to consider how the Bible is being used so far. Obviously it's an iconic book. It was a danger to society and was destroyed, and Carnegie, as a petty dictator, wants it to grow his empire. His reasoning is entirely Machiavellian. The Bible has the words to control people. He wants that control. He has to have the book. It would be difficult, either in real life or in reel life, to find a clearer explication of the iconic Bible.

Once his wounded leg's patched up, Carnegie tells his men they're going after Eli. They wonder about the fuss the boss is making over this one book. His response reveals his true motivations: "It's not a fucking book! It's a weapon! A weapon aimed right at the hearts and minds of the weak and the desperate. It will give us control of them. If we want to rule more than one small, fucking town, we have to have it. People will come from all over, they'll do exactly what I tell 'em if the words are from the book. It's happened before and it'll happen again. All we need is that book." At this point it looks like maybe the Bible did start the war after all. Isn't it a Good Book? Depends on who you ask.

Solara follows Eli out of town. After rescuing her from hijackers, he decides to allow her to come west with him. Pursued by Carnegie, they camp out in a cooling tower of a destroyed nuclear plant. Solara sees Eli reading the Bible and asks him to read it aloud. Instead, he closes the book and quotes Psalm 23. That night as she tries to sneak a look, Eli stops her and says that nobody touches the Bible but him. Keeping the Bible secret is essential to the plot—Eli has to keep everyone in the dark until the end. Again, the sexual implications serve to identify man and book. Solara creeps up to a sleeping man and uncovers his goods. The image comes from the book of Ruth.

Another shootout occurs at the isolated house of the cannibalistic George and Martha (Michael Gambon, Frances De La Tour) when Eli and Solara are ambushed there. Carnegie threatens Solara's life, forcing Eli to reveal where the Bible's hidden. Ironically appropriate for this book, it's hidden in a television. Carnegie then shoots Eli and leaves him to die, telling him to pray for him. Solara escapes by strangling the driver of her vehicle and, not having enough fuel, Carnegie, caressing the Bible, returns to town without turning back to chase her. Eli, like his namesake, experiences a resurrection. (Eli, in Hebrew, translates to "my God." The two most prominent biblical characters whose names begin this way are Elijah and Elisha, both of whom raise the dead.) Solara finds him walking west and gives him a ride in the commandeered armored car. She exclaims she can't believe he gave up the Bible. "I thought it was too important to you," she says.

"It was. I was carrying and reading it every day, got so caught up in protecting it, I forgot to live by what I'd learned from it." Eli experiences a kind of conversion here. The Bible as *Ding* isn't so important as what it says. The iconic book is, itself, useless.

Reinforcing this point, back in town Carnegie calls an engineer to pick the lock on the Bible clasp. Ironically, science is here at the call of religion. The lock is sprung, and Carnegie cries out. The Bible is in Braille, which he can't read.

At a colony of civilization on Alcatraz Island Eli identifies himself as having a King James Bible. "It's beat up," he says, "but it will do the job." Calling for reams of paper, he recites the Bible he'd memorized. The Alcatraz community has a printing press and begins to print the Bible once again. Eli dies and Solara returns home to complete her mission. Like Max Cady, Eli has become the Bible. Unlike Cady, his transformation is for the good of all. Or is it?

What is Solara's mission? Is it revenge for the way Carnegie abuses her blind mother? Is it to use the Bible to take over? Will the Bible lead to another war?

The Book of Eli is remarkable for being a major cinema release that revolves intentionally and completely around the Bible without being a Bible movie. The way Scripture's presented, although largely positive, has a great deal of negativity included in it. It apparently started World War Three. It's used to manipulate people. Its control over Eli blinded him (if it may be expressed that way) to its larger message. Only being shot and resurrected has made him realize that. Even so, he carries on the mission to make the book, and its potential dangers, available to humanity again. Scripture is intended to save civilization. Scripture, in the previous dispensation, destroyed civilization.

An even more obvious instance of salvation is presented. Eli becomes the Bible. The physical book is lost to Carnegie, feverish and dying in a town where nobody else cares. Memorizing the Bible is a remarkable feat. In the course of the film, and his life, Eli has become the book. He, in his very person, may bring salvation to the world. Or destruction.

The Unreliable Bible

Iconic books bring salvation. They also have a darker side. They can be abused, as we saw in Chapter 3. This chapter has considered deceptive scripture. Because the Bible is so iconic, it can be recognized even when quotes from it are false, or if another book is substituted for it. The Bible shifts shape easily. Any black, leather-bound book can be the iconic Bible if the situation's right. Any quote can be biblical. When such quotes don't come from Holy Writ they're as false as they are true.

We've seen a variety of deceptive scriptures here. There were false Bibles. Modern books may supplant the Good Book (*The Fog*). Ancient books that come from outside the Bible are just as powerful, if not more powerful, than Scripture itself. In the case of *Stigmata* a non-biblical Gospel wants to be admitted to the club. The Bible is only so big, and horror often brings its own scripture to the script.

There are also, in this Manichaean world, evil Bibles. For every Good Book there's a Bad Book. These Anti-Bibles take lots of possible forms. Grimoires, as we established in *Sleepy Hollow*, may stand in for the Bible. They may also be as powerful as Scripture itself. Read aloud they can raise demons or banish demons. Then there are those who seek the Devil's own Bible. Instead of leading to Heaven it leads to Hell. This is hardly the Bible you'll hear in church or synagogue, but it may be the Bible we see in horror.

Or the Bible can possess a person. That person becomes a "living" Bible. They may be either evil or good. The effect is the same—the Bible brings destruction. And possession is an idea that belongs to a world that includes many characters we've already seen. The Devil, demons, and evil humans populate both the nether regions and horror movies.

Ironically, the Bible in these situations maintains its function of salvation. Jules walks away in *Pulp Fiction*, while Vincent gets shot in the toilet. In the most extreme cases it can lead to damnation, and it's intended to do so. In *Constantine* demons want to go to Hell. Dean Corso wants to bring the Devil up here. *The Evil Dead* has an unintentional influx of, well, the evil dead. What they all have in common is a sacred/diabolical book that aids them in their quest. One person's damnation is another's salvation. This is horror, after all.

We now turn to the frightening realm of the diabolical world that's been glimpsed in this chapter. This is a universe built from biblical ideas. Baleful futures await as the Good Book predicts a cataclysmic end to the world. Ironically, the Bible itself almost completely disappears in this world it's generated.

5

The Diabolical World

She looked like an innocent little girl of about twelve. Living alone in a nearly abandoned house in rural Louisiana, she couldn't help but capture the attention of Dr. Katherine Winter, whose own daughter died at that age. The sky turns dark. The people of the local town of Haven are closing in with murderous intent. The girl, Loren McConnell, has been causing plagues. She turned the water to blood. Killed the fish, the frogs, the cattle, and brought lice, boils, and locusts. She must die. Wanting to help the poor child, Katherine finds herself raising a ritual knife above the screaming girl, about to plunge it in. She's found herself in the midst of "the reaping."

* * *

Much of silver screen horror draws on religion. Some of it draws heavily on the Bible specifically. It may do so while never showing an actual Bible. The films in this chapter are all based on the biblical world set in modern times (considering "modern" to include the seventeenth century), but that world may be quite different than popular perceptions. Scripture will appear in some of these movies, but not all. All of them, however, give us the opportunity to consider just how little the Good Book says about the Bad Place and just how much mythology people believe, based on celluloid.

Since Heaven isn't generally the subject of horror (but we'll consider it to close out this study), we find instead numerous films about Hell and its denizens. This chapter considers various diabolical minions. Rather like the popcorn in Chapter 1, this collection will start us off with an idea of what we will be up against in the nether regions. These movies paint a picture of a universe inhabited by the Devil, demons, and evil humans. We will look at *The Reaping* as featuring Satanists, *The Witch* with the Devil's familiars, *Prince of Darkness* as an example of Satan's son, and *Lost Souls* with the Antichrist/Devil.

Once the stage is set, we'll move on to the Unholy Trinity of horror: *The Exorcist*, *The Omen*, and *Rosemary's Baby*. It would be difficult to overestimate the influence these three films have had on the horror genre. Perhaps not as era-changing as *Night of the Living Dead* (1968), they all nevertheless came within a decade of it, with *Rosemary* being released the same year. These three films defined horror of the early-to-mid 1970s and all three are based on biblical concepts. Common knowledge back in those days stated they were just too scary for religious believers to watch. Today they seem pretty tame, but they revealed a new direction for horror based on the biblical vision of the end of the world (*Rosemary, Omen*) and the very scary idea of demon possession (*Exorcist*).

The *Exorcist* leads naturally enough into possession movies, the subject of the next chapter. We've already seen demons, and we'll see them in this chapter. Possession movies, however, almost constitute their own genre. Although demons certainly inhabit the diabolical world, we'll hold them at bay until after we've met the other hellish people in our neighborhood of horror. This diabolical world simply could not exist without the Bible.

Various Diabolical Minions

In many respects it would make sense to begin this chapter with the Unholy Trinity of *Rosemary's Baby, The Omen,* and *The Exorcist.* To do so, however, would naturally lead to the expectation of discussing possession movies after being primed by *The Exorcist.* Instead of frustrating expectations like that, we'll build anticipation up to this remarkable triad of movies by examining the various denizens of Hell. Also, the other films of this chapter haven't reached the iconic stature of this trinity, so the first shall be last and the last first. Many movies feature witches, Satanists, the Devil, and the Antichrist. This entire book could focus on such films alone. Instead an eclectic group of frightening figures awaits us here, and they'll show that the diabolical world is as complicated as Hell.

First off, we'll meet the Satanists. While not necessarily supernatural, these are the folks who take the Bible's Devil seriously enough to worship him. Also, *The Reaping* is a good example of how the Hebrew Bible can provide its own horror story. Then we'll look at one of Satan's familiars in *The Witch.* This beguiling film presents a world steeped in the Good Book, perhaps so much so that evil's inevitable. Then we'll find Old Scratch himself. There's no shortage of choices for Devil movies, but here we'll watch *Prince of Darkness.* Since John Carpenter's freshman (and best) effort, *Halloween,* simply couldn't fit into this book (no Bible at all), we'll use his Devil film from among the many that exist. Besides, Alice Cooper! And once we've met the unholy father we'll encounter the son in *Lost Souls.* This isn't a book of movie criticism, but this was the most disappointing flick in this book. Antichrist movies began in earnest with *The Omen*, but *Lost Souls* shows just how difficult it is to pull that off well. After we set the stage with these various denizens, we'll go old school with the original Unholy Trinity.

The Reaping (2007)

In a departure from the usual cinematic explorations of the Devil, demons, the Antichrist, and Revelation, *The Reaping* turns to the second biblical book of Exodus in the context of the plagues of Egypt. We've seen Exodus already in *Carrie* and *The Shawshank Redemption*. In the Bible the plagues are described in Chapters 7–11 of Exodus. The Israelites, who came to Egypt as a single family in a time of famine, have been enslaved by the Egyptians for centuries. Moses is sent as their savior, confronting the Pharaoh with a series of plagues—usually numbered at ten—culminating in the death of the first born. Unlike *The Ten Commandments*, *Exodus: Gods and Kings*, or even *The Prince of Egypt*, however, *The Reaping* is set in the present day.

Dr. Katherine Winter (Hilary Swank) is a professor at Louisiana State University. She was an ordained Christian minister, but now she's a scientist who specializes in explaining "miracles" empirically. We eventually learn that while she was a missionary in Sudan, a drought turned the locals against Christianity. They sacrificed Katherine's husband and their twelve-year old daughter to bring rain. Her fellow missionary, Father Michael Costigan (Stephen Rae) now lives in a Catholic institution, but he's discovered, via the unexplained burning of Katherine's face on his photographs of her, that plagues are underway. When placed in sequence the photographic burns form a sickle, a symbol of reaping, of evil.

Father Costigan telephones to warn Katherine, but she is being visited by Doug Blackwell (David Morrissey), a science teacher from the town of Haven, out on the bayou. The local river has turned red and he needs a scientific explanation. Katherine politely refuses, but Doug tells her they're blaming a little girl and they may try to kill her. Memories of her own daughter change her mind. Katherine, now an atheist, drives to Haven with her colleague Ben (Idris Elba). The river has indeed turned to blood, and the fish have all died. As they wade through the bayou Katherine encounters Loren McConnell (AnnaSophia Robb), the twelve-year old girl. When they make contact, Katherine has flashbacks and visionary experiences. Following the girl she winds up in a ruin. Doug finds her there and explains that this is the original Haven, wiped out by three hurricanes in a row. The locals decided to move the town to higher ground.

Meanwhile Ben's caught in the midst of dying frogs. In Exodus, for comparison, the water does turn to blood in the Nile, and the fish do die. The plague of frogs, however, involves an extraordinary number of living frogs overrunning the country. In *The Reaping*, a few dozen dead frogs fall into the already fouled water. To Ben, though, this looks pretty biblical.

That night Doug is grilling seafood for their supper. He turns his back for a moment and flies cover everything. Dinner is ruined. Then the cattle on a neighbor's farm start acting odd. And dying. Ben is convinced this is biblical—the flies follow the frogs and then the death of cattle, according to Exodus. Katherine explains that the ten plagues form a logical chain of events from algae turning the Nile red and killing the fish and frogs, which lead to flies on the decomposing bodies. This is an instance of the writers (Carey W. Hayes, Chad Hayes, and Brian Rousso) and director (Stephen Hopkins) having done their homework. As anyone teaching Hebrew Bible finds out, books explaining the plagues of Exodus in just this way are known by evangelical students. Ironically, such books often suppose such an explanation proves the Bible true, whereas, as in *The Reaping*, the result actually explains how natural occurrences are sometimes mistaken for miracles.

The locals are talking. The girl's mother, they say, is a worshipper of Satan. She sacrifices animals in her basement. Doug claims this is only a rumor. Back at his house, a thunderstorm knocks out the lights. Katherine finds Doug out at a grave in his yard. She learns that Doug's wife died young. They are both surviving spouses. They make love. Not gratuitously, as it turns out.

The next morning Katherine visits the McConnell house. She discovers a sickle symbol carved into a door jamb leading to the cellar. Finding Loren, she sees the girl's experiencing her first period. When she tries to clean her up she experiences a flashback to Loren's brother's death. Her blood ties into the blood of the bayou water and, of course, the Nile.

Meanwhile back in town, an epidemic of lice has broken out. All the kids are shaved. At the morgue Ben and Katherine learn that there really is an active Satanic cult in Haven. The sickle symbol was carved into Loren's brother Brody's back. In the Good Book the sickle is not, however, an evil symbol in this way. In fact the sickle isn't often used as a symbol in Scripture. Reaping does occur as a metaphor of death, but the sickle itself isn't highlighted at all.

The townspeople begin to break out in boils as the plagues continue to unfold. This is in keeping, mostly, with the biblical order of things. The plague of the death of the cattle was, according to Exodus, accompanied by hail, which comes in the movie in the form of giant flaming rocks at the end. Lice aren't one of the biblical plagues, except in the King James Version. The word that all the king's men translated as "lice" is better represented by "gnats." Gnats don't ratchet up horror like lice, however. In the popular imagination anything in too great a quantity can be a biblical plague.

Katherine calls Father Costigan. This is the beginning of the end. At this point the film moves back into apocalyptic territory, familiar from many horror films such as *The Seventh Sign*. The mythology here is completely fictional and not found in the Bible. There is, the priest says, a sect from before the time of Jesus. They brand their firstborn and sacrifice their second born, to bring forth the perfect child, one with the Devil's eyes. This child will bring the sect to power. God will send an angel—Katherine—to destroy the evil. The priest begs her to kill the child as fire breaks out in his room and burns him to death.

The townspeople are preparing a lynching. Katherine returns to the McConnell house and finds the ritual chamber in the basement with the accouterments of human sacrifice laid out. Loren's mother commits suicide and Katherine takes a ritual knife to kill the girl, invoking images of Abraham. The townspeople have arrived, however, also with murderous intent. A swarm of locusts arrives at Loren's bidding and attacks the locals. Locusts are actually a literal biblical plague, both in Exodus and elsewhere. They eat crops, however; they don't kill people directly as they do in *The Reaping*. Ben and Doug escape to the old town ruins. Ben, hiding in a crypt, discovers that children have been ritually killed in Haven for years.

Katherine arrives in the crypt to find Ben murdered. Doug warns her that nobody's safe when the girl is on the loose, and Katherine volunteers to kill her because Loren trusts her, again recalling Abraham. Outside the plague of darkness falls. As Katherine pins Loren down and raises the knife, she again experiences visions when they make contact. The townspeople are the real Satanists. They tried to sacrifice Loren, but couldn't. They need an outsider—Katherine—to do it.

The other residents of Haven arrive as Doug tries to convince Katherine to murder the girl. Katherine now realizes that the angel is Loren. The girl uses her powers to destroy those who are worshipping the Devil—the entire town. The plague of fire falling from heaven begins—the hail is described as fiery in Exodus—wiping out the wicked locals. When it's all over, only Katherine and Loren survive. Final girls. As they drive out of town, Loren asks about Katherine's baby. Her second child, conceived with Doug, the Satanist, is the one who will be born with the Devil's eyes and will initiate the end times.

Like other movies that take the Bible as their starting place, *The Reaping* reads the Bible as a magical book of predictions. The actual book that Father Costigan reads from as he warns Katherine isn't the Bible but most of the plagues are drawn directly from Exodus and are conjured by Loren as a means to punish the evil Satanists of Haven. The town name, of course, suggests Heaven, and that's part of the overall deception pulled on Katherine, as well as the viewers. This town is like Heaven, but the people all worship the Devil.

The plagues in Exodus were intended to free the Israelites from slavery. In *The Reaping*, the plagues are much more personal. Nevertheless, they fully rely on a biblical worldview where God intervenes in nature. The Satanists aren't supernatural, but Loren is.

In this world Father Costigan is an anomaly. He correctly discerns that something big is going down, but he gets the players wrong. He too experiences a plague of flies from his remote location. Yet, although the plagues are from God his "prophet" Costigan dies. This isn't entirely consistent with the universe of *The Reaping*. The sickle burned on the photographs is a warning from God, so why does God kill the priest? How did Father Costigan survive the uprising in Sudan? Perhaps he is a false prophet. He had, after all, misidentified Loren (or was he intentionally deceiving Katherine?).

However we understand his role, we have here a cinematic example of diabolical minions. The Bible is mentioned several times, but is seldom seen. This is a world that lives within the Bible in modern times. Evil is punished directly from Heaven and in true scriptural fashion. This view of the Bible as a template within which the diegesis of a film operates, tends toward an ultimate confrontation at the end of times. In *The Reaping* that confrontation is delayed with the twist ending. Viewers suspected Katherine and Doug were just having sympathy sex as two lonely young adults who'd lost their mates prematurely. The conception of a son with "the eyes of the Devil" is only mentioned after the sex scene when viewers likely have moved beyond that episode as a mere dalliance. The Devil's eyes, however, appears to be an oblique reference to the ending of *Rosemary's Baby*. (Horror films are notoriously self-referential.)

In the end, the nine classical plagues of Exodus took place. The "fiery hail" was taken more as fire than hail, but it culminates the divine attack on Haven. The "tenth plague" was the death of the firstborn. This takes a little mental calculus, but if the town routinely killed off second-born children, and some of the skulls in the crypt are dated from early in the twentieth century, it is a logical extension that the townspeople represent, as a whole, the firstborn. When they are killed by the fiery stones from the sky, the tenth plague is fulfilled. Yet, if Katherine's baby is the evil one, the smiting of the town has all been in vain.

Our next film moves us another step closer to the Evil One. Witches are standard horror fare, but the connection with the Devil is made exceptionally well in *The Witch*. By setting the story in a culture biblical from birth to death it introduces its horror slowly and demonstrates what might've happened yesteryear if there had actually been women who consorted with Satan.

The Witch: A New-England Folktale (2015)

The Witch is an example of biblically steeped horror with very little direct use of the Bible. The setting isn't in any way apocalyptic, and it takes as its starting point an entire society that prides itself on biblical observance. And that includes the belief in witches.

William (Ralph Ineson), a religious and upright man, head of a family of seven, is on trial in seventeenth-century New England. The charge against him isn't made explicit except his beliefs don't match those of the church, but he accepts exile from the town and builds a family home on the edge of the woods far away. The farm doesn't immediately prosper. The eldest daughter Thomasin (whose name ends in the word "sin," played by Anya Taylor-Joy) is on the troubled cusp of womanhood with no prospective husbands. While out playing peek-a-boo with the infant son Samuel (Axtun Henry Dube/Athan Conrad Dube), the child is stolen. The children have been forbidden to enter the forest. After a frantic search the baby is given up for lost. Unbeknownst to the family a local witch has kidnapped and murdered Samuel in order to become young again. There are real witches here.

The family, trusting the Lord will take care of them, attempts to carry on with a normal, albeit already difficult life. William reveals to his son Caleb (Harvey Scrimshaw)—who is starting to notice Thomasin as a woman since he too has no prospects for marriage—that he goes into the woods to hunt. Caleb sees his father is incompetent with a rifle, but William also reveals that he has set traps. The family cannot survive, he explains to his son, on the meager results of the farming. He must go into the forest.

With her mother Katherine (Kate Dickie) in deep mourning over the loss of Samuel, Thomasin is frequently scolded by her as she is given more and more domestic responsibilities. She must watch the younger children, Mercy (Ellie Grainger) and Jonas (Lucas Dawson). Mercy and Jonas tease the family goat, Black Phillip, until he becomes unmanageable. We should pause here to note that the order of this family is in accordance with Puritan understanding of the Bible. The father is clearly in charge and leads his family in prayer and makes the decisions. Katherine, as mother, is in control of the domestic situation, and children aren't to question their elders. Biblical through and through.

One day while Thomasin is washing clothes in the stream, Caleb comes to fetch water and Mercy has followed along. Thomasin wishes to get back at her unruly younger sister. Thomasin tells Mercy she's the witch who snatched Samuel—the family has decided it was a wolf that stole the baby—and that she'll snatch Mercy too, unless she behaves. This is a dangerous game, for in this period witches are taken very seriously. And, in the cinematic universe of this story, there really is an actual witch in the woods.

Witches, according to some views of the Bible, exist. This background led to the tragedy in Salem (mentioned above), some years after this story is set. The famous verse from Exodus 22:18 states, "Thou shalt not suffer a witch to live." In Salem (not in the movie) this caused a true-life tragedy many decades after Europeans had ceased hunting witches.

That night, after leading prayer before a meager supper, during which tense conversation flies, William informs Caleb that he will read the lesson from Scripture that night. The family must have a Bible, but we never see it. Caleb rises very early the next morning to secretly go check the traps. He's still a minor, and when Thomasin catches him sneaking out, she insists on going along into the forbidden forest. They find a rabbit in a trap but the situation gets out of hand. The dog runs off, the horse is spooked and also bolts. Brother and sister are separated. While Thomasin is found by her father, Caleb goes looking for the dog and finds the witch (Sarah Stephens) instead. She seduces him.

Katherine, meanwhile, blames Thomasin for the misfortune. They ought to send her away, she tells her husband in the night. The tension in the shrinking family begins to grow. One rainy night Caleb returns, stark naked, apparently bewitched. He's found by Thomasin. While he's in his sickbed, accusations of witchery are made by Jonas and Mercy. William stands before Thomasin and solemnly asks her if she loves God. If she loves the Bible. Here is another source of witchery for the family—the Bible that won't let them escape sin. Yet they must love it.

As Katherine tries folk remedies to nurse Caleb back to health, he suddenly awakes, sits up, quoting from the Bible. Parts of Song of Songs, a book of erotic poetry, are among the verses he quotes, smiling blissfully. Thinking him bewitched, the family has gathered to pray around his sickbed and Mercy and Jonas begin jerking and twitching, claiming Thomasin is a witch. Caleb coughs up a small apple and dies. Quoting Scripture here is taken as a sign of bewitching. We, the viewers, know that the boy has really been with a witch and was quoting the Bible out of context as a result.

Now that the witch accusation is in the open, William tries to get his daughter to confess. Mercy and Jonas accuse her, but she claims her younger siblings consult with the goat, Black Phillip, as their familiar. William, not knowing what to do, bars his children in the shed with the animals. Someone is a witch, but he can't divine who.

That night the witch does come. Old again, she attacks the children in the shed. In the morning William awakes to the damage, only to find Thomasin alone alive. Is she not a witch? Black Phillip unexpectedly charges him, puncturing his torso with his horns. Katherine emerges and attempts to kill Thomasin. Instead Thomasin kills her in self-defense.

The end of the film rather unexpectedly reveals that Black Phillip is the Devil. Thomasin signs his book and walks, naked, into the woods to join the other witches. Ironically the Bible isn't shown while the Devil's book is.

This movie fits here in the diabolical world since the Puritan outlook on that world included witches. Historically in New England, and Europe before that, this view was based on the Bible. If the Good Book said there were witches, then there were witches. Minions of the Devil, witches gain their power from consorting with him. In some cases the accused claimed to be possessed by the Devil. They sign his book, shown literally in this film.

Scripture doesn't contain many witch stories—in fact, there's only one. King Saul, Israel's first monarch, finds himself abandoned by advisors on the eve of war and he visits "the witch of Endor" to summon the prophet Samuel from beyond the grave. (Actually, in the Bible the dead go to Sheol, a sleepy place underground, and that's where Samuel is.) As with many Bible stories, this episode reveals only enough to inspire curiosity about the details. Plainly read, the "spirit" is really Samuel and "the witch" really did raise him from the underworld.

The Bible also has a prohibition against witchcraft, but this clearly isn't one of its main emphases. Nevertheless, even brief accounts in the Bible can be magnified to major social concerns. An entire mythology grew up around witches—that they fly, or astral-project, and they meet in witches' sabbaths to worship Satan. None of this is biblical, but it's a worldview based on cues from the Bible.

William and his family are pious. They pray—they may not show us a Bible, but the dialogue indicates that they have one on hand. And they know it well. Their outlook on life is beyond biblical, indeed, it's Calvinistic. Early on William tells Caleb that they can't be sure Samuel has gone to Heaven, indeed, none of them can be sure of salvation. Calvinism was a dominant form of Christianity in early New England. While based on the Bible, its theology is rather harsh. Like the belief in witchcraft, its worldview grew from Scripture but it's not the Bible's worldview.

Fearing that one or more of his children are witches, William has little choice but to figure out which. The Bible's explicit that witches should be put to death. That's really all it says about that. William's far from any community with which he might discuss the peculiar happenings in his home. This is what happens when one man is left to interpret the Bible on his own. All his children but one, his wife, and he himself, end up dead.

In some ways *The Witch* is commentary on the witchcraft trials of Salem. In both cases a society immersed in biblical concepts that aren't fully spelled out believes that witches are real. (We'll see this also in *The Conjuring*.) The end of the movie portrays an actual witches' sabbath and the Devil in human form. This entire quilt is stitched together from scraps of biblical fabric. The ending suggests that although the Bible powerfully controls society, the Devil possesses an even more powerful element in controlling nature. While the Bible-believing family lies dead his minion among them can actually fly.

Prince of Darkness (1987)

Since witches consort with Satan, we have to meet the Dark Lord himself eventually. In *Prince of Darkness* the Devil leads to an end-times scenario, but the apocalypse is averted by a priest luckily breaking a mirror.

Alice Cooper, who in the 1980s was often associated with satanic aspects of shock rock, is incentive enough to watch *Prince of Darkness*, although he has no lines in the movie. Actually, this film was touted as being a serious attempt at bringing science and religion into dialogue in the context of horror. It's an uneasy fit, but it brings us to a different biblical world with its own Bible. And it introduces the Devil. And his daddy.

Presupposing the ancient reign of Satan, John Carpenter's effort at theological horror offers an Anti-God that would make a Zoroastrian proud. In St. Goddard's Church, in an undisclosed city in California, the Brotherhood of Sleep has been keeping a secret. This powerful Roman Catholic order has an ancient reliquary—seven million years old—that contains a strange green fluid, recently awakened. A priest (Donald Pleasence) learning of the secret calls in Professor Howard Birack (Victor Wong), a philosopher-physicist, for help. Strange things have been happening that day—the sun and moon are visible together in the sky, ants are swarming, and a supernova's rays have recently reached earth from many lightyears away.

Dr. Birack agrees to help the priest and he brings several graduate students in the sciences to spend the weekend at the church, along with tons of scientific equipment. The homeless people of the neighborhood, led by Alice Cooper, begin to mass as the scientists arrive. Inside the church, the team visits a subterranean room full of crucifixes and burning candles. An ancient book—a palimpsest (an erased and rewritten book)—in Latin, Greek, and Coptic, stands open before the glass reliquary. The various scientists set up their instruments, not sure what they're looking for, as Dr. Birack and the priest privately discuss the matter. Just as there is matter and antimatter, it seems, there is God and Anti-God. The green fluid is the son of the latter. The Anti-God is revealed to be the father of Satan, so the green liquid is, in fact, the Devil. Or is it?

The ancient book is the Bible of this movie diegesis. It contains various biblical-sounding quotes: "I, Jesus, have sent mine angel to testify unto you this thing which shall be unleashed…. Mystery, Babylon the Great, The Mother of Harlots, and the Abominations of the Earth…. And the Prince of Darkness was himself sealed, that old liar, called the Devil and Satan, which deceiveth the whole world…. I saw a star fall from heaven unto the bottomless pit, and he was cast out as water from the flood." The frequent changes of voice and number reflect the confusion of this iconic book. It's 2,000 years old, and is a mix of differential equations and prophecies. Any student's nightmare.

The liquid starts leaking upward and sprays into the mouth of Susan (Anne Howard), one of the grad students. Now a carrier of evil, she infects others by spraying the fluid into their mouths. Lisa (Ann Yen), a theology student who is translating the book, is among her first victims. Students begin dying mysterious or gruesome deaths. Worms crawl up the window. Black beetles swarm. Those who've been killed, or at least some of them, come back to life and menace the living. The scientists can't get out since the homeless murder anyone who leaves the church.

Meanwhile Kelly (Susan Blanchard), another student, ingests the remainder of the green liquid and she apparently becomes Satan. She has to find a mirror, which the reanimated dead can't resist, to pull the father of the Devil from another realm back into this one. The priest is hiding in the room with the mirror and when he attacks Kelly with an axe, she simply regenerates and reaches through the mirror again. Catherine (Lisa Blount), the love interest in the movie, realizes what's happening and tackles Kelly through the mirror, falling in herself. The priest shatters the mirror with the axe, trapping them inside. The world is safe, for now.

Prince of Darkness wasn't particularly well received, and given its convoluted plot and ideas only partially developed, it's easy to see why. Nevertheless, it does populate the diabolical world with Satan, who, it turns out, has a dad. To make sense of that, we need to get an idea of who this "Prince of Darkness" is.

Satan is not a carefully delineated character in the Bible. Indeed, the unified character of "the Devil" doesn't fully emerge until the Middle Ages. We see him throughout this chapter because the Devil is irresistible to horror. There seem to have been many ideas about evil in biblical times and since there was no single church—or Jewish authority—there was no "orthodox" Satan. In the New Testament, where the majority of diabolical references are found, he's described in ways that only hint at who or what he is. Not all of the descriptions fit easily together. He's called the prince of the power of the air. He's the daystar, Lucifer, fallen from heaven. He's the tempter of Jesus and the father of lies. He's named Beelzebub, "lord of the flies" (we'll see this in *The Rite*, in the next chapter). He prowls about like a lion, seeking people to devour (as in *Sleepy Hollow*). In the book of Revelation he's somehow related to, but not the same as, the Beast. None of this is systematized in the Bible itself. (The actual title "prince of darkness" originated much later with the reformer Martin Luther and was reused by John Milton.) Nowhere in Scripture is he described as a red man with horns, cloven hooves, or a pterodactyl tail. In fact, he's not described at all.

Given this incomplete biblical picture, the figure of Satan has been endlessly interpreted and reinterpreted throughout history. Clearly he's a biblical character, but one with only incomplete development. This leaves plenty of room for recasting, whether in the Middle Ages or in horror films. *Prince of Darkness* suffers from not having a clear idea who Satan is either. Kelly seems to be pregnant, but then becomes "the Devil" herself, calling for her "father." This father is the Anti-God the priest describes. Neither the Bible nor the movie have a clear concept of who the devil this is.

In *Prince of Darkness* the big book of ancient languages stands in for a kind of Bible, but the actual Bible itself is strangely absent. When the priest prays for his life in the room with the mirror he's shown reading from an iconic book that could be the Bible, but his words indicate that it's not. It's more of a ritual book acting as a kind of ineffectual grimoire against the satanic forces unleashed in the church. A small book, possibly a Bible, appears at the death of an elderly priest at the beginning of the film, but it's not referenced in any way. The camera's not close enough to identify it.

While the Bible does contain prophecies about "the end of the world," they aren't nearly as prevalent as horror movies might have us think. We'll look at this in some detail among the Unholy Trinity. Of course, the Bible ends with the book of Revelation, which appears to focus on the end times. Biblical scholars tend to think it's actually a veiled account of Roman persecution in the first century, not predicting the last centuries. The first has become the last. That interpretation of the Bible continues to inspire horror movies, as we'll see.

Evil enters the world as Satan's son (*Rosemary's Baby*), the Antichrist (*The Omen*), and the Devil himself (*The Exorcist*). All of these movies reveal the diabolical world more clearly than Scripture does. The Bible offers different end games, but God is always, ultimately, in control. Horror begs to differ.

Lost Souls (2000)

Before we get to the Unholy Trinity, though, we have to get through *Lost Souls*. We met the Devil and glimpsed his father in *Prince of Darkness*. In this last stage-setting diabolical movie, we're about to meet him in yet a different guise. *Lost Souls* has a premise that fits nicely into this framework, however flawed the film itself may be. It's important to see how the diabolical world turns out when you don't do your homework, as in this case. Once we've seen how not to do it, we'll old school with the trio of movies that started it all.

Lost Souls is somewhat like a lost cause. Opening with a false Bible quote, "A man born of incest will become Satan and the world as we know it, will be no more," this flick could fit into the last chapter on deceptive scripture. Its focus on the diabolical world suggests it belongs here, however. What is the source of the intertitle quote? "Deuteronomy Book 17." Deuteronomy, which isn't divided into "books," doesn't mention Satan at all. As noted above, Satan is rarely mentioned in the Hebrew Bible. In reality, it would make much more sense to cite a New Testament book as the source of the fabricated quote, but Deuteronomy it is. False Bible quotes, as seen in *Pulp Fiction*, are hardly rare. There's nothing wrong with using them, of course, but "a man born of incest" singles out a crime where the child has no control. Classic blaming the victim. Also, why isn't the world constantly under the threat of the apocalypse with such a low diabolic bar?

Lost Souls again turns to satanic mythology for a story that seems to confuse the Antichrist with Satan. Setting Maya Larkin (Wynona Rider), as a former demon-possessed woman, against popular writer Peter Kelson (Ben Chaplin), this somewhat dreary movie begins with an exorcism. Father Lareaux (John Hurt) was the priest who delivered Maya from her demonic possession and, in a twist on the usual exorcism protocol, allows her to attend exorcisms as a laywoman. Convicted killer Henry Birdson (John Diehl) has requested such an exorcism. He's shown in his room in a psychiatric hospital scribbling columns of numbers on several pages of paper.

The exorcism fails, leaving Father Lareaux in a coma. Maya decodes the columns of numbers and comes up with the name Peter Kelson. Seeing him in a television interview, she realizes that he's the coming incarnation of Satan.

The movie plods on, giving hints that something isn't quite right with Kelson. He doesn't believe in "evil with a capital E." He declares that murderers can be explained without "third party" entities, such as demons.

Maya first visits him in his office, and then begins to stalk him. At supper with his remaining family (his parents are dead), which includes Father James (Philip Baker Hall), the priest who raised him, they say a conventional grace. Peter, who keeps his eyes open during the prayer, describes a dream he has about writing a book on XES. For a Devil-to-be, Peter doesn't even notice his obvious vices particularly well.

Maya tries to warn the diocese about Peter, but she's rebuffed by the church. Father Malcolm (Tom McCleister) says simply, "Maya, Satan is not what you think he is." Having various creepy visions, one involving XES, Maya tries to convince Peter that he's becoming Satan. Meanwhile, her supporter, Deacon John Townsend (Elias Koteas) attempts to shoot Peter at a publishing party after telling him that the time of transformation is near.

Peter, convinced that Maya is mentally unstable, finds her teaching in a parochial school and orders her to stop following him. She tells him, "You are about to become the Antichrist." Wait a minute—didn't the opening card say he'd become Satan? The confusion deepens here. The plot, already somewhat convoluted, isn't clear on the distinction between Satan and the Antichrist. It doesn't help that neither one, in the Bible, is a coherent character. They are, however, distinct evil entities. We'll discuss Antichrist further under *The Omen*, below. It seems that anything anti–God can stand in for Evil in this movie.

After their hostile encounter, Peter starts to notice things. He learns from a psychic that XES is a Greek number, 666. This also appears to be a movie mistake, since the combination would actually come to 611. Peter has his own doubts. In a church, the corpus falls from a crucifix to stare him in the face as Henry Birdson awakes from his coma. Dogs bark when Peter walks past. His blood type is impossible, based on that of his parents. Is he becoming Satan?

After a showdown with the escaped Henry in the late John Townsend's house, Maya reveals that Peter will transform on his thirty-third birthday, which happens to be the next day. In his apartment he finds a pentacle on the ceiling of his downstairs neighbor's residence and when he confronts his girlfriend about it, Maya accidentally shoots her. Convinced that he will become either the Devil or the Antichrist at the hour of his birth, he visits a church where Father James and his entire family are worshiping. They're revealed to be Satanists. We've seen Satanists in *The Reaping*, but *Lost Souls* tosses just about every diabolical minion in the mix. Satanists, witches (the pentacle), demons (the exorcism), the Antichrist, and Satan himself.

Driving to one of the tunnels in New York City, Maya shoots Peter as he turns 33 and walks away. Roll credits.

This entire movie is based on a biblical idea of diabolical minions, distorted and not exactly easy to follow. How does one distinguish Satan from the Antichrist? Clearly the Bible is a magical book of predictions here, but it presents an interbred diabolical world. Satan, Antichrist, and an ordinary human can all be the same guy. The film's Scripture foretells the coming of either Satan—whom the Bible itself states is already here—or the Antichrist. This antagonist to humanity tries to convince the world through a bestselling book that there is no such thing as Evil. He can't be killed until he actually transforms to Evil personified. Up to that point he's a regular guy dreaming about "xes." He doesn't read the Bible; in fact, nobody's shown reading the Bible—not even the priests. It's Maya's job to ID the Antichrist and to kill him, without the approval of the church.

Compared with *Rosemary's Baby*, *The Omen*, and even *Prince of Darkness*—in which the personification of evil is alive and well at the end, although perhaps trapped just on the other side of a mirror—*Lost Souls* simply has him shot point blank. Join the NRA and kill the Devil. Or Antichrist. This implies that the threat isn't dangerous if only someone will act on their conviction that evil persons should die.

More than that, the only Bible quotation in the movie is false. While incest is prohibited in Leviticus, it has nothing to do with supernatural evil. We considered 666 above (see *Pulp Fiction*), which derives from Revelation 13. The movie doesn't tie it to Revelation at all. The Bible occurs, misquoted, at the beginning and this misreading fuels the entire movie. It tries to introduce Satan, but somehow doesn't rise to the occasion, calling him the Antichrist, a slightly lesser evil, along the way.

There's no preexisting Christian mythology of a man turning into Satan. Satan is widely believed to be a supernatural figure, such as a fallen angel or God's ancient adversary. The Bible can be used to support those ideas. The Devil as a child of incest seems a bit insensitive since such children do exist, and through no fault of their own (remember *The Seventh Sign*). Biblical themes must be nuanced to be scary.

The Omen, by comparison, as we'll see shortly, was a successful end-time flick. Its story is contrived, to be sure, but the Bible does mention an Antichrist and a significant Christian mythology has built up around this figure. No matter how implausible, that mythology has been fully developed by devout believers. *The Omen*, in effect, simply says, "What if it went down this way?" *Lost Souls* says instead, "The Bible doesn't actually say this, but if it did, this is maybe what might have happened." The minions here fail to scare. It's too far removed from what the Bible actually does say to be believable.

There are limits to what even the Bible can save.

The Unholy Trinity

Three very influential movies probing the diabolical world in some depth emerged from 1968 to 1976. All were blockbuster successes and each played into—and even influenced—the Zeitgeist in exceptional ways. Not bad for horror. If you weren't alive in this time period, or have trouble remembering it, let me sketch a brief picture. The Vietnam War was underway. Lyndon Johnson lost influence to Richard Nixon and religion began to enter more openly into politics. Nixon's resignation left many feeling uncertain about the future when an American president could be caught spouting alternative facts. The best-selling nonfiction book of the entire 1970s was Hal Lindsey's *The Late, Great Planet Earth*—an Evangelical exposé of the coming Antichrist and the swiftly-following end of the world. Many Americans were convinced that this was well and truly the end.

Another of the decade's best-sellers was Billy Graham's *Angels: God's Secret Agents*. Yet another title, listed as fiction but featuring the dark angels, also hit it big early in the decade. It was a bestseller by William P. Blatty called *The Exorcist*. In the midst of the fear of political uncertainty and social revolution came movies that showcased the success of the forces of darkness. *Rosemary's Baby* suggested the son of Satan could be here, even now. *The Exorcist* showed how problematic demons could be in an age of science. *The Omen*, taking its script (not quite literally) from Hal Lindsey, showed how easily the Antichrist could access the White House. One of the reasons these three movies had such frightening potential is that the Bible seemed to be backing them. The '60s may have happened, but America was just about to elect its first Southern Baptist, born-again president. The biblical worldview was dominant. Unto that world a child was born.

Rosemary's Baby (1968)

Although it may seem difficult to believe, in the late 1960s and into the 1970s there was a very palpable religious fear throughout America. Self-proclaimed prophets like Hal Lindsey, and later Timothy LaHaye, were declaring that the end was near with a conviction that had many otherwise rational people convinced. Lindsey's *Late, Great Planet Earth* had a theatrical release and his open-collar, easy-going manner combined with his personal conviction persuaded many that the Antichrist was then alive and walking the earth. Fingering the Antichrist had become a kind of popular evangelical hobby, but one taken very seriously. This outlook made *Rosemary's Baby* one of the scariest movies of the day.

Rosemary (Mia Farrow) and Guy Woodhouse (John Cassavetes) are looking for a place to live in New York City. The young couple settle on the Bramford, where an affordable apartment has become available. Guy is a struggling actor and Rosemary has to wait to start a family until his job is more secure. She relies on her older friend Edwin Hutchins ("Hutch," played by Maurice Evans) for advice. Before the Woodhouses even settle into their new apartment Roman (Sidney Blackmer) and Minnie Castevet (Ruth Gordon) insinuate themselves into the younger couple's married life. Much older, the Castevets are grieving over the tragic suicide of Terry Gionoffrio (Angela Dorian), a young woman who'd been living with them and who'd briefly befriended Rosemary. Although Guy is at first cautious about getting sucked into the circle of a lonely, needy older pair, he soon warms to them as the couples socialize.

So far the story has little by way of biblical themes. That all changes when Guy gets his first acting break. A colleague who'd won the part in a play that Guy coveted inexplicably goes blind. Guy gets the part and is on the way up. Rosemary is disturbed by changes in Guy's personality. He spends too much time with the Castevets and working on his career. He placates her by offering to try to have a baby. Rosemary's overjoyed. On their romantic night at home, however, Minnie Castevet stops over. She's brought some dessert, laced with satanic herbs. That night Rosemary is raped by the Devil. Since she ate some of the drugged dessert she's not sure if it's a nightmare or reality.

Her pregnancy's difficult. She loses weight instead of gaining it and she's in constant pain. Minnie Castevet sets Rosemary up with her physician of choice: Dr. Sapirstein (Ralph Bellamy). He assures Rosemary that the pains will go away and that the baby's fine. Hutch, meanwhile, sends her a book that indicates the Castevets are really witches. Hutch suddenly takes ill and dies. Rosemary grows convinced that there's a conspiracy of witches who want her unborn child. The pregnancy pains have stopped but she no longer trusts Dr. Sapirstein. She makes an appointment with Dr. Hill (Charles Grodin), her initial obstetrician before Minnie had made arrangements for her. Rosemary reveals the witch conspiracy to Dr. Hill but he hands her over to Sapirstein and his associates, including Guy.

Back at the Bramford, the baby is born. The woman watching Rosemary tells her the baby died, but she can hear it crying through the walls. Arming herself with a butcher knife, she finds her way through a linen closet that used to connect her apartment to that of the Castevets. There she finds the faithful—the faithful of Satan. They're worshipping the demonic baby. They inform Rosemary that his real father is Satan and that now, at last, the Antichrist has been born. As the movie ends, Rosemary accepts her role as the mother of the child, at least so it seems.

As with the other films in this chapter the Bible frames the story that grows out from a religious world gone bad. The figure of Satan is a biblical character and the idea that an Antichrist will come also derives from Scripture. Neither is fleshed out fully.

Originally "Satan" was a title. "The satan," actually. He was a character from Iranian (Persian) mythology who was a prosecuting attorney among the council of gods. He wasn't evil. He was simply doing his job, like Sergeant Friday. Wandering about the world he locates those who are sinful and accuses them before the gods. In the Hebrew Bible, "satan" mainly occurs with the definite article. Also, he shows up very rarely.

By the time of the New Testament, however, there's a somewhat developed Anti-God called Satan. No "the." We see him as a character in the Gospels. He's evil, the father of lies, and God's true enemy. From that point on the character grows more and more into the Christian explanation for evil in the world. In the Bible, however, he isn't. Eventually he assumes the horns and goat legs of the Greek deity Pan. After some time he becomes a star in Hollywood. Films based on the Devil are too numerous for us to consider them all. This one, however, made the powers of darkness seem real with very little blood and gore and became the first of the unholy trinity.

Rosemary's Baby also follows the trajectory of the mythology of Mary. Rosemary, whose name includes that of the mother of Jesus, is the mother of the Anti-Jesus. The cross hanging upside-down over the black crepe of the bassinet made the connection clear. Yet Rosemary approaches the little fiend with a mother's love. There's some uncertainty concerning whether this is the same Antichrist we'll see in *The Omen*.

Again, the New Testament supplies the backstory. Although not a fully developed character in the New Testament either, the Antichrist becomes the future (or more likely, past, in the Roman world) enemy of God. He'll lead to the ultimate showdown between the powers of good and evil. The logic of *Rosemary's Baby* is that if the son of God had to be born of a woman, so did the son of the Devil. We'll explore this a bit more when *The Omen* rolls, shortly.

There's also a bit of confusion between Satan worshippers and witches here. In the Middle Ages witches were accused of having intercourse with the Devil (as we also saw in *The Witch*). The idea, while not biblical, also plays into the story of Rosemary and will reappear in *The Conjuring* (see Chapter 6). If witches have sex with the Devil, Rosemary appears to be implicated. Without the Devil and the Antichrist, there'd be no story here. *Rosemary's Baby* initiated a series of movies that explored this idea, based on the Bible, to a large audience of horror viewers. The story moves forward almost a decade later in *The Omen*.

The Omen (1976, 2006)

The Omen begins where *Rosemary's Baby* leaves off. Well, not exactly. The characters have changed, but the plot line still takes the biblical scenario of an Antichrist ("the" Antichrist) and moves it forward. The Bible does appear visually—only briefly—in *The Omen*, but the overall story springs from a growing mythology of the end of the world. Since it follows on from *Rosemary's Baby* and was part of the Unholy Trinity of horror of the era let's look for the mark of the Beast.

Of the Unholy Trinity the most obviously biblical is *The Omen*. It's the only film of the trio that shows an actual iconic Bible. Its entire storyline is drafted from a particular evangelical interpretation of scriptural end times. It all begins with a little boy.

Ambassador Robert Thorn (Gregory Peck) is going places in the political world. While in Rome his pregnant wife Katherine (Lee Remick) is taken to a Catholic hospital to give birth. Robert's called in and given the tragic news that the baby didn't survive. Katherine, sedated, doesn't know this and an unwed mother gave birth at the same time and she died in the process. Why not simply give the parentless baby to the Thorns? It would spare Katherine the pain of the truth. The future Ambassador is torn, but eventually decides to go along, for his wife's sake. They name the child Damien (Harvey Stephens).

Robert Thorn is made Ambassador to England and at Damien's fifth birthday party his nanny very publicly hangs herself. Large black dogs begin to appear. A new nanny, Mrs. Baylock (Billie Whitelaw)—a demonic Mary Poppins—arrives somewhat unexpectedly. Meanwhile the addict priest Father Brennan (Patrick Troughton) warns Robert that something is wrong. Thorn, an experienced diplomat, sees this as an attempt to ruin his political image by blackmail and he refuses to talk to Father Brennan. The priest won't give up. Finally Thorn agrees to meet him in a secluded, but public, location. Father Brennan tells the Ambassador that his dead child was switched for the Antichrist. He quotes a poem, "When the Jews return to Zion / And a comet rips the sky / And the Holy Roman Empire rises, / Then You and I must die. / From the eternal sea he rises, / Creating armies on either shore, / Turning man against his brother / 'til man exists no more." This will not end well. The priest indicates that the poem is from "Revelations" (note the plural), but it's not really in the Bible, except in the diegesis of the film.

After Thorn, unbelieving, storms away a literal storm begins. The priest is impaled by an aerial knocked from the church by the wind. Other signs, such as baboons raging against the car as Damien is driven through a safari-type zoo, and his refusal to enter a church, remain mysteries to the Thorns. Katherine is pregnant again and Mrs. Baylock is lurking, along with her satanic black dog.

A photographer, Keith Jennings (David Warner), decides that the Ambassador should be warned. Thorn visits the photographer's studio. Jennings reveals that photographs of the nanny and the priest indicate how they are to die—a kind of diabolical Instagram—before it happens. Since this also applies to Jennings' photo of himself, he insists on investigating alongside Thorn. They visit Father Brennan's room. Here's where the Bible first visually appears. In pieces. Pages torn from the Bible cover every interior surface of his room, even the windows, as if *An American Haunting* had taken place here after a glue explosion. The priest had intended to protect himself from evil. Whether or not the Bible succeeds in this is difficult to say. The priest didn't die while in the protected room. At the same time, the protection didn't extend to the churchyard. The iconic Bible is intended to save from evil—that much is safe to say.

Damien knocks Katherine Thorn off a ladder and down a couple of stories in their palatial foyer, causing a miscarriage. She will later fall again, this time from higher up in the hospital, courtesy of Mrs. Baylock.

Thorn, convinced that some evil has taken hold, travels to Damien's birthplace with Jennings. The hospital burned down long ago and the priest who suggested the exchange of babies was badly injured. He can't talk. He can barely move. He nonetheless points the pair to the cemetery where the mother is buried. On the road trip, Jennings reads from the Bible. He finds the false poem, "When the Jews Return to Zion." At a roadside café, in a typical evangelical scene of two men discussing the Bible at a public table, he reads more. Using Hal Lindsey's explanations of the end of time, he declares the Antichrist will rise from the world of politics. In the cemetery Thorn and Jennings unearth a jackal (anticipating *Pet Sematary*) before being menaced and chased off by black dogs. Convinced that his adopted son is the Antichrist, Thorn agrees to visit Carl Bugenhagen (Leo McKern, uncredited) in Megiddo, Israel, for instructions.

This is one of the instances of unexplained biblical illiteracy in the film.

Megiddo is described as being south of Jerusalem when it is actually well to the north. There seems to be no particular reason for this error other than failure to consult a map. Bugenhagen also says Christianity started in Megiddo, which isn't really the case since the final occupation of the site was nearly six centuries earlier than Jesus. It's never explained how an archaeologist like Bugenhagen became an Antichrist expert, but he's also an exorcist. (The archaeologist-exorcist was likely borrowed from *The Exorcist*.) Bugenhagen gives Robert seven ancient knives and explains how to kill his kid. Well, it's actually not his child, but a literal son of a bitch. Thorn is uncertain; what if this is a mistaken identity? What if the child is innocent? How can he kill a child? Disgusted, he throws the knives away, which sets up Jennings' famous beheading scene *a la* John the Baptist.

Wifeless, friendless, and armed with the knowledge that Damien will bear a 666 birthmark if he is the Antichrist, Thorn returns to England determined to kill the boy. He lures the demonic dog away and cuts Damien's hair to find the birthmark. The cutting of the hair while sleeping is a biblical trope going back to the Samson narrative. Before he can ritually murder Damien, Thorn has to dispatch Mrs. Baylock. Taking the boy kicking and screaming into a church, Thorn is about to kill the Antichrist as the police burst in and shoot the Ambassador.

The film ends with Damien under the care of the U.S. President, and ready to take over the world. The end intertitle quotes Revelation 13:18, bringing us back to 666.

As in *Rosemary's Baby* the biblical structure of the film lies in the pieced-together portrait of the Antichrist. During the 1970s, among many in the evangelical community, there was a strong belief that political events were aligned for the coming of a literal Antichrist. The founding of modern Israel as a nation was understood to be the fig tree coming to blossom foretold by Jesus, it was believed, in Mathew 24. In this mindset, 1948, the year Israel was established, had started the ticking of the end times doomsday clock. Hal Lindsey had published the enormously influential *The Late, Great Planet Earth* in 1970. In a subset of the evangelical culture, the Zeitgeist was just about ripe for an apocalypse. The Cold War continued to worry many, and the European Union, before the days of Brexit, was growing toward ten members—the correct number for the horns on the seven heads of the beast in Revelation 13. The entire Bible was scoured for prophecies to add to this amazing jigsaw puzzle falling together before true believers' eyes. *The Omen* takes its script from Scripture, understood as a kind of Bible code.

The figure of "the Antichrist," although it's been around for hundreds of years, isn't a developed character in the Bible. The groups of Christians concerned with end times had to cobble together a mosaic from lots of separate pieces having only their inclusion in the New Testament in common. For example, "the Rapture" isn't a phrase that occurs in the Bible and isn't really a biblical idea. The word "Antichrist" occurs only in the short letters 1 and 2 John, and there the phrase doesn't refer to "the Beast" in Revelation. Only by bringing these two ideas together (which early Christians did) was a composite character called "*the* Antichrist" developed. *The Omen* claims the three sixes represent the Devil, the Antichrist, and the False Prophet (the latter two from Revelation 13 and 16). In other words, the Antichrist is a post-biblical construction, based on the idea of the Bible as a magical book that can predict the future. The mythology is well-developed in Christianity, due in large part to the chronology provided by the *Scofield Reference Bible*.

David Seltzer, author of the novel *The Omen* as well as the screenwriter, went on record saying that the movie was especially scary knowing that the Antichrist was then alive and walking the earth. This is the "evangelical message" intimated earlier (in the Director's Commentary). That being noted, the movie takes a great deal of its imagery from non-biblical sources. Black dogs, for instance, are a perennial favorite of British folklore, but hardly biblical. More telling, the biblical city of Megiddo, the source of the word Armageddon (which is simply the name of the city in Aramaic with the word "mountain" prefixed to it), is the place where the seven knives (non-biblical) were unearthed. The number 666 is based on a reading of Revelation 13, as discussed under *Pulp Fiction* (see Chapter 4).

Additionally, a number of biblical images are scattered throughout the film for effect. The Samson hair-cutting motif has been mentioned already. Jennings' beheading, placing Thorn (whose name recalls the crown forced onto Jesus' brow) in the role of the Christ to Jennings' John the Baptist, was also mentioned above. Picking apart every biblical allusion here would be tedious and really wouldn't serve to indicate much more than what's already been suggested: *The Omen* is a non-biblical, biblically-based movie that continues the theme of the satanic child from *Rosemary's Baby*. It informs the discussion of the diabolical world by filling in details about the Antichrist. Not exactly the son of Satan here, but pretty damn close.

A word about the remake. To date, among the Unholy Trinity only *The Omen* has had a studio remake. (*Rosemary's Baby* and *The Exorcist* have been made into television movies or series, however.) John Moore directed the revamped *Omen*, which was released in 2006. In terms of cinematography, the new version is superior. In terms of the Bible—as well as the story itself—it's about the same. This is to be expected since David Seltzer is also credited with writing this script as well as that of the original. Mostly a scene-for-scene reshooting, the technology is updated (Robert Thorn [Liev Schreiber] carries a cell phone and Keith Jennings [David Thewlis] uses digital as well as film cameras) but even the actors' voicing is remarkably similar to the 1976 original. The casting of Mia Farrow—Rosemary herself!—as Mrs. Baylock was inspired.

Few of the new scenes, however, make the Good Book explicit. The remake begins in the Vatican Observatory with the sighting of the comet only verbally referenced in the original. Crosscut with scenes of natural and human-made disasters as the credits appear, the scene brings Cardinal Fabretti (Carlo Sabatini) before the college of cardinals and the Pope to inform them that Revelation 8:7 is being fulfilled. This is the Apocalypse. Interestingly, Roman Catholicism doesn't accept the evangelical interpretation of Revelation as a guidebook to the future. The setting in Rome is because the evangelical belief is that Catholics will somehow have something to do with all of this.

Scripture here is predictive, pure and simple. Another new scene has Robert Thorn attending the opera in London. The show is *Salome*, emphasized by a lingering close-up of John the Baptist's agonized, beheaded face. In case anyone missed the biblical reference to Keith Jennings' beheading in the original, this should make it explicit.

Otherwise the Bible appears in the same scenes: Father Brennan's room is papered with its pages, and Jennings reads from Revelation trying to find "When the Jews Return to Zion" while stopped at a roadside refreshment stand in Italy. Details differ but the storyline remains the same. It's a touch labored to think that somebody needs to have 666 explained to them in 2006 (Thorn doesn't get the reference) but we routinely suspend disbelief willingly for the sake of entertainment. And, of course, the entire artificial plot of "the Antichrist" is a biblical myth gone wild. The Bible's representation differs, albeit slightly, between films.

It may surprise some to find out that the Bible doesn't appear at all in the third and scariest member of the Unholy Trinity, *The Exorcist*.

The Exorcist (1973, 2000)

Who can forget the image of Regan MacNeil (Linda Blair), her head turning all the way around, projectile vomiting, and levitating above her bed as the Devil inhabits her innocent body and mind? Often cited at the very top of lists of horror movies, *The Exorcist* may not have been the first film to explore (or exploit) demonic possession, but it did set the standard by which all subsequent ventures would be measured. At the time of this writing a television series called *The Exorcist* is underway. Many now consider *The Exorcist* passé and not a little laughable. Remember the 1970s though. This was fear of a believable kind at that time.

Father Merrin (Max von Sydow) is a priest, scholar, and archaeologist. While digging near Nineveh in northern Iraq, he finds an image of Pazuzu, an ancient Mesopotamian demon. Pazuzu isn't named in the movie, but his iconography is unmistakable. Pazuzu isn't a biblical demon, but his identity, according to the movie, is a more conventional western one—he's the Devil. Or so he claims. Problem is, the Devil's a liar. Likely *The Exorcist* intends us to think this is the Devil—Pazuzu's a scary-looking demon whose image is just too good to pass up. In any case, strange things start to happen. As we'll learn, this old priest is also a monster-hunter—an exorcist.

Meanwhile in Georgetown, Washington, D.C., Chris MacNeil (Ellen Burstyn) is acting in a movie about campus protest. Her twelve-year-old daughter Regan is watched by Chris' assistant Sharon (Kitty Winn). They live next to Georgetown University where Chris occasionally notices the intense young priest, Father Damien Karras (Jason Miller) on campus. The priest is wrestling with guilt because his ill mother lives in a bad neighborhood in New York City and he's also struggling with his own faith.

Regan, when her mother's not home, has been playing with a ouija board. Chris has been hearing things in the attic at night, and when Regan shows her the ouija board the planchette moves all by itself. Regan explains that Captain Howdy talks to her through it, but Chris thinks it's just childish imagination. Events begin to bring Chris and Father Karras together.

The priest confesses to colleagues that he may have lost his faith. His mother dies alone in a psychiatric unit of a cheap hospital. Then during a party which brings Washington celebrities including Father Dyer (William O'Malley), Father Karras's friend, to Chris's house, Regan pees on the carpet in front of everyone and tells an astronaut "You're going to die up there." Medical tests ensue.

The doctors can only explain this as nerves, and they prescribe Ritalin. Regan starts using harsh language. Her bed begins to buck and shake at night. She masturbates with a crucifix. Her voice changes. Her head turns 360 degrees. Off camera, she kills Burke Dunning (Jack MacGowran), the director of Chris's movie, when he's temporarily babysitting her. Her room's freezing cold. The girl has to be tied to her bed. Out of medical options, Chris seeks out Father Karras, whom she finds through Father Dyer.

Father Karras doubts his own faith and certainly doesn't believe in demons. He agrees to see Regan, certain that he can demonstrate all of this is psychological. Despite his skepticism, the fact that Regan knows things she shouldn't makes him wonder. He records the "demon" to discover that on the tape, played backwards, she asks for Father Merrin. The demon claims to be the Devil himself. The Devil is a liar, of course, but something supernatural is definitely going on.

Although his health's poor, Father Merrin, who's back in the United States, agrees to the exorcism. Arriving at the MacNeil house, he sends Father Karras to the sacristy for a purple stole, holy water, and "*The Roman Ritual.* The big one."

Let's press "pause" here for a second. The size of the book matters, but it isn't the Bible. *The Roman Ritual* may look like the Bible—it may be a sacred book—but it isn't the Bible. It's the Catholic work that contains, among other rituals, the rite of exorcism. The Bible doesn't appear in this movie. Also while we're on pause, the American notion of demons (there are other notions elsewhere) derives from the Bible. We'll discuss this further below. Play.

When Father Karras returns the famous exorcism scene gets underway. "The power of Christ compels you!" the priests shout in unison as Regan levitates above their heads. This demon won't come out easily. Father Karras engages it in an argument, but Father Merrin suggests a break and dismisses his young colleague. Taking advantage of the uneven sides, the demon dispatches Father Merrin and is only defeated when Father Karras invites it inside him instead of Regan. The priest leaps out the window, killing himself and stopping the spiritual torment. Lest we fret over his soul, Father Dyer arrives and offers his dying friend the last rites.

For the possession genre, *The Exorcist* started the demonic ball rolling, but there are several noteworthy aspects regarding the Bible. Firstly, as mentioned above, the Bible doesn't appear. The iconic book, here standing in for the Bible, is *The Roman Ritual.* Rather like *The Book of Common Prayer* for Episcopalians, *The Roman Ritual* can function as an iconic book for Catholics, at least in horror movies. Demons are biblical monsters, but Scripture's advice on how to cast them out lacks the drama of "the power of Christ compels you!" Biblical phrases and quotations occur in the rite of exorcism. The scene couldn't have taken place without some iconic book. Here accuracy dictated that it not be the Bible itself. That doesn't hold for all possession movies, as we'll see.

A second noteworthy aspect is the identity of the demon. William Friedkin was likely justified in supposing that most viewers wouldn't be able to identify Pazuzu based on his iconography. In the movie the ultimate name he offers is "the Devil." The Devil and demons, although not fully fledged characters in Scripture, are different beings in traditional Christian teaching. There's only one Devil. Demons come in packs of legion. Even one of them is nasty enough to send a person back to mass. Possession by the Devil tends to occur in Catholic-themed horror.

A further observation is that the demon has designs on the priests from the beginning. When Father Karras first visits, it says, through Regan, that it wants to be together with him. It imitates his dead mother. When Regan calls out in a voice not her own, the demon is summoning Father Merrin. This battle's between the clergy and the demon, and Regan just happens to be the battleground. Who ultimately wins? At the end the priests are dead and we don't really know where that demon has gone. In the Gospels Jesus sends "Legion," the multitude of demons, into a herd of swine that drown themselves. It never explains where they go after that.

This possession movie involves a Roman Catholic monster. It's a priest killer. The MacNeils don't have any religious faith, and at the end, they are the survivors. Chris accepts a medallion from Father Dyer, but no profession of faith is made. Had she called in a Protestant, the film would've ended very differently.

The "Bible" (here *The Roman Ritual*) failed to drive out the demon. Only the prospect of getting two priests in one night is enough to lure him out. The iconic text failed in a time of need. Perhaps that's one reason the movie has the power to scare. If the ultimate cure doesn't work against pure evil, what can you do?

In the next chapter, we'll see that *The Exorcist* set the bar for all subsequent efforts at possession movies. It's not unusual for them to cite this film by name.

Diabolical Cast Call

The diabolical world in American imagination is a biblical world. In reality it's based on religious beliefs from a wide variety of traditions. Demons occur very rarely in the Hebrew Bible (Old Testament) and "the Devil" not at all. There's a late character called "the Satan"—a prosecuting attorney among the gods—who appears after Jewish contact with Zoroastrianism. The Satan isn't evil and the Hebrew Bible says very little about him. All the dead, for most of the biblical period, went "down" to Sheol, not Hell. Sheol was a resting place from which it was possible, but very difficult, to return. The dead weren't punished, but simply slept. Both bad and good went there. Sheol was the fate of all humans.

The one "witch" story in the Bible involves returning from Sheol. King Saul asks for his prophet Samuel to be brought up, which a conjurer does.

Witches, much later, were considered familiars of Satan, and we haven't even got to the Devil yet.

Zoroastrianism mainly developed in what was known as Persia at the time, in what we now call Iran. It was a strongly dualistic religion. Whereas the Hebrew Bible had no unified answer to the source of evil, Zoroastrianism believed in an Anti-God as well as a good God, well before *Prince of Darkness*. These entities struggled with each other constantly. The followers of good ended up in a place after they died that's an early version of Heaven, while those who followed evil ended up in an endlessly burning underworld. The region of Israel was ruled by the Persians in the sixth century BCE. Zoroastrian thought influenced Judaism, but it isn't fully reflected in the Hebrew Bible. This seems to be where ideas of Hell originated.

The New Testament was the product of a Judaism impacted by Zoroastrianism and the subsequent conquest of Israel by the Greeks (who introduced ideas such as souls) and then the Romans. During these centuries Satan (increasingly a name) developed into "the Devil." He was God's opponent, but he's never fully described. Demons existed in this world as well. The very earliest cultures had demons, but since they had no Devil and since demons weren't pure evil, they didn't match what they became in the New Testament. We'll talk more about demons in the next chapter.

The Bible also addressed the end of the world indirectly. Israel, remember, was constantly being overrun by foreign empires. The idea that someday all of this injustice would be repaid played into apocalyptic thinking. Scripture has no single roadmap for the end of the world. In the Hebrew Bible some prophets mention a coming cataclysm. Daniel, an apocalyptic book and the last book of the Hebrew Bible to be written, uses cryptic imagery to describe the rule by the Greeks. Jesus, in the Gospels, predicted end times here and there, but with no single narrative plan. Paul, for his part, mentioned some scenarios in some of his letters that indicated the end was coming and some would be "caught up" in the air. Revelation, the last book in the Bible, is a mysterious, symbolic description of the Roman Empire in the first century. Some came to see it as a prediction of the end of the world, although that's not what it was originally about. Neither Jesus, Paul, nor the author of Revelation mentions "Antichrist." This term comes from two of the small letters of John, but it was eventually applied to "the Beast" (probably Nero) mentioned in Revelation.

Within a century or so of the New Testament some of these original contexts had become hazy and the Roman Empire still held sway. Early Christians began to piece together when the oppression would end. The fully developed end of the world, however, didn't appear until the dispensationalism of the nineteenth century—just a couple hundred years ago. It was largely a Protestant concept, but it proved rich ground for horror movies.

The Bible is viewed in these movies in a predominantly Protestant light—specifically, an evangelical Protestant light. America's cultural Christianity is evangelical Protestant, and when horror draws on the Bible for the end of the world, or for diabolical characters, it has to fill in some very large blanks. This chapter has shown that the Devil's a useful and unifying character in this regard. He sleeps with witches, fathers children with jackals, turns into a green liquid, possesses little girls, and controls the homeless. In other words, the Devil can be just about anything a writer/director needs him to be. There will be Satanists around to worship him, and witches for female company.

When he gets around to orchestrating the end of the world—and note, often in horror it starts at the Devil's initiative—a character called the Antichrist will appear. Largely an evangelical construct, this Antichrist will be politically powerful and is sometimes thought to be the son of the Devil. He's only one of a cast of end-time characters; Revelation mentions "the beast" (from whom most Antichrist imagery is drawn) and "the false prophet." Neither of these two get as much air time as the Devil or Antichrist, who are sometimes played as the same character.

Although it took time, the idea grew that if God reigns in Heaven, the Devil must reign in Hell. Zoroastrians, Jews of the Rabbinic Period, and Jesus all thought of this region as fiery and a realm of punishment. All of this has been fruitful ground for horror films. What the Bible *doesn't* say, they're glad to direct in the viewer's imagination. All of this is more systematically developed in horror than it is in Holy Writ.

Now that *The Exorcist* has introduced the subject, let's move on to other demonic attacks in the next chapter. Iconic Bibles, whether the Bible or not, will be plentiful among the possessed.

6

Possession Movies

Ed Warren sets crucifixes up around the Perron house while explaining that demonic entities don't like it. "It pisses them off," he says. As the Warrens and their crew stake out the house, Lorraine finds an old noose in a crawl-space. The floor gives way. She falls to the basement where she sees the ghosts of the house's sordid past. "She made me do it," one ghost says as she murders her son. Lorraine runs for the basement stairs shouting, "I know what she did!" Ed grabs her, relieved she's unharmed. Lorraine's nearly hysterical—"I know what she did! She possessed the mother to kill the child. She visits Carolyn every night. That's what the bruise marks are. She's feeding off her!" One by one, the crucifixes fall.

*　*　*

Possession in Movies

Such was the impact of *The Exorcist* that, discounting knockoffs in the wake of its success, movies about demonic possession simply didn't move in new directions until after the turn of the millennium. Not that there weren't plenty of possession movies before that, but *The Exorcist* had a deep impact on the motif of exorcist as monster hunter. Remember *Constantine*.

Demonic possession movies are based inherently on the Bible. Without the biblical portrayal of demons the phenomenon would certainly not be widely known in our advanced, technological society. The iconic Bible itself may or may not appear in these movies, but the horror's distinctly biblical. The takeover of a body by a demon, although it occurs in many cultures, is just like biblical times when viewed through an American lens.

This chapter stands separate from the others in this book for two main reasons. One has to do with the character of demons. While demons are biblical, they're also pre-biblical and are complex enough to merit their own discussion. The second reason is numerical. Legions of possession movies exist. Frequently classified as the most terrifying of horror scenarios, being possessed grapples with the very meaning of horror. The demoniac maintains elements of her or his own personal identity while being controlled by something completely other. She's out of control, whether conscious of it or not. As a result, the theme has been revisited many, many times since *The Exorcist.*

We've run across demons in a few of the movies already examined— *Constantine* and *The Evil Dead*, for example. In some cases characters have been possessed. These movies, however, don't center on possession in the same way as the movies in this chapter do. As is true of most of the categories in this book, some overlap is to be expected. Some of the films treated in this section could fit elsewhere as well. What brings them together in this way is how demons react to the Bible (broadly understood, as an iconic book). Like a crucifix against a vampire, the iconic book is a major weapon for combatting demons. This use of Scripture—sometimes successful, sometimes not—will provide a fine example of how the average person understands the Good Book. So what are demons anyway? We'll explore that more fully once the movies are over, but for now, here's what we need to know—

Movie Demons

In the spate of reality television ghost hunting programs, many viewers have been exposed to demons as entities that have "never been human." They aren't ghosts, but they can haunt and act like ghosts. They're sometimes called "elementals," and they're always of evil intent. There's no good in them. Elementals were originally simply nature spirits, not necessarily evil. This understanding of demons is a modern, non-biblical explanation, phenomenon-based rather than literature-based (that is, the Bible's view). This ambiguity works well for possession movies.

Perhaps because books on possession have been appearing more frequently, there seems to have been a hunger for such films in recent years. Often they're "based on a true story" (*The Exorcist, The Exorcism of Emily Rose, The Rite, The Possession, The Conjuring*), crossing the thin line holding fiction back from reality. Even purely fictional movies (*Paranormal Activity, The Last Exorcism*) have intertitles or a shooting style that suggest they're "true." The goal here isn't to be comprehensive. This chapter alone could be as long as this entire book, and then some. This is merely a sampling of cinematic demons.

Possession movies began before 1973—a case could be made that *White Zombie* involved a form of possession. Since the starting point for this book is 1960 and since clearly the most influential possession of the early era of modern horror appeared with *The Exorcist*, that's the logical starting point. This chapter will begin with *The Exorcism of Emily Rose* since this movie raises the very question of what possession is. It departs from the assumptions and style of *The Exorcist*. Besides, it actually is based on a true case—dramatized and shipped overseas, but documented nonetheless.

The Exorcism of Emily Rose (2005)

Clearly not a simple knock-off of *The Exorcist*, *The Exorcism of Emily Rose* is framed as a courtroom drama with flashbacks of the possession and exorcism of the title girl. Like *The Exorcist*, *Emily Rose* is based on actual events, fictionalized for the screen. Anneliese Michel was a German woman who was diagnosed with epilepsy and who died (at the age of 23, not 19, as in the film) after undergoing a prolonged exorcism. Priests sought to cure her of what were thought to be spiritual symptoms, beyond her mere biological troubles.

Moving the action to the United States, *Emily Rose* opens with the visit of a medical examiner (Terence Kelly) to the isolated Rose household. Father Richard Moore (Tom Wilkinson) walks out of Emily's room and is with the family when the examiner tells them the death was not of natural causes. The film then shifts to the frame of the story. The prosecution for the court case enlists Ethan Thomas (Campbell Scott) a devout Methodist, for the trial. The defense, eager for a fight, assigns Erin Bruner (Laura Linney), an agnostic fresh off a Clarence Darrow–like murder case, to exonerate the priest on behalf of the diocese. Flashbacks punctuate the trial. Interestingly enough, although it would have made an excellent line of Bruner's defense, no swearing in scenes with the Bible are shown. Instead, the trial begins with Thomas showing the jury just how horribly Emily Rose (Jennifer Carpenter) died. He claims that as nothing but medical explanations would suffice, treatment with gambutrol (a fictional drug) would have cured her. She would still be alive.

Flashbacks show Emily's college acception, and her first demonic encounter alone at night in her dorm. Although a religious girl from a religious family, no Bible is shown in these scenes.

Meanwhile in court, Thomas is making a convincing case and Bruner can't find an expert witness to counter the medical explanation he's pursuing. She begins to have eerie visitations at 3:00 a.m., the traditional time for demonic activity. Father Moore later explains this to be in mockery of the tradition that Jesus died at 3:00 p.m. That tradition does exist, but it isn't in the Bible. According to the Gospel of Mark, the earliest account we have, Jesus cried out at the ninth hour before dying. The ninth hour translates to between 2:00 and 3:00 p.m. Crucifixion could last for days before killing a person, but Jesus died in a few hours, about mid-afternoon. The complementary tradition of late night demonic attacks, while not biblical, has a long pedigree. In the film Emily experiences attacks in the college hospital, in class, and in the college chapel at different times. Her boyfriend Jason (Joshua Close) follows her into the chapel and although they're in a church, no Bibles are shown. Jason takes Emily home to her family and Father Moore's called in to care for her.

When her father is called to the stand, the flashbacks show Emily being attacked at home. The religious iconography around the house demonstrates the family to be very pious, but no Bibles are seen. Upon cross-examining the witness, Thomas asks him, "Sir, do you often read the Bible?" After receiving a yes, he rejoins, "So do I." He then goes on to ask if Nathaniel Rose (Andrew Wheeler) read medical literature about his departed daughter's condition. This is the first mention of Scripture in the film. It's used here to compare with medical science. Which reveals the truth?

Since Erin Bruner has cast some doubt on epilepsy alone as the cause of Emily's symptoms, Ethan Thomas has brought a witness who diagnoses Emily's condition as psychotic epileptic disorder, thus accounting for the non-epileptic elements of the girl's experience. He too claims gambutrol would have cured her. Wanting to counter this scientific evidence, Bruner calls in Dr. Sadira Adani (Shohreh Aghdashloo), an anthropologist from Northwestern University, and an expert on possession. The professor testifies that possession, while rare, is a universally recognized human experience. Bruner makes the case that perhaps Emily could've actually been possessed since, as Dr. Adani opines, gambutrol would block the psychological benefit of exorcism, trapping the victim in the mental state of possession. Ironically Thomas, the Christian prosecutor, finds it inconceivable that the agnostic defense is suggesting actual possession as a cause for Emily's death.

The focus of the trial shifts to science versus religion rather than whether gambutrol could've stopped the attacks. Which belief system is accurate? At this point Bruner might've pointed out that swearing on a Bible—which doesn't happen in the film—is a tacit statement of the power of spiritual beings. Is it any more rational than believing demons torment a girl? Swearing on a Bible also indicates we live in a biblical, if diabolical, world. This was a missed opportunity for the defense.

Erin Bruner gets a break when her assistant discovers there was a psychologist present for the exorcism. Dr. Graham Cartwright (Duncan Fraser) had requested confidentiality, but has now decided he will testify on scientific grounds that Emily was not epileptic. Bruner visits Father Moore in prison where the Bible is first shown in the movie. The priest is reading the Scriptures when she arrives. No reference is made to it. With Cartwright's testimony to corroborate the priest's account, and his tape recording of the rite, they're sure to win. When Cartwright is killed in a freak accident, all they can do is have the priest tell what happened.

When Father Moore describes the exorcism he mentions using *The Roman Ritual*, the same text as in *The Exorcist*. Indeed, as he prepared for the exorcism a demon attacked him the night before. We're shown *The Roman Ritual*, black leather with a gilded cross on the cover, falling to the floor. We have seen this foreshadowing of doom several times before—a sacred text on the floor spells trouble. The ersatz Bible of Catholic-based possession movies, *The Roman Ritual*'s powerless before this demon.

As the actual exorcism is played out, no Bibles appear. Those present use *The Roman Ritual*. Emily breaks free of her restraints and runs to the barn. There bats, snakes, and rats become active. Father Moore insists on having the name of the demon, but Emily keeps counting to six. She finally names herself Belial, Lucifer, the Devil in the flesh. The horses, terrified, escape. The exorcism fails.

Consider once again the identity of the demon. As in *The Exorcist* the demonic being identifies himself as the actual Devil. In the biblical world, there's a distinction made between "the Devil" and demons. Neither is fully drawn out and advanced demonologies wouldn't come along until the Middle Ages. Possession movies face a great temptation to make the demon the ultimate enemy of God. Too great a temptation to pass up, especially in Catholic possession movies. Why settle for a lesser evil?

Demanding the name of a demon is based on Jesus' most famous exorcism, that of the Gadarene Demoniac (Mark 5). When the demon torments this man, Jesus demands his name. This is the famous "Legion" (also a horror film title)—the only demon named in the Gospels in the context of an exorcism. In both Judaism and Christianity, having the name of the demon became an essential component of the rite of exorcism. Intercut back to the movie.

Cartwright misses his day in court. When he tries to explain why to Bruner a car speeds by and kills him. Erin visits Father Moore in jail once again to find him reading his Bible. When she explains that Cartwright is dead and the case is lost, he slips a letter from the Good Book. He hands it to Erin. As we've seen before, a sacred text often requires additional material to be effective. The Bible hasn't been able to save the priest, but perhaps this modern scripture can. This is Emily's final communication. Read to the court the next day, the letter reveals Emily had a vision of Mary and chose to die possessed so that others might believe. She receives the stigmata (see Chapter 4), which Thomas claims to be self-inflicted.

After all this, the jury returns a guilty verdict but recommends that the sentence be time served. In essence, they believe the medical explanation, but they haven't ruled out the demonic either. Standing at Emily's grave in the rain, Father Moore and Erin Bruner conclude their relationship. She remarks on the epitaph, chosen, we're told, by the priest. Emily quoted it to him the night before she died. It comes from Paul's letter to the Philippians: "Work out your own salvation with fear and trembling." Although the Bible has been silent in this film, it has the final word.

Three end cards follow, the first stating Emily's grave is frequently visited as a shrine. The second claims that Father Moore went into seclusion after these events. The final intertitle suggests Erin had an anthropologist study this and write up the case notes that led to this movie. All three are intended to suggest this isn't just a fictional account.

It's true that the grave of Anneliese Michel has become a destination of tourists, but probably not for the reasons suggested in the film. The biblical quotation on her stone is "Es ist vollbrächt" ("It is accomplished," Jesus' last words in John 19:30). There seems to be little doubt that Michel was epileptic and that medical help likely might have prolonged her life. The case of Anneliese Michel was studied by an anthropologist, but the movie takes considerable liberty with the story.

Comparison with *The Exorcist* is informative. Neither movie features the Bible. Clearly Catholic priests know the Bible, but to fight a demon *The Roman Ritual*, the prescribed text, is followed. The biblical monster isn't banished by the Bible. *Emily Rose* switches the focus to the larger question in our present-day world: can we accept the reality of demons? If we trust science we can't believe in demons. If we believe in demons, not even the Bible can help us.

From here we'll move on to some non–Catholic examples of possession movies. *The Last Exorcism* features a Protestant exorcist. *The Possession* will give us a Jewish one. In *Paranormal Activity* there's demonic possession in a completely secular context. With *The Rite*, we'll return to another Roman Catholic example. *The Conjuring* is included here because of the strange combination of demon and witch and ghost that occurs in it. As such it will also serve as the final movie of the chapter, before we try to get to Heaven.

The Last Exorcism (2010)

Radically different from both *The Exorcist* and *The Exorcism of Emily Rose* in a very basic way, *The Last Exorcism* is a Protestant possession movie. The Protestant branch of Christianity is generally traced to Martin Luther and his 95 Theses nailed to the door of the Wittenberg Castle-Cathedral in 1517. In reality the movement had many roots in different locations but the end result is that organized Christian groups emerged that envisioned their religion as sometimes having very little in common with Roman Catholicism. Especially among Reformed traditions like Presbyterians, and later, Baptists, ritualism itself was considered wrong and the practices of Catholicism were rejected. The result is that Protestants simply don't have ancient rituals for dealing with demons. Taking the Bible seriously, Protestants tend to believe in demons, but they didn't develop a formal rite to expel them. This was clearly demonstrated by the Methodist Ethan Thomas's blank dismissal of possession in *The Exorcism of Emily Rose*. Protestants don't have their own version of *The Roman Ritual*.

None of this relates directly to the Bible, of course. Protestants tend to believe the Bible alone is key for salvation, and thus we would expect a more biblical outlook in an exorcism movie featuring Protestants. Clearly part of the tension of cinematic treatments like *The Exorcist* and *The Exorcism of Emily Rose* is the dramatic power of *The Roman Ritual*. In fact, it serves as a stand-in for the Bible and most people would have trouble telling the difference. (Remember *Constantine* reading the last rites from a Bible, where the rite doesn't appear. It's found in *The Roman Ritual*.) *The Last Exorcism* is a new departure in this regard.

The Rev. Cotton Marcus (Patrick Fabian) is a preacher like his daddy. In the first several minutes of the film the Holy Bible is everywhere. The movie is of the "found footage" variety, shot in documentary style, giving it the appearance of being a true story. As the film crew of two follows him around, they reveal that Cotton is a charismatic preacher and that he began doing exorcisms when he was ten. He's an accomplished magician and show-man. He also doesn't believe any of it. Although he knows and quotes from the Bible, he confesses to the camera that he's not so sure about God and he definitely doesn't believe in demons. He stopped believing when he realized that medical science was helping people more than showmanship and because a child about the age of his son (Justin Shafer) was accidentally killed by well-intentioned exorcists. The story's obviously aware of Anneliese Michel.

The point of the documentary is to be an exposé—Cotton will take the crew on an exorcism to demonstrate that it's all for show. Before they go to a randomly selected request for deliverance, they stop in to see Cotton's father (John Wright, Jr.), a true believer and his son's biggest booster. Claiming 150 demonic notches on his Bible, Reverend John Marcus pulls an ancient demonology book, *Hortus deliciarum*, from his safe. Obviously an iconic book to be used alongside the Bible, it's one of "only about twenty" and it names and illustrates the various demons known to the Latin-reading literati. The Latin makes it sound like the Bible and the book's age and leather binding reinforce that connection.

Cotton explains that the Roman Catholics get all the press because of "the movie" (*The Exorcist*), but that all Bible-reading Christians have to believe in the Devil if they believe in God. Satan was a fallen angel and the demons are the 300 followers who were thrown from Heaven with him, thus the book has a finite number of fiends to list. This is a case of the Devil you know. Exorcism, Cotton privately tells the camera, is a scam.

The randomly selected letter takes Cotton, journalist Iris Reisen (Iris Bahr) and the cameraman (Daniel Moskowitz) to Idlewood, Louisiana. Note the names here: Cotton Marcus recalls Cotton Mather, one of the most influential early American Protestant ministers. Iris Reisen makes us think of "reason" and the camera shows the superstition and poverty of the locals as they talk about the UFO landing site and how the Gates of Hell are physically located by the Sweetzer Farm. In his letter Louis Sweetzer (Louis Herthum) explains that he thinks the Devil himself has possessed his 16-year-old daughter Nell (Ashley Bell). Nell's brother Caleb (Caleb Landry Jones) doesn't want the exorcist with his camera crew to be there at all.

Covertly preparing his illusions, Cotton gets the family ready for an exorcism. Using his father's book, he identifies the demon as Abalam. Abalam appears in the early modern grimoire *The Lesser Key of Solomon* as a demon king. *The Lesser Key* is an actual grimoire. No demons, apart from Legion, give their names in the Gospels (any others that may be named in the Bible are few, and disputed). Unlike *The Exorcist*, however, *The Last Exorcism* is all for show—Cotton doesn't believe in demons and he simply fabricates the connection to Abalam to show the film crew that he can.

During his rigged exorcism, Cotton uses the Bible, not *The Roman Ritual*. Iconically, he presses the Bible to Nell's head to cast out the demon. Strangely for a Protestant, he also uses a crucifix—engineered to give off a puff of smoke—to convince the family that the demon has left Nell. Caleb, who early on figures out this is a hoax, approves. Apart from the question of if the Bible really "works" we also have to ask if it can work for someone who doesn't believe in it. Of all the movies we've watched, here the Bible comes the closest to being a mere prop.

Paid handsomely for his "services," Cotton drives to a hotel five miles away with the crew. In the middle of the night Nell shows up. She makes sexual moves on Iris and then vomits. Cotton takes her to the hospital and has to explain to Louis that the exorcism worked, but Nell requires medical help as well.

Expelled from Louis's circle of trust, Cotton calls on the Sweetzer's minister, Pastor Manley (again, notice the name; played by Tony Bentley). The pastor isn't welcome at Sweetzer farm, but he will come if he's invited. Back at the farmhouse Nell has slashed Caleb's face, indicating that she did kill the animals Louis claimed she had while she was possessed. Cotton and crew stay with Nell as Louis drives his son to the hospital. Iris discovers that Nell's pregnant. She's been chained to her bed so they release her. Convinced this is a case of traditional southern incest, Cotton and Iris discuss the best way to ensure Nell gets help. Now that she's free, however, she prowls creepily around the house, speaking Latin, and filming herself killing a cat while naked.

The crew's worried. Nell drew the dead cat spattered with blood beforehand, but she also drew the crew. Dead. They lock Nell in her room until father comes home. Louis claims it was Abalam who impregnated Nell, just like the book said. When Cotton refuses to do another exorcism, Louis orders them off his property, intimating that he's going to shoot Nell. With no other options, Cotton agrees to a second exorcism. That night in the barn, Bible in hand, he tries for real. Contorted into impossible shapes and knowing the name Abalam (which she hadn't heard), this looks like it might be the real thing. Until she says "blowing job" instead of "blow job." Cotton then surmises she's suffering guilt, not possession. She confesses that local boy Logan Winters (Logan Craig Reid) is the father of her unborn child. Pastor Manley is called in to deal with this all-too-human crisis. He enters with a huge Bible under his arm, and the crew leaves. As they go we're shown the local pastor, Bible open, praying for the newly forgiven Nell.

At the diner where Logan works, however, Cotton and crew learn the boy's gay. Not only that, but Pastor Manley lied about not seeing Nell for years. They head back to the farm where Manley's overseeing an outdoor satanic ritual and Nell's giving birth to a demon. It seems that possession was the case, after all. Cotton steps forward to stop the demon, Iris is hacked to death by a Satanist, and the cameraman is beheaded by Caleb, who's a member of the sect. They end up just as prophesied by Nell's drawings.

First we need to sort out what's happened here. Caleb, knowing the possession and pregnancy to be demonic, objects to his sister's exorcism until he learns Cotton's a charlatan. Louis is also correct that his daughter's possessed. Two Bible-bearing clergy differ on the point. Manley knows Nell is bearing Abalam's son, and Cotton wrongly rationalistically rejects demons. Cotton's fate is left open to interpretation, and indeed a sequel was released three years later. (It doesn't feature Cotton Marcus, however.)

How about the Bible? What's its role? If used correctly, the movie implies, it can exorcise demons. This is the fear Caleb has. Cotton Marcus uses it as a prop only and even when he begins to wonder if the demon might be real, he doubts. At the second exorcism he becomes convinced this was a case of simple fornication guilt, not demonic possession. In his final scene, heading into the fire, he has no Bible with him. Pastor Manley, whose Bible is red, is also using the Bible as a prop. He has to convince Cotton and Louis that he's sincere. Nobody in this movie really believes the Bible except Cotton's aged father and Nell's family. In its lack of effectiveness, it's almost anti-iconic. The demonology book *Hortus deliciarum*, meanwhile, contains the truth.

Hortus deliciarum is, in reality, the title of an actual twelfth-century manuscript, but it isn't a demonology. The film's correct that it's rare, but it's actually more of a choir book, with the distinction of being one of the first books known to have been written by a woman. In other words, the effective text in *The Last Exorcism* is false while the real text (the Bible) is ineffective.

Protestants, when faced with demons, would have little recourse but to turn to the Bible. Although Scripture doesn't drive the demon out in this instance, we're led to believe that, in the right hands, it would've done so. The Bible should be able to drive out demons, but in *The Last Exorcism*, it doesn't.

Our next demon departs from Christianity altogether and comes to us from a Jewish context.

The Possession (2012)

Opening with a scene of a demonic attack centered on a dybbuk box, *The Possession* takes us from Catholic and Protestant demons to the Jewish variety. The title card indicates that this movie, like *The Exorcist*, *Emily Rose*, and *The Rite*, is based on a true story.

Clyde (Jeffrey Dean Morgan) and Stephanie Brenek (Kyra Sedgwick) are recently divorced. They have two young daughters, Hannah (Madison Davenport) and Emily (called "Em," played by Natasha Calis), who feel that their father's always been distant. He tries to spoil the girls on his weekends, compensating for his divided attention. While shopping at a yard sale to furnish the new, isolated house he's purchased, he lets Em select a strange box with Hebrew letters carved into it. It's difficult to open—and intentionally so—but Em manages to find the hidden lock. The contents are strange and somewhat reminiscent of the Holocaust. Em slips on a ring she finds inside and begins to experience episodes of strange events.

Shuttled back and forth between mother and father's houses, Em is not thriving. Her parents believe that the circumstances of the divorce are manifesting psychologically. Her teacher, after an incident with the box at school, opens it at night and is violently killed. Clyde has begun to suspect something unhealthy about Em's attachment to the box and he takes it to a remote dumpster and tosses it in. When Em realizes it's gone, she acts as though Clyde is beating her and she runs off into the night in search of it. The "woman" inside, once she finds the box, flies into the girl's open mouth in the form of a swarm of moths, and Em's now fully possessed. Stephanie, and the court, believe Clyde was actually beating Em that night and he's denied further visitation rights.

Distraught, Clyde tries to find out what's really happened to his daughter. He visits a professor—apparently of religious studies—at the university where he coaches basketball. The professor (Jay Brazeau) explains that the box is from the 1920s or '30s, likely from Poland. It's a dybbuk box. Clyde asks what a dybbuk is. The professor indicates it's a dispossessed spirit, a demon. The box was meant to trap the demon and the inscriptions say, basically, "warning, deadly—do not open."

Here again we see a conflation of demonic beings. The Hebrew Bible has no single word for "demon" and there is no unified description of what a demon is in the Bible. "Dybbuk" isn't a word from Scripture. In Judaism the idea of a dybbuk developed over time and it represents an evil spirit first attested in early modern Judaism. This Jewish variety of demon clings to a person and can be exorcised. Not nearly as commonly exploited in horror as Christian demons, they represent another form of possession by another form of demon. A dybbuk is a human soul denied entrance to the realm of the dead because of sin. It seeks a living body instead.

Clyde watches Jewish exorcisms—some of which feature unnamed books—on the internet and decides that his daughter is indeed possessed. Locating a gilt-edged Tanach that includes both English and Hebrew words, Clyde defies the court order and visits Em when his ex-wife's out on an errand. A word about the Tanach: this is the Jewish Bible. In many Christian traditions it's called "the Old Testament." Tanach is a kind of acronym for the first letters of the three sections of the Hebrew Bible: the "law" (Torah), the prophets (Nevi'im), and the "writings" (Chethuvim). Other than the order of the books it's pretty much identical to the Protestant Old Testament. This is an exotic Bible for many American viewers, but it's the same old Scripture.

Clyde begins reading, in English, words from Psalm 91. Some of the

Hebrew inscription on the box is also from this Psalm. It's often considered a "protection psalm." Em stares maliciously at her father and the book flies from his hands and smashes into the wall. The Bible, at least in the hands of a novice, is ineffectual against a demon. Once again Holy Writ ends up on the floor and bad things follow.

Ejected from the house by Stephanie, Clyde knows he has to find help for his daughter. He drives to Brooklyn to find Tzadok (Matisyahu), a Hasidic Jew who's agreed to meet him. The men of the synagogue, seeing the dybbuk box and learning it's been opened, refuse to help. Tzadok, however, feels obligated to assist and returns with Clyde. He discovers the name of the demon, which they must know to pull it back into the box. The name was inscribed behind the mirror on the inside lid. It's Abyzou, the "taker of children."

Em's been hospitalized and the family has to find an isolated ward for the exorcism. They go to the physical therapy room where Tzadok explains the candles, water, and olive oil used in the ritual. He pulls out his book, written in Hebrew. Even in high resolution frame-by-frame stepping through the Blu-ray disc doesn't reveal the title; in a theater it can't be read. Clyde opens his book and reads along in English. Although it isn't the same Tanach he had earlier (it has no gilt pages), the language is biblical. Clearly the intent is to suggest the Bible being read simultaneously in Hebrew and English.

Em resists and escapes. When Clyde finds her he insists the demon take him, which it does. This horror trope isn't unique—we saw it in *The Exorcist* and *Stigmata*. Tzadok realizes the apparently peaceful scene isn't right. He begins the ritual again, calling out the name "Abyzou" until he's able to force the demon out of Clyde. Protecting Em with his book and prayer shawl, Tzadok forces the demon to crawl out, trapping her once again in the box. Tzadok drapes his prayer shawl over the box, and places his book on top. The Bible has defeated the demon at last. The final scene frees it again, of course. This is horror, after all.

Here we find the Bible directly in a position of power over demons. This demon is different from Catholic demons but it's controlled in much the same way—a ritual including candles, anointing, and reading from a sacred book. Catholic, Protestant, and Jew all use the Bible to attempt to exorcise demons, although the exact form may differ from case to case. In the diabolical world, demons also differ. Some are fallen angels, some are the Devil, some are spirits of the evil dead. It's a standard of exorcism rites that a demon must be named to be expelled. This goes back to biblical accounts of Jesus (who was Jewish) demanding demons to identify themselves before casting them out.

We're still no closer to learning what a demon really is. A dybbuk is a distinctly Jewish demon, a dispossessed soul and not a fallen angel. *The Last*

Exorcism told us there were 300 demons who were fallen angels, in a Protestant context. Emily Rose's demon was Catholic and identified itself as the Devil, not technically a demon. All of this grows even more complex when there's no religion at all to help against a secular demon.

Paranormal Activity (2007)

It could be argued that *Paranormal Activity* isn't a possession movie. It's clear, however, that a demon has invaded Katie (Katie Featherston) and although it may be purely secular, this is nevertheless a possession film. It's of interest here because of the contemporary, non-theological explanation—popularized by reality TV ghost-hunting programs—of what a demon is.

The opening intertitle makes a statement that implies the picture is, in fact, true. Since it presents itself as raw footage, it can't state that this is based on a true story without destroying the illusion. The movie's presented as if it's simply the series of files downloaded from the camera. Verisimilitude. No big name actors. But also no Bible.

Katie is a college student who has moved in with her boyfriend Micah (Micah Sloat). The entire movie's cinéma vérité style: of the found footage species. The young couple have been bothered by paranormal activity so Micah has purchased a video camera to try to capture evidence and thus figure out what's going on. Spooky things happen, particularly at night, in their San Diego house. Obviously there's some tension between the two, but the camera also picks up unusual things as the couple sleeps.

Despite Micah's light mockery, Katie calls in a psychic (Mark Fredrichs). She reveals to him that these kinds of things have happened since she was eight. The phenomena have followed her when she's moved houses. Sensing this isn't a ghost, which he specializes in, the psychic suggests this might be a demon. Demons, he explains, aren't dead humans, like ghosts are. In fact, nobody knows what demons are, but they're to be handled by a professional. He warns the couple not to try to communicate with it. Since he can't work with demons he gives them a referral and leaves.

Micah doesn't really believe the psychic or respect his approach and he wants to purchase a ouija board. Katie absolutely refuses and makes him promise he won't buy one. Meanwhile the nighttime events increase in intensity and fright. Borrowing—not buying—a ouija board, Micah earns Katie's wrath while keeping to the letter of the law. When they're out of the house, the planchette moves on its own before scorching something that can't be read into the board. Katie, without remembering it, climbs out of bed and stares at Micah for hours while he sleeps. The viewer knows by now that the focus of this demon is Katie. She wants to call Dr. Avery, the demon specialist—tellingly not a priest. After a daytime attack, she ignores Micah's ruling on the matter and calls the demonologist. Dr. Avery isn't available, so she calls the psychic to come back.

The oppression in the house is so great that the psychic can't stay. He promises to try to help, but anxiously leaves. Micah wants to find a hotel, but Katie says she thinks they'll be safer staying at home. She smiles at the camera after Micah steps out of frame. That night she murders him and comes back into their bedroom to destroy the camera that's been watching over them for three weeks.

End cards state that Micah's body was found shortly after and that Katie has been missing ever since.

A completely secular demon possession movie, *Paranormal Activity* has spawned several sequels (currently five). The demon's never explained in this initial chapter. Micah reads a book, *Devils, Demons and Witchcraft* by Ernst and Johanna Lehner, which is mostly pictures, but he's duly impressed at how bad demons can be. This isn't an iconic book—paperback and merely informative (not performative)—it can educate but can't exorcise. Micah's choices, in reality, are limited. Without a ritual specialist, or even a religion, what can you do against demons?

Like *Ghost-Hunters* and various other reality television shows, in *Paranormal Activity* demons are divorced from their biblical origins, or perhaps taken to their pre-biblical state. They aren't explained. They simply are. And what are they? Non-human, disembodied entities. No Bible shows up, is quoted, or is even referred to in *Paranormal Activity*. Not even *The Roman Ritual*. The demon is capable of knowing what the couple's doing and leaving physical signs of its presence. Interestingly, Micah and Katie aren't married and when they have sex (off camera) Micah says that what Katie does is wild enough to be illegal in 20 states. Indications may be that in a world with no rules, demons can be a real problem with no solution. Horror can be conservative in that way.

Paranormal Activity represents a new stage in possession movies, fueled by the fact that demons defy explanation. Protestants and Jews have the Bible to help them, and Catholics rely on *The Roman Ritual*. When there are no iconic books, there's no place to turn for help facing demons that can't even be defined.

The Rite (2011)

The Rite, although it brings us back into the familiar Roman Catholic realm that started it all, is interesting to compare here. While this book doesn't focus on the discrepancies between written and cinematic versions of stories, it's worthy of note that this film was based on a successful non-fiction book (Matt Baglio's *The Rite*). While *The Exorcist* was also based on a book, William Blatty's work is generally classified as a novel. The film (directed by Mikael Håfström) deals, as does Baglio's book, with subtleties. For the purposes of cinematography *Exorcist*-style contortions appear, and as in many other possession movies, characters make reference to *The Exorcist* in the film itself.

The story follows Michael Kovak (Colin O'Donoghue), a young man who wants more out of life than being a mortician. He wants to go to seminary, but he's not sure he believes. Indeed, after four years he decides to drop out. Father Matthew (Toby Jones), however, is convinced the boy has what it takes and sends him to a course on exorcism in Rome.

Still doubting, and struggling with the idea of celibacy, Michael's sent by Father Xavier (Ciarán Hinds), his instructor in Rome, to see the unconventional exorcist Father Lucas Trevant (Anthony Hopkins). Father Lucas explains that demons are the Devil's foot-soldiers. The priests equates them with the Devil—"demons, diablo, the Devil" he says to Michael, indicating that they're essentially the same. There's a blurring of categories, or at least terminology, that's unusual for a Catholic priest. Catholic possession movies, especially, tend to make the offending demon the Devil himself. He's the big-name draw.

While at Father Lucas's house, Michael's unexpectedly drawn into the exorcism of Rosaria (Marta Gastini), a pregnant 16-year-old. Although intense, the exorcism doesn't include impressive displays such as viewers probably expect. In fact, it's terribly informal. Father Lucas' cell phone goes off in the middle and he stops to answer it. There's a black book present, with gilt-edged pages, but it's neither opened nor read from. In later scenes it appears to be *The Roman Ritual*. No Bibles show up for this Catholic ceremony. It isn't clear that the demon has been expelled—it hasn't revealed its name—but Rosaria has some relief and when she's sent home Michael questions whether there was anything non-medical going on there at all. A sick girl needs a doctor, not an exorcist. Even the rite seems to have failed. Father Lucas explains that exorcism's a long process and until you get a demon's name, you can never really cast it out. In horror the first exorcism never works.

Back at school a fellow student and journalist, Angeline (Alice Braga), asks Michael to share what happened at Father Lucas' house. For confidentiality purposes, Michael refuses. The next lecture in the course reveals that demons take orders and each has a separate name: Beelzebub, Leviathan, Baal. Father Xavier instructs the students to get a demon's name to gain some control.

Finding Rosaria's bracelet in his pocket, Michael returns to Father Lucas's house to find out how it got there. While he's there the girl's exorcism continues. No books are present this time. Michael concludes she was impregnated by her father. The three nails she spits up, he surmises, were her attempt to harm her unwanted baby. Her possession reveals itself in more dramatic form this time with some of the standard contortions.

Michael, although still doubting, now can't keep away. His next visit catches Father Lucas going on a house call to a young boy, Vincenzo (Andrea Calligari). Plagued by nightmares, the boy woke up with heavy hoofmarks embedded in his torso. He calls his demon "the mule," from his nightmare. Father Lucas performs an exorcism—no books, no script—and finds a frog inside the boy's pillow. Rosaria's bracelet, as well as the bracelet of a corpse Michael had prepared in his father's funeral home at the start of the film, featured frogs. When Michael finds a frog in Father Lucas' bag, he thinks it's all a trick by the priest (with echoes of *The Last Exorcism*). Father Lucas implies that "the trick" may itself be a trick orchestrated by demons since they're liars.

Rosaria's much worse. She's hospitalized and restrained. She believes she's possessed, but Michael has no faith. In this third exorcism, the Bible is quoted, and mentioned, for the only time in the film. Michael says, "You know the Bible," to which the demon replies "Quite well." When Rosaria and her baby die inexplicably, Michael decides to grant Angeline her interview. Back at his dorm room, like a plague scene from Exodus, frogs are everywhere. Learning his father's had a stroke, Michael prepares to fly home. When his flight's delayed he calls and talks to his father. Disconnected, Michael calls back right away only to be informed by a doctor that his father died six hours before the phone call when they just spoke. Michael's being stalked by the demon. He sees the mule and returns to the seminary.

Accompanied by Angeline he returns to visit Father Lucas, but the priest has now been possessed. He's sitting in his exorcism room, singing from a hymnal and he tells Michael that Father Lucas isn't there. Michael, still doubting, and not a priest, prepares for the exorcism. This time he goes by the book—*The Roman Ritual*, not the Bible. This demon mocks and fights. Now that he believes in the Devil, Michael believes in God and the demon must finally give its name—Baal. Michael's now a monster-hunting exorcist.

About Baal. Father Xavier had talked about demon names earlier: "Beelzebub, Leviathan, Baal." Beelzebub, literally "lord of the flies," is most likely a corruption of Baalzebul, "prince Baal," a title used among Israel's northern neighbors in ancient times. Baal (whose personal name is Hadad) was considered by many to be the powerful deity who controlled the weather.

In other words, Baal wasn't a demon, but a god. Baal's mortal enemy was Leviathan, or Yamm ("the sea"). The three names cited by the good priest are all Canaanite deities. In the Bible Baal is Yahweh's rival. (Yahweh is the personal name of Israel's God). Leviathan is the sea serpent, according to one of the Psalms, made by God for the fun of it. Of the three names given, only Beelzebub is potentially a demon's name in the Bible. It may also refer to the Devil, however.

In the world of the movie Baal's a demon. Among some evangelical Christian groups it's believed that Canaanite gods were "real" since Israel's neighbors worshipped demons. Scholars know that this isn't really the case, but the movies inform us that the Devil and demons are the same. *The Rite* is a good example of this: "demon, diablo, the Devil" turns out to be Baal, a ruse by any other name.

Michael, after his successful exorcism, returns to America to become a priest. The end cards tell us he's still casting out demons. So is Father Lucas.

Our focus on the Bible highlights the fact that books are largely absent from *The Rite*. Although it's a Catholic setting even *The Roman Ritual*'s generally unused in the exorcism scenes. The expulsion of demons is a power play between belief and doubt and tends to become a shouting match between the insistent exorcist and the sly Baal.

Tellingly, in *The Rite*, the exorcism isn't successful until *The Roman Ritual* is used and the demon's name is known. The iconic book, in some measure, works in this instance. Rosaria isn't ever really freed, but the demon seems to have its designs on the priest, just as in *The Exorcist*. Even Vincenzo's mule comes to haunt future priest Michael. To drive the demon out of the priest the Bible's stand-in, *The Roman Ritual*, finally performs. It's almost as if doubt regarding the efficacy of, well, "the rite," has arisen since *The Exorcist*. At the end, however, the iconic book backed with faith defeats a demon.

The Conjuring (2013)

Our final possession movie offers varieties of minions of the diabolical world, together with demons and possession. *The Conjuring* is a possession movie, but it crams so much in that it's difficult to tell who's really doing the possessing.

The Conjuring brings together several horror themes: ghosts, witches, haunted houses, demons. And it claims to be based on a true story. In a somewhat new approach to horror, this film presents several different entities of apparently different species. It's also a complicated blend of reality and fiction, an increasingly popular move in horror cinema. Let's begin with the reality.

Ed and Lorraine Warren were real life ghost hunters. In the paranormal community, this movie was highly anticipated far in advance of its theatrical release. Even before *Child's Play*, the haunted doll Annabelle had a reputation as a "possessed toy." *The Conjuring* begins with the story of Annabelle, but she is only loosely tied into the plot. The Warrens handled the actual Annabelle case and were also involved in the Amityville investigation. Their work has been controversial and has been consistently challenged by skeptics. As of this writing Lorraine Warren is still alive, but Ed died in 2006.

As Roman Catholics, the Warrens were self-taught paranormal experts. The title card for the movie states that Ed was recognized by the Catholic Church as a demonologist. Lorraine also claims to be clairvoyant. *The Conjuring* is based, loosely, on their investigation of the haunting of the Perron family in Rhode Island.

Now this is no place to tease apart the tangled threads of real versus fictional components in movies, but the mixing of several elements here makes this flick a special challenge. The Perron entity, "in reality," is cited as being a witch. In the movie the witch is demonic—so much so that an exorcism is called for. But that's getting ahead of the story. The cinematic treatment's complicated by its factual base, in a similar way that *An American Haunting* is.

The movie begins with a couple of young women being haunted by Annabelle. The Warrens (Vera Farmiga and Patrick Wilson) indicate that the doll isn't actually possessed, but it's a conduit for a demonic presence. The doll (in real life a Raggedy Ann) is taken and locked in the Warren's paranormal museum in Monroe, Connecticut. Meanwhile, the Perron family—a truck driver, his wife and five daughters—move into a house in Harrisville, Rhode Island. Nighttime events begin to torment the daughters, along with demonic signs (things happening around 3:00 a.m., horrid smells, raps in groups of threes). The mother, Carolyn (Lili Taylor), wakes up with unexplained bruises.

The Warrens lecture to college audiences, showing tapes of an exorcism. A book is shown open in the hands of a priest—likely *The Roman Ritual*, but not explicitly identified. Carolyn Perron's in the audience. Things have gotten out of hand at the Perron home. Carolyn begs the Warrens to come to their house. After witnessing a number of things there themselves, the Warrens set up an investigation with full ghost-hunting paraphernalia. The activity's so intense that they take it to Father Gordon (Steve Coulter) to request permission for an exorcism. The Catholic Church must approve exorcisms in advance (as we know from *The Exorcist*.) The complication is that the Perrons aren't religious and the children were never baptized.

The house's history stretches back, according to the movie, to a "witch" executed in 1692. Mary Eastey, one of the innocent victims hanged at Salem, is said to be the ancestor of the witch that sacrificed her child in the house. This more recent witch, Bathsheba Sherman (Joseph Bishara), cursed the land. Murders and suicides followed in the house. A dead boy named Rory (Nate Seman, uncredited) is using a mirrored music box as a conduit. Also, a demon is involved. At this point the movie plot works only if the Salem witches were really witches—an unintentional slight on the real-life tragedy of the innocent victims of the state next door. It also complicates what's going on in the Perron household.

When the exorcism—an emergency in this case—takes place, we have Carolyn clearly possessed and tied to a chair. Ed tells Lorraine to "get the book," which is black leather, with gilt edges and a red ribbon marker. These are all visual cues for a Bible, but the Latin that Ed reads indicates it's *The Roman Ritual*. The title on the spine is illegible but it's two words. The mind fills in "Holy Bible." Ed performs the rite with the book open all the time, but can't get the demon to give its name. Desensitized audiences know that the first exorcism never works in possession films. Carolyn, freed after her chair falls from the ceiling, seeks to sacrifice her youngest daughter April (Kyla Deaver). Again we see elements of the Abraham and Isaac story as the mother raises the huge scissors above her daughter.

Once Carolyn's identified by name—Bathsheba—and she's faced down by the Warrens and her husband Roger (Ron Livingston), the evil spirit's vomited out. Like a dog we'll have to return to that vomit. When the Warrens walk out in the sunshine, Ed still has the book in his hand, closed, and the danger's averted. Temporarily. A sequel was released in 2016, and a prequel spinoff (*Annabelle*) in 2014, which in turn had another prequel (*Annabelle: Creation*) in 2017.

To understand how the Bible works in *The Conjuring* we need to clarify some of what's happening here, if possible. In the opening interview of the movie, Ed Warren tells Annabelle's owners that a demon is a non-human entity—the standard ghost-hunting definition, as also seen in *Paranormal Activity*. Demons can't possess toys, however, so these conduits are best kept locked up. Then there are multiple entities in the Perron household including demons, witches, and ghosts. The climactic exorcism scene physically hurls out the entity. The story reveals the culprit to be a demon, but the name of the demon indicates that she's a possessing witch. In the biblical world witches didn't possess people in the way demons did. Some confessed "witches" in seventeenth-century New England claimed to be possessed by the Devil, and some of the "afflicted girls" of Salem were deemed to be possessed by witches.

In early America, at least, you could be possessed by a witch. The idea slowly died out, but has been revived by *The Conjuring*. Ed does mention, when setting up religious items around the house (no Bibles) that a witch has connections with Satan, but somewhere in the confusion the witch and demon have become mixed up. It's this Bathsheba that's expelled. Witch, demon, or possessing ghost?

The book used in the exorcism is never named. Like the iconic Bibles we've seen throughout this book, it looks like Scripture and most people probably can't tell the difference without a title being shown explicitly. Even that might not make a difference. In any case, the book-based exorcism doesn't work. The "Bible" is helpless to save the family from the witch/demon/ ghosts that torment(s) them. Only the direct confrontation from family, armed with the witch's name, frees the possessed. Knowing the name, obviously, is necessary to end a possession.

This is an appropriate place to bring the possession discussion to an end. Evil entities of various sorts are confused and conflated. Religious books, unnamed, can't help. We've reached the apotheosis of horror. All kinds of entities are out to get us and the Bible won't help. Worse, it can't help. And this is based on a true story.

Demons

Demons are complicated. They don't come from a single source. Many cultures around the world have them. Even within Catholic culture they seem to shape-shift to match the fears of the time. America, being heavily influenced by the Bible, draws its main understanding from Scripture. So the first question is, how did the Bible view demons?

Demons were recognized from the earliest writing cultures. The Sumerians, who invented writing, knew of demons. They weren't, however, unremittingly evil to them. Of the ancient views of "non-human entities," these Mesopotamian demons come the closest to being what would later be known as "elementals." They're like forces of nature which, depending on where you happen to be standing, may harm you or not. They seem to have been a personified way of explaining disasters. What they don't have, though, is a constant, consistent backstory. They were a *Ding* that people recognized. Where exactly they came from would never truly be settled. As people started writing, demons were already there. They didn't possess people like later biblical demons. The main thing that distinguishes them from "monsters" is that they appear to be part human and walk on two feet instead of four.

Pazuzu, whom we saw in *The Exorcist*, was one such demon. Despite his fearsome appearance, with snake penis and all, he wasn't really totally evil. In a non-monotheistic world evil doesn't have to originate from beings opposed to the "one true God." Most divine beings have some good and bad in them. Demons tend toward the negative end of the spectrum, but they aren't the embodiment (enspiritment?) of evil. They're semi-divine beings whose presence often creates disaster for humans.

The Bible appeared many centuries later than the earliest Mesopotamian writings. Some of the characteristics of demons seem to have carried over from contact between ancient Israel and their neighbors to the east. The biblical worldview, although not monotheistic at first, eventually limited the power of deities apart from Yahweh, the god of Israel. Some of those other deities ended up reconceptualized as demons. Demons were part of the biblical outlook from the beginning. Part of the scenery.

In the Hebrew Bible (a.k.a. "Old Testament") fallen angels don't really exist. "Sons of the gods" fornicate with "daughters of men" in Genesis 6, but the Bible doesn't explicitly call them fallen angels. A brief passage in Isaiah 14 mentions the fall of the daystar (the Babylonian king at the time the passage was written) who will later be conflated with Satan. The connection isn't made in Isaiah. There is no unified story of the origin of demons in the Bible. Most of the time "angel" is simply a messenger in the Good Book. They may have been a class of servant deities originally. There's no full story of angels falling and becoming demons. In fact, there's no single biblical Hebrew word for "demon." When a person's oppressed by a supernatural entity, it's generally called an evil or unclean spirit.

The real problem began when monotheism took hold. A world with lots of room for spiritual beings bottlenecked to one single deity. Evil still existed in the world and if you've only got one God either that divinity can't control evil (God isn't all-powerful) or that divinity is part evil. One way out of this dilemma is to say there are other powers—but not gods—fighting against the good God. We saw in the last chapter that the Devil was one such entity. Demons, conveniently, were on hand to accompany the Father of Lies.

Many ideas about demons emerged in what's called in some Christian circles "the Intertestamental Period." Jewish scholars call it "Early Judaism." As the Christian name implies, there are sources that aren't in the Bible that appear between the time of the "Old Testament" (traditionally around the fifth century BCE, but in reality a few centuries later) and the New Testament (beginning around the 50s of the Common Era with Paul's early letters). The Apocrypha mentioned in our introductory documentary came from this time period and so did lots of other documents largely overlooked by those only interested in what actually made it into Holy Writ. Those other non-biblical documents, however, tell us quite a bit about the world of demons.

Israel at the time of the New Testament was quite a cosmopolitan place. It had been influenced by (actually, conquered by) Assyria, Babylonia, Persia, Greece, and Rome, each culture bringing their own gods. Although Israel was monotheistic by then the culture was especially heavily influenced by the Greeks after Alexander the Great. To complicate matters, the Greeks believed in *daimons*, which gave us our word "demon." *Daimons*, however, were nature spirits, and they were generally good. The word was borrowed to describe evil entities of various descriptions. Since demons aren't uniformly understood and may reflect beliefs about different beings in different cultures, they present special challenges for historians of religion.

The most dramatic demonic possession stories that inform American culture are from the New Testament. We're told in the Gospels of a man who lives among the tombs. He runs around naked. He's so wild he can't be restrained. Jesus casts a legion of demons out of him. They go into a herd of swine that run down a hill and drown themselves in the Sea of Galilee. Then again, we hear in Acts of a demon that overpowers and beats the exorcists who try to cast it out. These beings are all the more frightening for not being clearly described.

One of the most difficult tasks for modern people is to separate all that we believe about demons from the biblical world so that we can look at them objectively. Like "Satan" and "the Antichrist," demons aren't unified characters in the Bible. For example, in Isaiah 34 what we would call demons are treated as spirits that haunt the desert. The prophet doesn't even call them "demons." When Old King Saul is in a murderous mood the Good Book says an "evil spirit" was tormenting him. We'd likely call it a demon (or psychological disease). In the New Testament demons are often a way of explaining epilepsy. At the same time, Jesus and others have conversations with them. They're never described with any physical characteristics in the Bible (they are, after all, spiritual beings). We don't know what they look like. Eventually they're relegated to the rank of fallen angels. Beings in league with, but separate from, the Devil. All of this becomes solidified after the Bible became a *Ding*.

Possession movies often treat demons as biblical, although what the Bible's referring to by the word remains unclear. The problem is the Bible doesn't have a unified idea of what demons are. The best that we can do in describing biblical demons is to say that they're beings that torment humans. They may be the personification of evil. Sometimes they're fallen angels or organized followers of Satan. Their origin is mysterious. No matter what they are, they're always scary. Especially since they can possess people.

Are the Devil and demons separate entities? It's pretty hard to tell with no empirical way to test them. What is taught—or at least has been taught—to budding theologians in the movies is that evil has a hierarchy just as good does. If Heaven's arranged with God on top and angels between humans and deity, spiritual symmetry demands the Devil on bottom and demons between humans and Satan. In the Catholic Middle Ages elaborate demonologies were worked out. Some of the demons named in the Middle Ages appear in horror cinema. Abalam, Abyzou, Baal, and Belial are all named in the episodes we've watched. So is the Devil himself.

Traditionally, calling a demon the Devil is like calling a crab a lobster—they're two different things. Witches, purely human, were understood to consort with the Devil (we saw this in *The Witch*, as well as in *The Conjuring*), but not to have been demons. If horror's our guide, lines are blurred. It doesn't help that demons can be different entities to different people.

The origins of these ideas of a dualistic universe go back to the Zoroastrianism, and ancient Persian (Iranian) religion. Zoroastrians saw the world as starkly divided into good and evil. If there was a good God there had to be an evil god. Demons became anti-angels in Judaism, but before that happened people used demons to explain why bad things happen to good people. Evil spirits and even the evil dead could possess a person. Demons were misfortune. Fit into the elaborate scheme of Christian medieval theology they became fallen angels with names and personalities—always nasty. This became official teaching. Protestant literalists (*The Last Exorcism*), when push comes to shove, accept this demonology as well.

Movies, however, inform us about the Bible and also about the spiritual world. When you want to heighten the possession of a young (usually) girl dramatically, you make the demon the worst of the lot—the Devil. We saw this in *The Exorcist*, *The Exorcism of Emily Rose*, *The Last Exorcism*, and *The Rite*. The most over-the-top conflation (*The Conjuring*), however, avoids this identification. Invoking the Devil is pretty much to be expected in the horror world. Who wants to be haunted by a lesser demon when there's a more powerful one readily at hand? And that means the Devil possesses people—something that never happens in the Bible. Cinema's our guide here, however. This sampling of possession movies tends to show that shift between demon and Devil as viewer orthodoxy. Evil by any other name.

This viewer experience, however, is split. The secular demon's an entity that has never been human and no books work against it. The classic demon should respond to the iconic Bible or its stand-in, *The Roman Ritual*. It'll take more than one try, but the demon from Hell has to obey the rules. Sometimes a substitute's offered and that temporarily works as well. As further possession movies get cranked out we'll find more and more cases where the exorcism, and by extension, the Bible, just don't work. The Bible's a relic and even what it indicates demons might be, can't be taken at face value. They're entities that have never been human. "Reality television" tells us so. The idea, ironically, seems to go back to Ed and Lorraine Warren, devout Catholics. In classifying demons as spirits, they gave the world an entity that acts like a ghost, only worse. It has no idea what it means to have lived and lost. When they explain the origin of demons, they go back to fallen angels.

So, what do demons have to do with the Bible? In some ways, the Bible is their origin story. Being sensitive to the malleable image of what the Bible is, recognizing it in *The Roman Ritual* is essential when you have to face demons. As we expect in horror, categories, and boundaries are crossed. The point is made perhaps most eloquently in *The Rite*. Exorcism can work, but there's no guarantee that the effects will last. Indeed, the Bible is sometimes absent, as we saw in *The Exorcist*. Other times the Bible is there, as in *The Last Exorcism*, but it's powerless to save.

Possession movies continue to be made. "Based on a true story," they feature a religious monster that once responded to the commands of the Bible. Like vampires with crucifixes, they've acquired resistance to the Good Book over time. The story may be true, but without a Bible that works there's little hope of banishing them for good.

7

Heavens Above

There's somebody else in the house. Doors securely locked, children and servants abed, as night falls Grace Stewart can't understand how the music from the piano drifts through the house. Reaching for a shotgun, she bursts into the shadowy conservatory only to find it empty. She slams the keyboard cover and locks it. As she slips out of the darkened room, the door slams in her face. Calling for Bertha Mills, she demands the key for the locked room. Bursting back in, she finds the keyboard cover open once more. The secure haven she's made is no Heaven after all.

* * *

Where can we possibly go from demons? In what develops from the ancient worldview of the Bible, the opposite of Hell is Heaven. For pretty obvious reasons, Heaven isn't featured in horror very often. It does, however, appear. On the other hand, it may not be surprising to find the Bible in Heaven. And this is one of the great ironies of horror: even Heaven itself can make us afraid. This can happen in several ways, generally mediated by the Good Book.

In modern times we know that all that's above our heads is outer space. Infinity. Surely we've lived beyond the need for a Bible in the space age. One way that Heaven's addressed in horror is via aliens. Surprisingly, horror that features space creatures doesn't always ignore the Bible. Quite apart from the Blob, which can be understood as an alien (at least in the original 1958 version), other space and alien horror also occasionally brings the Bible into focus.

Heaven is where you go after you die. The problem is you have to die to get there. Those who haven't gone into the light yet, according to parapsychology, are ghosts. We haven't seen too many ghost movies in this book, but the Bible does occur in one where the characters are waylaid on the way to Heaven. When you're stuck here, you might try to find some bliss cinematically. When you do you might find that bliss interrupted by a demon.

164

Another locus of Heaven, at least in modern terms, is here on earth. Or at least in a parallel dimension. This chapter will close with the religiously rich, complex world of *Hellraiser*. Others have suggested that the sequels delve further into religion, but the Bible's right there in the first installment. Kind of a popcorn moment, but that only brings us full circle. The Cenobites may not be aliens, but their view of Heaven complicates what Hell is supposed to be, and makes them an appropriate ending to this book. We'll begin our exploration of Heaven, however, with those literally from above our heads— space aliens.

Alien Bibles

As has become clear throughout this book, genre is often in the eye of the beholder. Two categories of "genre fiction"—horror and science fiction— often have a blurry line between them. The reason is pretty obvious. Both may contain elements of the fantastical and both may be frightening. Science fiction is often placed in the future, but it's presumed that fear will continue into that future. And eventually, contact with others will be made. The potential for fear is great.

Often considered the originator and pinnacle of space horror, *Alien* brought these two sources of discomfort forcefully together. When we learned that a temperature-controlled, pristine home with many mansions didn't exist above the clouds, what we found was space, dark and cold. And uncaring. Astronomers gave us an infinite universe full of a near vacuum where even light was rare. No one could hear you scream. Reaching the nearest star to our sun would take four years traveling at the speed of light. Not only was there no Heaven above with its angels and harps, the Earth was terribly isolated. As horror fans know, isolation is key.

The Bible in these circumstances faces special limitations. First of all, in films set in the future, books are often lacking. For that reason many alien horror movies with the Bible take place on Earth. Also the very lack of Heaven challenges what the Bible promises. Technology that allows either humans or aliens to traverse it suggests that a 2,000-year-old book might not be the best manual to follow. And yet it remains.

The Fourth Kind (2009)

Like demons, aliens are particularly scary in movies if you believe in them. Or at least in the possibility that they exist. Although widely panned,

The Fourth Kind was an effectively executed horror film. For someone watching it late at night, with no background reading, it certainly seems real. The intercut "actual footage" makes it seem that the events were based on true occurrences, as actress Milla Jovovich tells you with a completely sincere, straight-at-the-camera confession as the movie opens. Split screens with "reenactments" and "actual footage" only add to the effect. Intercut throughout with "dramatizations" of the events, the viewer is convinced of the verisimilitude of the story.

That having been noted, the Bible functions as evidence of what's come to be known as the "ancient astronaut" concept. The idea isn't new. Zecharia Sitchin has been arguing for years that the Sumerians knew of alien contact. Even the short-lived television drama *Project U.F.O.*, which ran from 1978 to 1979, began with the words "Ezekiel saw the wheel. This is the wheel he said he saw." The words in the authoritative voice of Jack Webb, accompanied by an artist's reconstruction of Ezekiel's spare description, were pretty convincing. The idea is that ancient civilizations were indeed visited by aliens and hints of this remain in their writing and arts. This is the basis behind *The Fourth Kind*.

The title, by the way, is based on the UFO encounter designation rating devised by J. Allen Hynek, a UFO skeptic who eventually became a true believer. Despite the carefully honed public laugh reaction, UFO reports are fairly common. What makes a sighting a close encounter of the first kind, however, is proximity. The usual figure is 500 feet—close enough to see some detail. A close encounter of the second kind involves physical trace elements—scorched ground or stalled cars, for instance. The third kind involves seeing an occupant, whether alien or robotic. Hynek's scheme, of course, had been used successfully in movie titles before. *Close Encounters of the Third Kind*, which was in part based on alleged actual incidents, makes the point of going through the three categories.

Although Hynek (who had a cameo in *Close Encounters*, by the way) stopped at three, *The Fourth Kind* followed the convention that extended the possibilities. Close encounters of the fourth kind involve alien abduction. Set this scenario in the remote community of Nome, Alaska, and you've got a solid basis for horror. Olatunde Osunsanmi's *The Fourth Kind* involves the abduction of several of Dr. Abigail "Abbey" Tyler's patients. Tyler (Milla Jovovich and Charlotte Milchard) uses hypnotherapy to help her clients access memories suppressed by aliens. The backstory is that Tyler's husband was murdered, leaving her with two children, Ronnie (Raphaël Coleman) and Ashley (Mia Mckenna-Bruce), to raise on her own. The memories she raises are frightening—her clients claim to see an owl watching them sleep, but then it's not an owl....

The film begins with the real-life director, Olatunde Osunsanmi interviewing the "real" Dr. Tyler (Milchard) at real-life Chapman University. Later hypnotized back in the movie diegesis by Dr. Abel Campos (Elias Koteas), she tries to recall the murder of her husband. She wants to carry on his research. She meets three patients who have seen the owl. In abductee literature this is known as a screen memory—the owl is covering for an alien encounter.

Tyler is shown praying—saying Grace before a meal with her family. She's a believer. That night she picks up a book on Sumerian by Awolowa Odusami that her husband had been reading. The author's phone number is inside on a slip of paper.

Working to get behind the screen memories, Tyler finds herself in trouble as Tommy (Corey Johnson/Pavel Stefanov), one of her clients, kills his family before committing suicide. He utters some words of Sumerian before the killing starts, surrounded by the police with Abby in attendance. At home that night she tape records her thoughts.

The next morning her receptionist, transcribing the notes, tells her that she needs to hear what's been captured on the recorder. Abby hears other voices and her own screaming. It seems she has been a victim too. She's evaluated by her colleague Dr. Campos. They learn that her husband Will was investigating ancient astronauts, and she calls the author of the Sumerian book, whom her husband had telephoned before his "murder." Dr. Odusami (Hakeem Kae-Kazim) flies to Nome and explains the Sumerian to Tyler, based on the voices on her tape.

Dr. Campos is skeptical. While Dr. Odusami is explaining that Sumerian is a language unrelated to any other and that artwork shows anomalies, images of various artifacts are flashed on the screen. They appear to represent aliens. Some of the objects are Sumerian clay tablets, but one is a fleeting close-up shot of a page of the Bible. The passage? The first page of Genesis. Dr. Odusami states that "Genesis came from the ancient Sumerian epic of creation." Interestingly, the Bible is shown in a museum case along with Sumerian artifacts.

For those who haven't spent years reading about the first eleven chapters of Genesis, this is part of the "primeval history" section of the Good Book that comes before the story of Abraham. The first three chapters of Genesis tell stories about the creation of the world. Chapter four is about Cain and Abel. Chapter five contains a genealogy of the antediluvians—those who lived before the flood. The flood story goes from Genesis 6 through 9. It starts off with a strange passage that still has people guessing. The "sons of the gods" (the Hebrew often uses the plural word "gods" to refer to the singular god of

Israel, Yahweh) see the beautiful "daughters of men." They come down and intermarry with them apparently creating the *nephilim*, or "fallen ones." Then the Bible goes on to say there were giants on the earth in those days. It doesn't state, but implies, that the giants are the children of this divine-human coupling. Yahweh then decides to shorten human lifespans to 120 years. The flood is the first part of this divine euthanasia program.

What in the world is going on here? Biblical scholars still debate it, but popular culture provides an elegant solution. The sons of the gods are aliens. This is a biblical version of what might be classified as a close encounter of the seventh kind (built on to Hynek's original three). Human alien hybrids in the Bible. Cue the *X-Files* theme music. Immediately after this very strange episode, Yahweh chooses Noah to build an ark.

In *The Fourth Kind* the view of the Bible is as quick as an alien one-night stand. The point the movie makes is that Sumerian is an alien language. Sumer, in actuality, was an early civilization in southern Iraq. In real life Sumerian is an example of a language isolate—a language that has no known relation to any other. The other languages of antiquity such as Hebrew, Aramaic, Akkadian, and Ugaritic, are all related and are known as Semitic languages. Although the wedge-shaped (cuneiform) sign-system of Sumer was borrowed to write the slightly later Akkadian, the two languages aren't related. Long before *The Fourth Kind* Zecharia Sitchin and others began to suggest that ancient aliens were involved. A reconstructed version of the story goes like this: Sumerians were civilized by aliens. They were the first human culture to build and live as a complex civilization. They invented writing, the wheel, mathematics, and many other human firsts. This abrupt jump-start of culture suggests to some that outside help was involved. It would also explain why Sumerian is unrelated to other languages. As unlikely as all of this sounds, it makes for good stories. And scary movies.

It also ties in to the idea of demons. Some proponents of this alien hypothesis—among those who tend to be evangelical Christians—see these aliens as demons in disguise. They turned humans on to alien sex and the worship of pagan gods. Was it accidental that *The Exorcist* began in ancient Iraq? These demonic presences, then, continue to exist and trouble our world. They occasionally come around in flying saucers to confuse us. Or maybe that's how they travel, and we've mistakenly assumed demons can't fly.

So, how does the Bible function in *The Fourth Kind*? It is an authoritative text. In fact, it contains—hidden in plain sight—the answer to a mystery. The strange story of sons of the gods is really about alien visitors. It's a reliable historical record, even if misunderstood. This Bible does offer a kind of salvation—it saves from the misperception that the *nephilim*, the fallen ones, are deities. Yes, they're stronger and more technologically advanced, but they're physical beings just like us. For the Bible tells us so.

But then, as Abby undergoes hypnosis and the Sumerian is translated, in broken fashion, the alien claims "I am" then "savior." After garbled words, "father." This is obviously during the abduction of Ashley, her daughter, that takes place following her realization that aliens were involved. The tape recording then goes on to have the Sumerian alien declare, "I am ... God." Abby, in an interview with Osunsanmi, declares they can pretend to be God, but they aren't. The Bible, despite its prescience, can't save us from aliens from the heavens.

The Good Book here is a *Ding*. A *Ding* in a museum case. It's inert and outdated. An artifact that can only save if outside material—Sumerian texts—helps to interpret it. Even then, ancient astronauts come down and abduct, regardless of belief. When it comes to literal heavens, the Bible is merely another specimen behind glass.

Signs (2002)

Okay, it has to be admitted up front that the Bible in *Signs* is only implied. This is dangerous territory since it could easily be construed as an argument from silence. After all, the Bible doesn't appear in most horror movies. *Signs*, however, is included here as a diegesis formed from the Bible where aliens step in. The Bible's in the backstory.

There are legitimate reasons for including it in this viewing. Graham Hess (Mel Gibson), the father of the family around which the movie circles, is a former minister. In fact, other characters keep calling him "Father." We learn that Hess left the church after his wife died in a horrific accident, leaving him with two small children. There is a shadow on the wall of their home where a crucifix used to hang. Hess refuses to pray, even when an alien invasion is confirmed. Even when he sees an alien in his corn field. Even when aliens break into his own house. It's not surprising then, that we see no Bibles. Like every stand-in for God, Bibles have been expunged from his life.

The film as a whole revolves around religion. In the context of a Christian family (it isn't specified to which denomination Hess belongs, but since he's called "Father" and he was married, Episcopalian is a safe bet) one of the expected signs, if you will, would be the Bible. M. Night Shyamalan, however, doesn't let us see one. Its absence is felt in scenes such as the death of Graham's wife. He's called out to his wife's last moments as she's pinned between a car hood and a tree. If ever there's a moment a Bible was needed, this is it. In this scene, as at the end of the movie, he is wearing a Roman clerical collar, and priests in horror are inseparable from their Bibles. Or at least *The Roman Ritual*. Not Father Hess.

This is a movie about faith, after all, and it's far more about humans than about aliens. In fact, it can be understood as a kind of retelling of the biblical book of Job. What's missing from the film, however, is any vestige of Holy Writ. The Bible here is implied.

At several points we've seen that other books may represent the Bible. Often these books are "iconic"—widely recognized and frequently leather-bound and old. In *Signs*, Morgan Hess (Rory Culkin), Graham's son, buys a book at the local bookstore after the invasion begins—*We Are Not Alone: Evidence of the Extraterrestrial*, by, among others, Dr. Bimbu. This movie prop book does not represent an actual published book. It's treated, however, as the exclusive authority on aliens in the movie. When Graham first discovers Morgan and Bo (Morgan's little sister, played by Abigail Breslin) reading the book, he makes fun of the name Bimbu—five letters and beginning with "Bi" just like Bible—suggesting that the book is by a crackpot. When he sits down to look, however, it's clear the book is prophetic. It shows their very house being attacked by aliens. Graham takes the book away from the children at this point.

After he encounters an alien locked in Dr. Reddy's pantry (Reddy is played by M. Night Shyamalan), Graham becomes a believer. After that Bimbu's book is gospel. Graham asks Morgan what the book says about the situation in which they find themselves. There is no question that it is author-itative.

Unlike other iconic books pinch-hitting for the Bible, though, *We Are Not Alone* is a modern, paperback book. It certainly isn't old, but it's the only book in a minister's house that is treated as knowing what the future holds. Either this is a nihilistic statement—unusual in a movie that is ultimately about regaining lost faith—or it's an iconic book that serves in the place of *the* iconic book for most clergy. In this one instance, the absence of the Bible may tell us something about the way scary movies see Scripture. This is an implied Bible. If the Bible isn't or can't be shown, an alternative may be used. This is pervasive in movies where the idea of the Bible is required, but Holy Writ is absent. What is the Bible doing here? Nothing. So the movie implies.

Getting Lost

Ghosts share at least one thing with aliens: some conservative Christians believe them both to be demons. The Bible has only one bona fide ghost story. When Saul, the first king of Israel, requires advice the only prophet he can turn to, Samuel, has already died. This is a problem because Saul had banished all the necromancers from his kingdom. Fortunately, one remained. This otherwise unnamed woman—the "witch" of Endor (which gave its name to a moon in the *Star Wars* franchise)—is able to bring Samuel up from the underworld. The Israelites, at this point in the story, didn't have a Heaven yet. That was to come a few centuries later.

Samuel's ghost tells Saul he's about to die in battle. This story has particularly spooky resonance with a ghost movie of trapped spirits in another time of war.

The Others (2001)

Unlike most of the other movies in this book, *The Others* is partially a foreign film. Listed as a Spanish-American production, it was shot in English, with a clear interest in capturing American distribution. It worked. The movie performed remarkably well in the American market. It also had an iconic Bible.

There's no way of describing this atmospheric, gothic film's use of the Bible without a necessary spoiler. Famous for its twist ending, *The Others* is a straightforward ghost story. Its use of the Bible is somewhat intensive as the main characters have all become lost in limbo.

Grace Stewart (Nicole Kidman) awakes with a scream. The opening credits had featured an illustrated children's catechism book being read by candlelight. We're told this is the island of Jersey, 1945. The Second World War has ended, and three servants, Bertha Mills (Fionnula Flanagan), Edmund Tuttle (Eric Sykes), and Lydia (Elaine Cassidy) approach the door of Grace's gothic mansion offering their services. Grace, awaiting her husband's return from the war, is somewhat neurotic. She recites the house rules: doors are to be kept closed and drapes drawn. Her children Anne (Alakina Mann) and Nicholas (James Bentley) cannot be exposed to the light because of a rare condition.

Grace teaches the children catechism lessons. Anne is preparing for her first communion. This is important since Anne, reading a story of early Christian martyrs, declares that they could've kept believing in their hearts while denying Christ with their lips, and spared their lives. This leads Grace to insist that had Anne done this, she would've ended up in children's limbo—one of the four Hells, along with the Hell of the damned, Purgatory, and the bosom of Abraham. Grace warns them that they want to avoid children's limbo—it's very hot and at the center of the earth and it never ends. Sensing that sister and brother are distracting one another, she separates them to do their lessons alone, but not before reminding Nicholas that he can squeeze his rosary if he's afraid.

A child's weeping brings her back to their separate rooms, but neither has been crying. Anne tells her there's a boy in the house. That night the boy, Victor, touches Nicholas while the children are in bed. His screams bring Grace, who the next day punishes Anne for lying about the boy nobody else can see. Her punishment? To read the Bible aloud. Scripture is being used here as punishment. In the effort to get her children to Heaven, Grace has resorted to using the Good Book punitively. This isn't Bible abuse as we've seen in Chapter 3; the intention is to avoid limbo, so although Anne doesn't want to be punished, it's for her own good. For three days she has to read Holy Writ aloud.

Concerned, Bertha Mills asks how long the punishment will go on. She has to learn to ask for forgiveness, Grace replies. "It's about time she learned to read the Bible," she comments. And can Bertha stop Lydia from running about overhead? It's giving Grace a headache. When she spots Lydia and Bertha outdoors, and still hears the running, Grace demands Anne tell the truth. There are others in the house, Anne insists.

Bertha, as the nanny, listens to the children talking about how their mother dismisses ghosts as nonsense but still believes in the Bible. Grace says, Anne declares, that "all this stuff about ghosts is rubbish, and then she expects us to believe everything written in the Bible." The seven-day creation and the flood stories they don't believe. Or that the Holy Spirit is a dove.

Meanwhile Grace discovers a book of the dead—an album of photos taken of the dead to preserve something of their souls. She tells Bertha to get rid of it. Here the Bible isn't shown, but it's discussed and contrasted to a "book of the dead." Remember, the Good Book's a book of life. The Bible, which the children have a difficult time believing, is a book unlike the much more parsimonious picture book of dead people, or even ghost stories. The Holy Spirit can't be a dove, since "doves are anything but holy."

Grace is conflicted. She can't believe in the others, yet the evidence all points that way. Bertha suggests the dead can be mixed up with the living. "The Lord would never allow such an aberration," Grace declares. The living and dead will only encounter one another at the end of eternity; "it says so in the Bible." That's the last direct mention of Holy Writ in the movie.

How is the Bible functioning here? It's being read and believed in by the dead. As the servants reveal, Grace and the children, as well as the servants themselves, have been ghosts all along. Lost in limbo. Grace is trying desperately to get her children into Heaven. They study the catechism, read the

Bible, and have religious discussions. Scripture is intended to save them, but it's too late. They're already dead. In limbo.

This use of the Bible is somewhat pivotal here and demonstrates how intimately connected Scripture is with the concept of going to Heaven. As we've seen above, however, it's ineffectual. Had Grace wanted to avoid limbo, she would've had to have applied what she knew of the Bible before she smothered her children and shot herself.

Alternative Heavens

Sometimes Heaven can't wait. Tormented individuals try to find their own relief while here on earth. The results are often horrific. One way to "get high" is represented in the quasi-possession movie *Lovely Molly*. Another way involves solving a puzzle-box because nothing else will fulfill insatiable appetites in *Hellraiser*. In both of these films, strongly based on religious hauntings, the Bible appears as popcorn—small bits—as we reach our fingers to the very bottom of the bucket.

Interestingly, our last two movies deal with adults moving back into their childhood homes after their parents' departure. Books on religion and horror often focus on the *Hellraiser* series. Not addressing sequels becomes difficult in this instance since the storyline grows considerably over the course of the films. The basic idea, and a simple Bible reference, however, make the original *Hellraiser* an appropriate final stop on the way to Heaven. Especially since it looks a lot like Hell. But first, what to do when life gives you nothing but misery and bad memories?

Lovely Molly (2011)

Edgar Allan Poe once wrote, "the death of a beautiful woman is, unquestionably, the most poetical topic in the world." It is no surprise, then, that horror frequently takes up the trope of the young woman in distress. *Lovely Molly* leaves the question of its namesake's (Molly, played by Gretchen Lodge) actual demise open, but it strongly implies her death. The story revolves around a young woman who doesn't find wedded bliss to be Heaven. Instead she relies on heroin to get high. Oh, and there's a demon stalking her that might just be her father.

Bliss is a word with connotations of Heaven. Indeed, according to the *Oxford English Dictionary* the earliest usage of the word was a synonym for Heaven. Since there's no literal Heaven above, finding your true love and entering into an exclusive, committed relationship is often presented as a kind of Heaven on Earth. At Molly's wedding, which opens the film after a self-taped but failed attempt at suicide, we find a Bible. This is, like *Hellraiser*, a popcorn appearance of the Good Book, but its significance runs through the film. In the charismatic, Baptist ceremony, Pastor Bobby (Field Blauvelt) is shown in a fleeting scene, holding his Bible closed. There's contemporary music, and clapping in the church. No Catholic Tridentine mass, this. The camera records some uncertainty about Tim (Johnny Lewis), the groom. Not everyone in the family is enthusiastic about him.

Moving back into Molly's childhood home, the couple begins experiencing paranormal activity at night. Doors unlocking and opening. Alarms going off. But no intruders are found. Tom is a truck driver and that means Molly's going to be spending a lot of time alone in this isolated house. Hints are dropped that something unpleasant has happened here before. We might stop to consider that Roger Perron in *The Conjuring* was also a truck driver.

To help cope with her loneliness, Molly—who has started using heroin again as a form of self-medication—arranges a visit from Pastor Bobby. She's wearing a provocatively revealing wrap, and when she catches the minister's eyes straying to her underwear she begins to question him about carnal vices. When was the last time he was really drunk? (Before he was saved, but it's not appropriate to talk about it.) Is he gay? Since he's not, does he miss sex with women? And here he is on a pastoral visit without a Bible to save him!

There's quite a lot happening in the scenes with Pastor Bobby. Charismatic Christianity is extremely devoted to the Bible. In the wedding scene, however, the pastor's Bible is closed. He admits to being buzzed at Molly's reception, and the minister imbibing wine at her home raises its own set of questions. Molly is the Delilah to this Samson. The one thing that any charismatic knows can save him—the Good Book—passes so swiftly that you can barely see it. Meanwhile Molly has found ecstasy through opioids.

And she's also being oppressed by a demon. The film doesn't state the identification directly, but the suggestion of Orobas is confirmed by her deceased father's infatuation with horses and the iconography of the demon found buried beneath the floor of the shed. Pastor Bobby is defenseless against this denizen of Hell. In fact, the reverend becomes Molly's victim. Apparently responding to a call from Molly one rainy night, he sees her as she exits the house naked. He winds up dead in the bathtub. The last we see of Molly, after she dispatches her husband, is her unclad body leaving the house once more into the welcome arms of what looks to be a horse demon in the shadows of the night.

Lovely Molly is a bleak movie, even for horror. The completely ineffectual Bible is shown, closed, at the start of the couple's life together. It is supplanted by heroin used to cover a past of childhood abuse in the very house where Molly seeks wedded bliss. Molly's version of Heaven is Hell. A similar understanding of the Good Place is found in Clive Barker's nightmare.

Clive Barker's Hellraiser (1987)

In some ways, *Hellraiser* is a strange choice to end this movie screening. Like *The Wicker Man*, it's a British film. Although it relies heavily on religious imagery, it doesn't visually show the Bible. The Good Book appears as the tiniest possible bit of popcorn in an aural reference near the end of the film. Books addressing religion and horror, however, often dwell on *Hellraiser*. Besides, it has quite a lot to say about Heaven. Or is it Hell?

To begin with the obvious, "cenobite" is a religious (but not biblical) term. Monasticism—the idea that you could lead a more holy life by separating from society—began in its classic form in Late Antiquity. You had basically two choices: live by yourself utterly alone (eremitic monasticism) or live in an isolated group, or community (cenobitic monasticism). There seem to be some hermits in the Bible, such as perhaps John the Baptist, but the movement only began after the New Testament. Cenobites were a type of monk.

These days a web search for "cenobite" will more likely bring up the *Hellraiser* series as a first hit rather than actual monks. Led by Pinhead, these unsavory monsters are "demons to some, angels to others," but to find them you first have to solve a puzzle.

Larry Cotton (Andrew Robinson), a milquetoast guy, wants to move back into his childhood home. Religious and profane imagery mix in what his brother Frank has been using as his upstairs hideout. Larry's daughter Kirsty (Ashley Laurence) meanwhile has found a place of her own. Larry's second wife Julia (Clare Higgins) has a secret. She's had an affair with Larry's brother Frank (Sean Chapman/Oliver Smith). "It's never enough," Frank complains to her after sex, in a flashback.

Blood from Larry's lacerated hand on move-in day reconstitutes his dead brother. Julia discovers him in his secret room. Frank hasn't left the house after all. Frank had solved, before his death, a puzzle-box that opened the realm of the Cenobites. In the midst of candles and kneeling as if in prayer, he's suddenly pierced by hooks and dismembered, becoming a puzzle himself as Pinhead (Doug Bradley) makes clear by arranging the pieces of his face on the floor.

Resurrection is a biblical theme, as we saw in an early bit of popcorn, *Pet Sematary* (see Chapter 1). But now that Frank's been raised, he needs more blood to reconstitute his body. Julia brings strangers home to supply the need. When she demands an explanation, Frank shows her the puzzle box. "It's dangerous. It opens doors," he warns. "Doors to the pleasures of Heaven or Hell, I didn't care which." It leads to "Pain and pleasure indivisible." In other words, there is a basic confusion here. Good and evil, pleasure and pain, Heaven and Hell. They are all, in Clive Barker's world, very close to each other. Not very biblical, of course, but good horror.

Frank, never satisfied, wants Kirsty as well. She finds the puzzle-box and manages to escape him. Out on the street, Kirsty passes two nuns. They turn and stare at her. She faints and awakes in a hospital. Locked in her hospital room she solves the puzzle-box. A monastic world with screams and baby cries lies behind the walls. Chased back into her room by a monster, she meets the Cenobites. When she asks who they are, Pinhead replies with his famous "demons to some, angels to others" quote.

Quickly piecing it all together, Kirsty offers to give them Frank—who has escaped them—for her own freedom. Pinhead agrees, warning her "We'll tear your soul apart," if she fails to keep her word. Back at the house even more confusion reigns. Frank and Julia kill Larry and Frank is wearing Larry's skin. Who is he? Bad Frank or good Larry? When Kirsty arrives, she's fooled. Frank then kills Julia and Kirsty runs upstairs to hide. A falling statue of Jesus nearly gives her away. All of this is very interesting, but where is the Bible? Its appearance in this film is audible, not visual. And it's like a final bit of popcorn.

Kirsty backs into Frank's secret room and he follows her. The Cenobites appear. Hooks pierce Frank's body, pulling him into a cruciform pose. "Jesus wept," he leers before being pulled apart. Did you hear it? You might've missed it. As Evangelicals of the King James only version like to note, "Jesus wept" is the shortest verse in the Bible. The smallest Bible bit possible brings *Hellraiser* into the biblical world, between Heaven and Hell.

A brief note, however, on chapters and verses. It is a common misconception that everything between the covers of the Bible is Holy Writ. Scripture has had a long and complex history. Even its role as "the Holy Bible" is far more complicated than it seems at first. The original texts were written in Hebrew and Greek (with a little Aramaic). They were composed as separate pieces—now commonly called "books" and eventually brought together in a collection. That collection read continuously from book to book, once they were bound together. Taken all together, this compilation of books was difficult to navigate. Eventually, centuries later, chapter divisions were added. In other words, chapter numbers aren't part of the original. It wasn't until the sixteenth century that verse numbers were finally added. They were put in to make any specific place easier to find. In fact, there's even a puzzle-box-like code used to pinpoint exact locations in any Bible. It works like this:

> An eight-digit number is assigned to each verse. The first two digits (01 through 66, with the books of the Apocrypha following on from that) designate the Bible book. The next three digits (001 through 150) are the chapter, and the final three digits (001 through 172) are the verse number. As is to be expected, this system follows the Protestant Bible order of books. 19119172, then, would be Psalms 119:172—the final verse of the longest chapter in the Bible. All of this came centuries after the Good Book was compiled.

Only in a context where chapter and verse can be cited is there a shortest verse in the Bible. Significantly, this shortest verse, the one used in *Hellraiser*, is from the story of the resurrection of Lazarus by Jesus. Frank, who has been raised from the dead quotes it just before his second death. The idea of a second death comes from Revelation.

In future components of the franchise, the *Hellraiser* series will continue to explore religion and suffering and sexuality. There's plenty of room for blurred categories here. Demons live in Hell, but angels dwell in Heaven. The Cenobites are both. And neither. The brief glimpse of their world in this celluloid vision mixes the monastic Heaven with the monstrous Hell. The Bible functions here not to send Frank to Heaven or to Hell, but to a mixture of both. It's a place to which he doesn't want to return. His last words are from the Good Book.

Let's finish the movie. To further complicate things, the Cenobites have no intention of letting Kirsty go. As she reverses the puzzle back into a box she shouts "Go to Hell!" Pinhead dissolves, screaming. Then, in a city scene characterized by open fires—suggestive of Hell—Kirsty throws the puzzle-box into the blaze. The doorway to Hell—or is it Heaven?—is destroyed. Or it would be, were the box not rescued by a dragon in league with the Cenobites.

Pirates of the Caribbean: Dead Men Tell No Tales (2017)

One final piece of popcorn. As this book was being completed, the fifth *Pirates of the Caribbean* movie was released. It nicely ties in many of the themes we've seen in this chapter, and since it appeared at the start we'll view it quickly in closing. In a throwback to the original film of the franchise, the enemy monsters are ghosts. Once more the Bible appears, this time in the context of the heavens.

Carina Smyth (Kaya Scodelario), an astronomer accused of being a witch, is seeking "the map that no man can read." She determines it is the nighttime sky—the heavens. This she does with her father's diary, clearly an iconic book. Along the way Captain Jack Sparrow (Johnny Depp) finds himself in Hangman's

Cove where he's being forced to marry Beatrice Kelly (Hannah Walters), the sister of another pirate. Significantly, the scene occurs in the skeleton of a whale, evoking the Jonah tale. As Sparrow is headed into what is obviously the opposite of marital bliss, the priest (Jonathan Elsom) says, "Put your hand on the Bible," as he tries to get Jack to say "I do." Holding the Good Book up, he repeats the injunction while no one in the scene pays any attention to what he says. The wedding is broken up by Captain Barbossa (Geoffrey Rush).

These two senses of Heaven match the perspective of horror quite well. Heaven's not what it appears to be. Sparrow's life is in danger and the solution is "Heaven" in two senses of the word—a forced marriage, and in finding the Trident of Poseidon, which will literally save him from the ghosts. To find the Trident, he must look to the heavens. The marriage, it's strongly implied, will be Hell.

Unlike typical horror, the movie ends with the status quo restored. The Trident is found on an island that contains a map of the heavens, and Jack and crew are delivered. Captain Barbossa is the one who sacrifices his life in the process. But as the franchise has revealed, resurrection is nearly as common as death. The Bible, as in most horror, is ineffectual. The priest is completely ignored, and the Bible, instead of saving Sparrow, threatens to condemn him to Heaven.

Heavenly Frustrations

Heaven was a biblical concept that probably originated with the Zoroastrians. An intentionally dualistic religion, it gave us not only the Devil and Hell, but also Heaven. Had Judaism, and subsequently Christianity—the religions of the book, the Bible—grown into world religions without Zoroastrian influence, ideas of what happens after you die would have been very different. The Semitic Sheol was no Hell, but it was no Heaven either.

When Heaven shows up in horror, it's not Bible-based. Many are surprised to learn that the Bible really doesn't say much about Heaven either. It's not in the Hebrew Bible ("Old Testament") at all. Early inklings appear there, associated with the three-layer universe mentioned above. The picture's very hazy: literally above our heads is where God dwells. Dead people, however, go to Sheol, beneath the ground.

Under the influence of the Zoroastrians, the New Testament begins to offer a blissful afterlife. Only fleeting shots—like the Bible in much of horror—are offered. New Jerusalem. Gates of pearl. Streets of gold. No death. No crying. Mansions. Heaven as a place where all desires are met is only an idea that evolves over time. The Bible is the *Ding* that gets the concept started, but like Hell Heaven doesn't come into its own until later. If everyone dies and some are good while others are not, justice demands a bifurcated afterlife. So the thinking goes. And Heaven becomes, in the popular imagination, where you get everything you want. Horror calls that into question.

Horror spends comparatively little time in Heaven. That's not at all unexpected. When the good have to face what comes after life, however, the Bible may offer cold comfort. Over our heads are no pearly gates or cloud-top mansions. Our own atmosphere gives way to the barrenness of space, whence those once thought to be angels come. They visit us in the dark, with malicious intent. Even though the Bible warns us, we don't know enough to decipher it. Dr. Abigail Emily Tyler doesn't even seem to have a copy in her house. Instead, the Bible is in a museum case. Things in museum cases are artifacts, not living things.

When Graham Hess loses his wife he also loses his faith. No Bibles are seen in his house either. The truth about visitors from above comes in a secular book that has a prophetic element to it. It has his own house illustrated inside. Salvation comes here not through the Bible, but through baseball. Graham's dying wife prophesied as well, "Swing away Merrill. Merrill … swing away."

Those who died while still here, just after World War II—when UFO sightings first became big news—sometimes lose their way. Grace Stewart wants nothing more than for her children to make it to Heaven. Stuck in a limbo where the war's over but never truly ends, the family is bereft of a father and the Bible can do nothing to save them. You can't get to Heaven by reading the Bible after you're dead. It's too late. Heaven is like a mist that you can't grasp. Hope for it is always there, but at the end of the day the family's at home in limbo. "This is our house," they say, resolved to their fate.

The popcorn pieces of the Bible in *Lovely Molly* and *Hellraiser* show earthbound sinners seeking to make their own Heaven. If wedded bliss can't do it, heroin might help. Or sadomasochism. The results are blurred. Chemicals released in the brain that free endorphins only last so long. "It's never enough," says Frank Cotton.

Indeed, *Hellraiser* brings us back to that liminal world where Heaven and Hell are hard to distinguish. Those who meet the Cenobites will be tortured to death and taken to extremes. That's what Heaven and Hell are all about. They are the places of extremes. Heaven is pleasure in extremis. How much pleasure can one take? One subset of popular culture declares it must be boring. Pinhead disagrees. You can't tell Heaven from Hell in his world. And quoting the Bible is salvation to some, and damnation to others.

So what can we say about the Bible in horror when the movies are over?

Conclusion

The Bible is no stranger to cinema. Lurking in movies of all kinds as a symbol of respectability and rectitude, it's at home in horror. It's so common that we don't often stop to think how strange this is. An entire cultural sphere—including several American subcultures—can be expected to recognize and process the iconic meaning of a religious book at a glance. The cultural resonance of this book is so great that other books can be substituted for it and its meaning is largely unaffected. You don't even have to be able to read the title. This is why the Bible's been called a *Ding* throughout this book.

But what is this Bible? First of all, it's the Protestant Bible. (When Catholics need a sacred book, they have other options like *The Roman Ritual.*) More than simply Protestant, this is the Evangelical Bible. It's a book that predicts the future. It alone leads to salvation. It is, in every sense of the phrase, the Good Book. This is our *Ding*.

American culture, as technically inclined as it is, still believes in magic. This has been the case from the beginning and that supernatural effect has often been focused on that same iconic book. The Bible magically saves. That's the underlying American belief. This *Ding* is everywhere: songs, novels, political speeches, on the Internet, in libraries, and even in horror. Movies are but one element of pop culture to explore, but they are a bellwether of how we, as a culture, view the Good Book.

We gather in front of the big screen in large numbers. We see the same message at the same time. Few of us read the books biblical scholars write. As a culture we encounter the iconic Bible and its interpretation in a darkened room filled with strangers. Horror, which relates closely to religion, tells us many things about Holy Writ. We've merely begun to look at the results here, but this is what we've found. This *Ding*, this iconic book, is magical and holds out hope when the forces of darkness gather.

In contrast, this non-iconic book you're holding has looked at a sampling of horror and horror-related movies that make use of this iconic Scripture. Other horror movies also use the Bible, but those discussed here are particularly instructive. In some—like popcorn—the Bible appears in a single scene, usually to establish the character of a person or community. This happens across time from 1960 up to movies in the new millennium. It makes a difference if it's open or closed. A writer or director wishing to reveal the nature of a person, or monster, can use the Bible.

Consider *Van Helsing* again: Frankenstein's monster—one of the earliest and most pervasive of movie monsters—is declared human on the basis of a Bible in his lair. For all the faults of this swashbuckling horror adventure film, the development of Frankenstein's creature is compelling. Sympathetically portrayed, he only wants to exist. Like all of us, he didn't ask to be born. Finding himself alive he turns to the Bible—not the alchemical works of Paracelsus that his creator might have used to bring him into being—to find meaning and consolation. The book appears merely for seconds, but it informs the self-sacrificial nature of this "monster."

In other examples (*Psycho, The Wicker Man, Pet Sematary, Lovely Molly*) the iconic Bible portrays respectability. Upright, decent church folk carry it, read it, and draw consolation from it. It sets the stage for horror by contrasting with it. Ironically, the Bible as a book contains many horror stories. Iconic books can pull off this dual identity. The Good Book contains salvific secrets, but it also tells of inhuman treatment of others. It even has monsters. And it rests among other iconic books, some of them equally powerful.

With the iconic Bible we've seen that aspects of abuse of power creep in. Seldom is the use of the Bible utterly pious. It can be used to influence people, or even manipulate them. It spells out punishments and serves to hide weapons. It *is* a weapon sometimes. Paul of Tarsus refers to the word of God as the sword of the spirit. Horror uses that sword. Literally, even, in the world of pirates.

The iconic Bible isn't always what it seems. Let's face it, it's a big book with many boring parts. Lots of people never read it. At the same time false quotations are easily ascribed to it. It's common to hear someone say "the Bible says," only to follow this up with words from some other source of wisdom. Horror movies do that too. And they conflate iconic Bibles with other big, leather-bound books. These are common in vampire movies (which haven't been addressed here). These books sometimes become evil, or Anti-Bibles. This feels a more natural fit for horror. Books of the dead, grimoires, and even Bibles written in Hell. And people can become Bibles. The end results are seldom good. The living Bible tries to kill you. Then it tries to destroy the entire planet. Bibles may be implied, as well as explicit. When horror touches religion, the Good Book is never far away.

The dualistic outlook of good and bad in our culture borrows heavily from the Bible. The Bible, in turn, borrows heavily from Zoroastrianism here. Not surprisingly, horror tends to focus on the diabolical side of this equation. Movies feature the Devil, his father, his son, his associates. Three of the defining modern horror movies—*Rosemary's Baby, The Omen*, and *The Exorcist*—participate in this world of evil beings. Much of what contemporary Americans believe about demons derives from movies about possession. We're never given a clear view of demons in the Bible. They develop into fallen angels, possessing spirits, elementals, entities that were never human. They take over human bodies—generally those of young ladies—and they make what is sacred utterly repellant.

According to the script we've been shown as cultural consumers, the Bible—or some holy book—should be able to drive demons out. More often than not, however, it fails. Exorcisms succeed when someone else offers to be taken by the demon. This in itself is a biblical motif with Legion, the many demons of the man living among the tombs, leaving him to enter a herd of swine. The iconic books are seldom effective. If they were there'd be no real drama. All you'd have to do is remember to bring your Bible with you.

Demons, which are very common in horror, push back. We find them not only in possession movies proper, but in various guises throughout horror. Constantine fights demons, as does Ash in *The Evil Dead*. It may be a demon plaguing the Bell family of Tennessee, and lovely Molly. Is Jack Torrance possessed? Perhaps even those who resurrect from the dead when buried in a secret pet cemetery may actually be victims of possession. The Reverend Meeker's conversion to the religion of the Blob may reflect this as well. It's hard to say.

Dualism pervades into the few horror films that explore Heaven. In biblical thought Heaven is as far from Hell as you can get. Yet even the poor Lazarus in the Gospel of Luke can look across the gulf into Hell. The rich man sees him in the bosom of Abraham and asks for him to be sent over with some water. This junction between Heaven and Hell is found in horror's Bible as well. It's referenced directly in *The Others*.

In a world where a physical Heaven is lacking, the beings from the other side are decidedly disturbing. They may know the Bible, quote it, read it aloud, but nothing helps. The Bible doesn't get you into Heaven. And even if it does, you still can't tell it from Hell. Thus spake Pinhead.

By far the majority of horror movies contain no Bible. It is, however, rare to find a book analyzing horror cinema that doesn't mention religion in at least a passing way. Some make the point openly and centrally—religion and horror aren't that far apart. Religion, in America, often involves the Bible. For those attuned to Scripture from childhood, noticing Holy Writ in horror films comes somewhat naturally. As a cultural artifact, an iconic book, it can be used to suggest many things. The Good Book may represent the hope of Heaven or salvation from Hell. It may stand in for God. This iconic book plays an important role in society, as in the genre. And yet, surveys show many Americans know very little about it. It will, however, tell them how to vote.

This book offers a sampling of horror films and how they present the Bible. American culture has high biblical awareness and low biblical literacy. What people believe about the Bible may come from clergy or parents, but it also comes from popular culture. Movies are a powerful medium. The ideas they present so forcefully seep into perceptions of reality. For a few years many people could quote Ezekiel 25:17. They quoted it incorrectly, however. The point is movies reflect, and even direct, the way we think about things. Religion is experiential. Many people come to know it through culture. Religions have sprung up around *Star Wars* and *Avatar*. Vampire communities flourish, especially noticeably in the period after *Interview with the Vampire* was released. Movies influence religious sensibilities.

"Horror and moral terror are your friends. If they are not, then they are enemies to be feared," Colonel Kurtz informs Captain Willard in *Apocalypse Now*. This quote stands as the epigraph at the start of this book. The Bible, this *Ding*, often accompanies horror. If we don't know it, it can also easily become an enemy to be feared. It, like Colonel Kurtz, controls people.

Answering "why" this may be won't lead to any satisfactory answers. We have instead explored here the question of "what." What this *Ding* is doing here. Scripture has a scripted role in horror cinema. It's a book that's supposed to save you but, this being horror, it can't. It is a friend of horror.

Now we need to define this *Ding*—what is this Bible, according to horror? We've already seen that, overwhelmingly, the Good Book is the Protestant Bible. More than that, it's the Protestant Bible as interpreted by evangelical Christianity. Roman Catholics may use a Bible in horror, but they use it just like their evangelical co-religionists. We even occasionally see the Jewish Bible, but it functions just like its evangelical counterpart. This is the Bible *Ding*.

What is this evangelical Bible doing in horror? First of all, it functions largely as "prophecy." It magically predicts the future. That future's generally a bleak and inevitable apocalypse. This Scripture also gives rules that both humans and supernatural beings must obey. It's a book of immense power—so immense that it can represent God himself (and yes, for evangelicals he tends to be a he). Other iconic books may slip into this role if they look or sound biblical. Horror, however, has the last laugh. Holy Writ doesn't really work against the forces of evil. This *Ding*, this deity, can't save. It can deceive and be deceived. Or even destroyed.

Think about this a moment. Biblical scholars—those who devote their professional lives to understanding this book—do not explore it as any kind of magical text. Most of them aren't monster slayers in their time off. They take Scripture seriously enough to sink their entire life's work into it. There's no magic there. Some study the Protestant version, while others look at the Catholic, Jewish, or various Orthodox Bibles. They look at it rationally, logically. That's not the Bible we see in popular culture. The *Ding* movie directors and writers show us is a book powerful like no other.

Consider the fact that a dropped or thrown Bible leads to an attack. Clearly such assaults are part of the horror genre but the thrown Bible is a trigger. Scripture itself isn't often the object of attack. When it is, in the singular instance here of *An American Haunting*, there is no recourse left. Those who throw the Bible down have invited their fate. In horror, it's never slow in coming. There's a conservative subtext here since some Fundamentalist groups insist the Good Book should never be placed on the floor. Horror often flaunts this, however, since Holy Writ is a poor rescuer.

Fear relies on challenging certainties. This powerful *Ding* can be—and in horror often is—overcome by other iconic texts. Grimoires of immense power may out-perform Holy Writ. Monsters that become objects of worship in their own right can accommodate the Bible. Demons can defy it, even if it sometimes stands in for God. For them it's an enemy to be feared. It's not their friend. The struggle is eternal.

Horror movies often use, and help define perceptions of, the Bible. This book has tried to make some order out of this chaotic world. You can see the Bible a lot more than you might think, if you know where to look. We are becoming a more secular culture, but as long as there's horror, it's safe to count on the Bible's enduring presence. Just don't rely on it to save you.

A Note on Sources

One of the more embarrassing social moments is when you show up at an event and find someone else is wearing the same shirt or dress, or leather mask, that you are. After this book had been completely written, I discovered Cynthia J. Miller and A. Bowdoin Van Riper, *Divine Horror: Essays on the Cinematic Battle Between the Sacred and the Diabolical* (Jefferson, NC: McFarland, 2017). Not only was the title similar to what I'd originally selected independently, but many of the movies featured were those I'd examined here, although I analyze them from quite a different perspective. This book, unlike *Divine Horror*, focuses on the Bible, and I note that this book was written without the benefit of its insights. While I don't list tons of articles here, the same fact applies to Mary Ann Beavis, "'Angels Carrying Savage Weapons': Uses of the Bible in Contemporary Horror Films," *Journal of Religion and Film* 7 (2003). In a case of convergent evolution, I wrote the full draft of this book before I became aware of Beavis' article. To me this confirms the validity of the approach. These two resources affirm what I'd independently noticed, and demonstrate that religion, and specifically the Bible, find value and validation in horror.

No book arises, of course, without other books behind it. Instead of a traditional bibliography these credits list books that were influential in my thinking about horror, monsters, and the Bible. They are divided by chapter, but with some overlap. Since many of the topics raised early in this book are addressed at points later, this list of sources is heavily front-loaded. The books mentioned early on apply to many of the other chapters in the book. Where it seems appropriate to do so the reader is referred back to a relevant previous section. After the Previews each section notes sources (principally books) that address the subjects of that chapter specifically.

Previews

There are many books on horror cinema since the topic has become fashionable among academics in the last few years. Some of the resources I found especially helpful are these that follow. Andrew Tudor has been influential in analyzing horror among film specialists. His *Monsters and Mad Scientists: A Cultural History of the Horror Movie* (Oxford: Basil Blackwell, 1989) is a useful resource. He offers a systematic analysis of the various threats represented by the genre and their relative frequency in the movies. Peter Hutchings, *The Horror Film* (Inside Film series, Essex UK: Pearson Education, 2004) who made the point about genre instability in a way that confirmed my approach to the topic, is the film critic who suggests people find their own paths through horror (p. 31). Kendall R. Phillips, *Projected Fears: Horror Films and American Culture* (Westport, CT: Praeger, 2005) focuses on ten seminal exemplars in the field. Douglas L. Cowan's *Sacred Terror: Religion and Horror on the Silver Screen* (Waco: Baylor University Press, 2008) was the book that made me realize just how much the scary movie industry had to do with religion. He doesn't mention the Bible very much, though. Another early book in my thinking on the subject is the edited volume by Christopher Partridge and Eric Christianson, *The Lure of the Dark Side: Satan's Western Demonology in Popular Culture* (Sheffield: Equinox, 2009).

A number of useful histories and analyses of horror in general, which tend to be naturally idiosyncratic, include the following: David J. Skal's *The Monster Show: A Cultural History of Horror* (2d edition New York: Faber and Faber, 1993), and Wheeler Winston Dixon, *A History of Horror* (New Brunswick: Rutgers University Press, 2010). Both contain analyses of much of horror cinema, but even I can say I've seen some movies that neither of them mention. The collected coven of horror films is truly massive. For film analysis in general I found Colin McGinn, *The Power of Movies: How Screen and Mind Interact* (New York: Vintage, 2005) helpful. Carol J. Clover's *Men, Women, and Chainsaws: Gender in the Modern Horror Film* (Princeton: Princeton University Press, 1992) has been enormously influential. Intended as a study of gender in horror, it has come to be used to analyze horror in general and it gave the academic discussion the concept of the "final girl." Cynthia A. Freeland's *The Naked and the Undead: Evil and the Appeal of Horror* (Boulder, CO: Westview Press, 2002) continues the exploration of gender and horror. A very recent contribution, *Why Horror Seduces*, by Mathias Clasen (New York: Oxford University Press, 2017), takes up the question of why we watch horror, which I leave unaddressed here.

A more theoretically heavy tome is Judith Halberstam's *Skin Shows: Gothic Horror and the Technology of Monsters* (Durham: Duke University Press, 1995). Provocative and engaging from a Catholic angle is Edward J. Ingebretsen, S.J., *Maps of Heaven and Hell: Religious Terror as Memory from the Puritans to Stephen King* (Armonk, NY: M. E. Sharpe, 1996), although it isn't specifically about movies. His *At Stake: Monsters and the Rhetoric of Fear in Public Culture* (Chicago: University of Chicago Press, 2003) also explores the gender aspect of horror, specifically focusing on homosexuality fears. Exploring race in horror, which I don't really address here but nevertheless noteworthy, is Robin R. Means Coleman, *Horror Noire: Blacks in American Horror Films from the 1890s to Present* (New York: Routledge, 2011). Coleman makes the point that zombies were part of African-Caribbean religion (vodun, or voodoo) before becoming "monsters."

General books on horror have been helpful, including Adam Rockoff's *The Horror of It All: One Moviegoer's Love Affair with Masked Maniacs, Frightened Virgins, and the Living Dead...* (New York: Scribner, 2015) and Jason Zinoman, *Shock Value: How a Few Eccentric Outsiders Gave Us Nightmares, Conquered Hollywood, and Invented Modern Horror* (New York: Penguin, 2011). These two books, written by industry insiders, give fun and informative views of how horror has developed, and continues to develop, into an American cultural standard. Religion and film is handily addressed by John C. Lyden's *Film as Religion* (New York: NYU Press, 2003). He suggests that movies can be a form of religion. He has a chapter on horror and thrillers, which he classifies as quite similar. Even more insightful is S. Brent Plate, *Religion and Film: Cinema and the Re-creation of the World* (Short Cuts, New York: Columbia University Press, 2009).

Routledge has published quite a bit on religion and movies. Christopher Deacy, *Screening the Afterlife: Theology, the Afterlife and Film* (Milton Park: Routledge, 2012) has useful, if brief discussions of some horror films. Adele Reinhartz has been writing academic treatments of the Bible and film for some time. Her *Bible and Cinema: an Introduction* (London: Routledge, 2013) is a useful summary. She addresses *The Shawshank Redemption* (as does Deacy), but not horror. A more recent treatment, which tends a little toward the belief end of the spectrum is Crystal Downing, *Salvation from Cinema: The Medium is the Message* (New York: Routledge, 2016).

Monsters in general are addressed in any number of books including Stephen T. Asma, *On Monsters: An Unnatural History of Our Worst Fears* (New York: Oxford University Press, 2009), Timothy K. Beal, *Religion and Its Monsters* (New York: Routledge, 2002), Richard Kearney, *Strangers, Gods and Monsters* (New York: Routledge, 2003), David D. Gilmore, *Monsters: Evil Beings, Mythical Beasts, and All Manner of Imaginary Terrors* (Philadelphia: University of Pennsylvania Press, 2003), Jeffrey Jerome Cohen, ed. *Monster Theory* (Reading Culture, Minneapolis: University of Minnesota Press, 1996—a collection of scholarly essays, generally technical), W. Scott Poole, *Monsters in America: Our Historical Obsession with the Hideous and the Haunting* (Waco: Baylor University Press, 2011—non-technical and quite enjoyable),

Brenda S. Gardenour Walter, *Our Old Monsters: Witches, Werewolves and Vampires from Medieval Theology to Horror Cinema* (Jefferson, NC: McFarland, 2015—well written and accessible). On the more theoretical side there is Sarah Alison Miller, *Medieval Monstrosity and the Female Body* (Routledge Studies in Medieval Religion and Culture, New York: Routledge, 2010). The essays in Robert K. Martin and Eric Savoy's *American Gothic: New Interventions in a National Narrative* (Iowa City: University of Iowa Press, 1998) helped set the mood.

The observation about monsters as a threat from space in the case of *The Blob* (1958) came from Tudor, *Mad Scientists*. I had noticed this when I was growing up, but had never tallied the films to see how common it was in that era.

To get an idea of just how many subgenres of horror there might be see Chris Vander Kaay and Kathleen Fernandez-Vander Kaay, *Horror Films by Subgenre: A Viewer's Guide* (Jefferson, NC: McFarland, 2016).

Many of these sources were used throughout the movie sections listed below. Their notes may refer you back here.

Author's Commentary

Since I taught biblical studies for nearly two decades, listing all the books that formed the thoughts behind this chapter would be a fool's errand. I have, however, read a number of books that address specifically the role of the Bible in American culture that perhaps fall outside the realm of the standards of biblical scholarship.

Mark Pinsky's *The Gospel According to the Simpsons: The Spiritual Life of the World's Most Animated Family* (Louisville, KY: Westminster/John Knox Press, 2001), now available in a second edition, is the standard source for the Simpsons and Christianity.

For surveys on American Bible-reading habits see Philip Goff, Arthur Farnsley, and Peter Thuesen, eds., *The Bible in American Life* (New York: Oxford University Press, 2017).

Publications on early American lay beliefs about the Bible in easily accessible format are rare. The paucity of sources is a real issue, and, frankly, those who study Bible tend to be interested in the larger figures. Still, Jon Butler's books, *Awash in a Sea of Faith: Christianizing the American People* (Cambridge: Harvard University Press, 1992) and *New World Faiths: Religion in Colonial America* (New York: Oxford University Press, 2008), both address the vital point that Christians in America maintained magical beliefs alongside their biblically-based faith. The general view seems to be that magic and Christian faith are mutually exclusive. In reality, when that assumption is tested it falls apart. Butler has done his homework and this book has benefited from it. Also see Owen Davies' *America Bewitched: The Story of Witchcraft after Salem* (Oxford: Oxford University Press, 2013).

Mark Noll, whose name is synonymous with the field of American religion, presented a masterful *In the Beginning Was the Word: The Bible in American Public Life, 1492–1783* (New York: Oxford University Press, 2016) that surveys the topic of the title. The subject was also the focus of a series of books by the Society of Biblical Literature (SBL), including Ernest F. Frerichs, ed. *The Bible and Bibles in America* (The Bible in American Culture series, Atlanta: Scholars Press, 1988), Philip Culbertson and Elaine M. Wainwright, eds., *The Bible in/and Popular Culture: A Creative Encounter* (Semeia Studies 65, Atlanta: SBL, 2006), Mark A. Chancey, Carol Meyers, and Eric M. Meyers, eds., *The Bible in the Public Square: Its Enduring Influence in American Life* (Atlanta: SBL Press, 2014). An earlier book co-edited by Noll (Nathan O. Hatch and Mark A Noll, eds., *The Bible in America: Essays in Cultural History* [New York: Oxford University Press, 1982]) addressed this topic as well.

For H. P. Lovecraft some good sources are: Don G. Smith, *H. P. Lovecraft in Popular Culture: The Works and Their Adaptations in Film, Television, Comics, Music and Games* (Jefferson, NC: McFarland, 2006) and S. T. Joshi, ed., *Dissecting Cthulhu: Essays on the Cthulhu Mythos* (Lakeland, FL: Miskatonic River Press, 2011). W. Scott Poole (*In the Mountains of Madness: The Life and Extraordinary Afterlife of H. P. Lovecraft* [Berkeley: Soft Skull Press, 2016]) makes the point that modern horror movies wouldn't be what they are without Lovecraft's influence. He is also discussed in many of the books cited in Chapter 1. For references about belief in the *Necronomicon*, see these sources.

Books like Mitch Horowitz's *Occult America: White House Séances, Ouija Circles, Masons, and the Secret Mystic History of Our Nation* (New York: Bantam Books, 2010) and Owen Davies's *America Bewitched* (cited above) demonstrate that magical belief persists in the United States.

The idea of an "iconic Bible" has been around for some time. The term originated with esteemed religion scholar Martin Marty in an essay in Gene M. Tucker and Douglas A. Knight, eds., *Humanizing America's Iconic Book* (Biblical Scholarship in North America 6. Chico, CA: Scholars Press, 1982). The study of the concept took a large step forward with the efforts of James W. Watts, and he published the early results of this conversation in a combined issue of the journal *Postscripts* in the form of his edited book *Iconic Books and Texts* (Sheffield: Equinox, 2012), which he kindly sent me. This book owes a debt of gratitude to Watts and his efforts.

"Texts of Terror" is the title of an influential book by Phyllis Trible (subtitled *Literary-Feminist Readings of Biblical Narratives* [Overtures to Biblical Theology] [Philadelphia: Fortress Press, 1984]).

Timothy Beal and I have a fair amount in common. He has written both on monsters (see the note on Previews) and the Bible—*The Rise and Fall of the Bible: The Unexpected History of an Accidental Book* (New York: Mariner Books: 2011). Like Beal I was raised in a religious household, studied the Bible, went into academia, and became interested in how the Bible was perceived in wider culture. Likewise, although I studied for my masters at Boston University, Stephen Prothero came to the school after I graduated and began writing books that fascinated me. Primary among those used here is *Religious Literacy: What Every American Needs to Know—and Doesn't* (San Francisco: HarperOne, 2008). Another significant book on this topic is Paul C. Gutjahr, ed., *The Oxford Handbook of the Bible in America* (New York: Oxford University Press, 2017).

Scholars who directly address book magic in early America include Owen Davies with *Grimoires: A History of Magic Books* (New York: Oxford University Press, 2009), and less so, Brian P. Levack, ed., *The Oxford Handbook of Witchcraft in Early Modern Europe and Colonial America* (Oxford: Oxford University Press, 2013) but this a good resource for witchcraft in the time period. Books on early witchcraft are many; Stacy Schiff, *The Witches: Salem, 1692* (New York: Little, Brown and Company, 2015) is one of the more recent studies. See also Paul Boyer and Stephen Nissenbaum, *Salem Possessed: The Social Origins of Witchcraft* (Cambridge: Harvard University Press, 1974), considered a classic in the field. Returning once again to the question of gender, and ranging wider than Salem, is Carol F. Karlsen, *The Devil in the Shape of a Woman: Witchcraft in Colonial New England* (New York: Vintage Books, 1989). She discusses possession by witches.

For magic in general I can recommend Randall Styers, *Making Magic: Religion, Magic and Science in the Modern World* (New York: Oxford University Press, 2004), Ronald Hutton, *The Triumph of the Moon: A History of Modern Pagan Witchcraft* (Oxford: Oxford University Press, 1999), Sabina Magliosso, *Witching Culture: Folklore and Neo-Paganism in America, Contemporary Ethnography* (Philadelphia: University of Pennsylvania Press, 2004), Claire Fanger, ed., *Conjuring Spirits: Texts and Traditions of Medieval Ritual Magic* (University Park: Pennsylvania State University Press, 1998), Hugh B. Urban, *Magia Sexualis: Sex, Magic, and Liberation in Modern Western Esotericism* (Berkeley: University of California Press, 2006). Further observations of contemporary witches may also be found in Alex Mar, *Witches of America* (New York: Sarah Crichton Books, 2015).

For American belief in the Devil, see http://news.gallup.com/poll/193271/ americans-believe-god.aspx (accessed 23 December 2017). This is also a representative survey of American supernatural beliefs. Colonial diaries are discussed by Beth Barton Schweiger in *The Bible in American Life* (Goff, Farnsley, and Thuesen, cited above).

The quote "thou shalt not suffer a witch to live," comes from Exodus 22:18. Further biblical condemnation of witches comes from Deuteronomy 18:10–11.

Chapter 1

Most books on "the Bible and film" focus on Bible movies, but some useful information may be gleaned from them. Among those that stand out are J. Cheryl Exum, ed., *The Bible in Film—The Bible and Film* (Leiden: Brill, 2006). As an edited volume, however, the contributions are uneven and some of them are in German (appropriate for Hessians, in the next chapter). Also collected essays, *Close Encounters between Bible and Film: An Interdisciplinary Engagement*, Laura Copier and Caroline Vander Stichele, eds. (Atlanta: SBL Press, 2016) has a high concentration of useful pieces. Another effort in this genre, focusing on the Bible, is David Shepherd, ed., *Images of the Word: Hollywood's Bible and Beyond* (Semeia Studies 54, Atlanta: SBL Press, 2008). Gary Yamasaki, *Insights from Filmmaking for Analyzing Biblical Narrative* (Minneapolis: Fortress, 2016) is one of the latest volumes on the topic. It is, however, concerned with interpreting the Bible rather than understanding it. Adele Reinhartz has written extensively on the topic; her ideas are gathered in *Bible and Cinema: An Introduction* (details in Previews). In *Film as Religion* John Lyden (details also in Previews) suggests movies can *be* religion. Unlike most writers on the topic, he has a chapter on horror and thrillers. A book that I acquired for Routledge, Ronald Green, *Buddhism Goes to the Movies: Introduction to Buddhist Thought and Practice* (New York, 2013), also addresses religion and horror, among other topics of religion and cinema in eastern Asia.

Popcorn was also a horror movie from 1991, which I very much wanted to see. It is now very difficult to locate for a reasonable price and isn't available on my movie subscription provider account.

For the horror films analyzed in this chapter the books listed under "Previews" above apply. Helpful books on Frankenstein and his creature include: Susan Tyler Hitchcock, *Frankenstein: A Cultural History* (New York: W. W. Norton, 2007), Roseanne Montillo, *The Lady and Her Monsters: A Tale of Dis-*

sections, *Real-Life Dr. Frankensteins, and the Creation of Mary Shelley's Master-piece* (New York: William Morrow, 2013), and Lester D. Friedman and Allison B. Kavey, *Monstrous Progeny: A History of the Frankenstein Narratives* (New Brunswick: Rutgers University Press, 2016). All three of these are outstanding treatments of the topic. They are non-technical and surprisingly engaging.

The comments on Hitchcock and Hammer Studios draw from Skal, *Monster Show*, Jones, *Horror*, and Dixon, *A History*, all cited in the Previews section. The edition of Stephen King's *Pet Sematary* is the New York, Pocket Books edition (2001).

For pirates any number of interesting treatments can be found. The reference to Davy Jones as based on Cthulhu was from an article I read in *The Atlantic*, I believe. Perhaps it was *Time*. I do recall it was in the waiting room of a medical office. In either case, I read the article long before I thought of this book and failed to make a note of it. No amount of googling brought the exact article back. The resemblance is so commonly noted that it's now reflected all over the Internet. Many internet sources today repeat the connection since the web brought Cthulhu, dead but dreaming, back to life. Neil Rennie's *Treasure Neverland: Real and Imaginary Pirates* (New York: Oxford University Press, 2013) is a useful introduction that incorporates the *Pirates of the Caribbean* universe, albeit briefly. For information on the pirate's code, the movie franchise's wiki was useful: http://pirates.wikia.com/wiki/Code_of_the_Pirate_Brethren, accessed 12 August 2016.

Jon D. Levenson, *Death and Resurrection of the Beloved Son: The Transformation of Child Sacrifice in Judaism and Christianity* (New Haven: Yale University Press, 1993) is a good source on the subject of resurrection.

Chapter 2

The observation about Thomas Edison can be found in Jones, *Horror*, cited in the Previews section.

Biblical scholars have addressed cinema quite frequently, but horror less so. John Lyden's *Film as Religion* actually has a chapter on thrillers and horror, and Douglas Cowan's *Sacred Terror* addresses the larger topic of religion and horror. Cowan's work was seminal in my thinking as I began this project.

Being in the public domain, Washington Irving's writings may be found in many different editions. The quote from "The Legend of Sleepy Hollow" in this chapter is taken from The Modern Library edition (*The Legend of Sleepy Hollow and Other Stories* [New York: Random House, 2001], page 295. Brian Jay Jones' biography is a fairly thorough source on Irving's life (*Wash-*

ington Irving: The Definitive Biography of America's First Bestselling Author [New York: Arcade Publishing. 2011]). Further Hudson Valley folklore can be found in Jonathan Kruk, *Legends and Lore of Sleepy Hollow and the Hudson Valley* (Charleston: The History Press, 2011). The Bible passage about condemning witches is Exodus 22:18.

For a full treatment of the "Wandering Jew," see George K. Anderson, *The Legend of the Wandering Jew* (Providence: Brown University Press, 1965). This otherwise comprehensive volume suffers for lack of a subject index.

Revelation has been a contentious book from the beginning. Commentaries on the book are too numerous to list here and books about Revelation are legion. A fairly recent and insightful offering is Elaine Pagels, *Revelations: Vision, Prophecy, and Politics in the Book of Revelation* (New York: Penguin, 2012). The title here raises the point made in the text above about the title of the book itself. Revelation, as a title is in the singular. Because of evangelical interpretations of the signs of the end times—such as we see in *The Seventh Sign*—the book is frequently, if incorrectly, cited as "Revelations."

There are several books about how "the end of the world" developed in modern Christianity. It is mostly an American idea, although it had its roots among an obscure British sect known as the Plymouth Brethren. One of the Brethren, John Nelson Darby, devised a "roadmap" for the end of the world based on his division of time into dispensations. Scholarly treatments of his disciple Cyrus Scofield are very difficult to locate. One of the readable, if decidedly polemical, accounts is Joseph M. Canfield, *The Incredible Scofield and His Book* (Vallecito, CA: Ross House Books, 2004).

Chapter 3

Abuse of the Bible in general has been a popular topic for writers like John Shelby Spong, *The Sins of Scripture: Exposing the Bible's Texts of Hate to Reveal the God of Love* (San Francisco: HarperSanFrancisco, 2005) and before that, Phyllis Trible, *Texts of Terror* (cited above in the Author's Commentary section). For a more political use of the Bible inspiring terror, see Chris Hedges, *American Fascism: The Christian Right and the War on America* (London: Jonathan Cape, 2007).

My general statement that some suggested Kevin Smith was an unlikely horror director came from reviews that I read about *Red State* shortly after its release. Since I wasn't working on this book at the time I didn't note who specifically made these statements, but as an auteur Smith isn't widely known for horror.

Brent Monahan, author of *An American Haunting* (in book form, *The Bell Witch: An American Haunting* [New York: St. Martin's Griffin, 1997]), was teaching a course on how to deliver online classes via Sakai at Rutgers University in 2011, when I was working as an adjunct in the Religion Department. I arrived early and only after we'd talked for several minutes did I realize that he was the author of the book. He answered my email questions from time to time following our close encounter.

Otherwise the resources for this chapter are largely the same as for Chapter 2.

Chapter 4

The reference to the origin of *giallo* from Italian pulp fiction comes from Hutchings' discussion of the genre in *The Horror Film* (details in Previews). Other information on *Pulp Fiction* was derived from this wiki: http://www.imfdb.org/wiki/Pulp_Fiction (accessed 29 October 2016).

Interestingly, the idea of false scriptures hasn't received much academic attention at all. Many sources are available on other texts from the ancient world, however. A good place to start is Marvin Meyer, ed. *The Nag Hammadi Scriptures* (New York: HarperCollins, 2008). For a direct discussion of *Stigmata* and the hidden gospels, written by Philip Jenkins, see: http://www.bibleinterp.com/articles/hiddengospel.shtml (accessed 16 November 2017). This followed his cautionary book on the subject, *The Hidden Gospels: How the Search for Jesus Lost Its Way* (New York: Oxford University Press, 2001).

Although H. P. Lovecraft isn't the direct basis for any of the movies discussed in this book his influence on horror films in general has been impressive. The reference for the quote about the *Necronomicon* being "a bible of black magic" is Dixon, *A History* (cited under Previews), p. 161.

The reference to *The Fog* remake referring to religion less than the original comes from Douglas Cowan, *Sacred Terror*. The idea of a "final boy" is a play on Caroline Clover's trope of the "final girl" from *Men, Women, and Chainsaws* (see Previews for details on these books).

The "Gnostics" are a current topic of spicy debate. Various works by Elaine Pagels may be consulted on them. A rather authoritative treatment on the current state of the debate is David Brakke, *The Gnostics: Myth, Ritual, and Diversity in Early Christianity* (Cambridge: Harvard University Press, 2012). A translation of many of their sacred texts may be found in Marvin Meyer, ed. *The Nag Hammadi Scriptures* (noted above). For a balanced discussion of stigmata see Ted Harrison, *Stigmata: A Medieval Mystery in a*

Modern Age (New York: Penguin, 1996). As with demons, academic books on stigmata are somewhat rare.

Chapter 5

A list of the best-selling books of the 1970s may be found on Berkeley's website: https://www.ocf.berkeley.edu/~immer/books1970s (accessed 16 May 2017). The statement that *The Late Great Planet Earth* was the best-selling book of the entire decade is available on PBS: http://www.pbs.org/wgbh/pages/frontline/shows/apocalypse/explanation/doomindustry.html (accessed 16 May 2017). The point is also made in Matthew Avery Sutton, *American Apocalypse: A History of Modern Evangelicalism* (Cambridge: The Belknap Press of Harvard University Press, 2014). This is a very good source for understanding much of the end time mythology that drives modern evangelicals.

The character of Satan has been constructed from many sources over a long period of time. The way the Devil is represented isn't stable either historically or in the present. A good source is W. Scott Poole, *Satan in America: The Devil We Know* (Lanham, MD: Rowman & Littlefield, 2009). One of the best treatments is Jeffrey Burton Russell, *Devil: Perceptions of Evil from Antiquity to Primitive Christianity* (Ithaca: Cornell University Press, 1987). This is part of a series of books by Russell that cover Evil in different historical periods. Kathryn Gin Lum, *Damned Nation: Hell in America from the Revolution to Reconstruction* (New York: Oxford University Press, 2014) looks at ideas of where the Devil lives. Elaine Pagels, *The Origin of Satan: How Christians Demonized Jews, Pagans, and Heretics* (New York: Vintage Books, 1995) is more interested in a somewhat theological genesis of the idea. Susan R. Garrett, *No Ordinary Angel: Celestial Spirits and Christian Claims about Jesus* (New Haven: Yale University Press, 2008) also addresses the Devil.

Matthew A. Killmeier's article in *Divine Horror* (see the Preview notes) makes sense of John Carpenter's *Prince of Darkness* better than other treatments.

For the Antichrist see Robert C. Fuller, *Naming the Antichrist: The History of an American Obsession* (New York: Oxford University Press, 1996). Two excellent sources on the "Rapture" are Barbara R. Rossing, *The Rapture Exposed: The Message of Hope in the Book of Revelation* (New York: Basic Books, 2004) and Amy Johnson Frykholm, *Rapture Culture: Left Behind in Evangelical America* (New York: Oxford University Press, 2007). A recent treatment may be found in Sutton, *American Apocalypse* (noted above).

A note about *The Exorcist*: the movies treated in this book are theatrical releases. *The Exorcist* was rereleased in a fuller version in 2000, and it is that theatrical release I used as the basis for the discussion here. Since it provides a fuller explanation of what the demon is, it makes good sense to include the extra ten minutes in this discussion. The footage was shot for the 1973 production, but cut from the original release. It was later restored as a rapprochement between Friedkin and Blatty (see Zinoman, *Shock Value*, for details).

Chapter 6

Demons aren't a topic covered too often in book-length academic treatments. Russell's *Devil* (details in Chapter 5) remains one of the best resources. For a more technical, literary exploration see Ewan Fernie, *The Demoniac: Literature and Experience* (New York: Routledge, 2012). Francis Young, *A History of Exorcism in Catholic Christianity*, Palgrave Historical Studies in Witchcraft and Magic (New York: Palgrave Macmillan, 2016) is one of the most recent explorations that deals explicitly with exorcism.

For demons in Mesopotamia, the most accessible sources are Jeremy Black and Anthony Green, *Gods, Demons and Symbols of Ancient Mesopotamia: An Illustrated Dictionary* (Austin: University of Texas Press, 1992), and Jean Bottero, *Religion in Ancient Mesopotamia* (Chicago: University of Chicago Press, 2001). Many more technical works exist on Mesopotamian religion, but these two should answer basic questions about demons in context.

Malachi Martin's controversial classic in the field, *Hostage to the Devil: The Possession and Exorcism of Five Contemporary Americans* (San Francisco: HarperOne, 1992) remains a popular source. A book of one of his associates was made into a possession movie (not covered here): Ralph Sarchie and Lisa Collier Cool, *Deliver Us from Evil: A New York Cop Investigates the Supernatural* (New York: St. Martin's Griffin, 2001). Matt Baglio's *The Rite: The Making of a Modern Exorcist* (New York: Image/Doubleday, 2010) is also a popular treatment, and the basis of the movie discussed in this chapter.

The anthropologist who studied Anneliese Michel's case is Felicitas D. Goodman. Her book *How about Demons? Possession and Exorcism in the Modern World*, Folklore Today (Bloomington: Indiana University Press, 1988) is still one of the most reputable sources on the topic. Her book on Michel is *The Exorcism of Anneliese Michel*, conveniently published in English by Wipf & Stock (Eugene, OR: 2005).

On current evangelical approaches to possession see Sean McCloud, *American Possessions: Fighting Demons in the Contemporary United States*

(New York: Oxford University Press, 2015). An excellent source on Jewish demons, and exorcism in general, is J.H. Chajes, *Between Worlds: Dybbuks, Exorcists, and Early Modern Judaism* (Philadelphia: University of Pennsylvania Press, 2011).

Finding factual, non-contradictory information on Ed and Lorraine Warren is frustratingly difficult. They were a fascinating couple who pioneered ghost hunting as well as demon-busting; they referred to themselves as demonologists. Their own assessment of the Perron case involving a witch comes from *The Providence Journal* (http://www.providencejournal.com/breaking-news/content/20130718-film-the-conjuring-depicts-familys-reported-experience-with-paranormal-activity-in-burrillville-farmhouse-in-70s.ece accessed 23 June 2017). Various books by the Warrens, co-written with—ahem—"ghost writers," are available. The point about demons being fallen angels, according to the Warrens, came from Gerald Brittle, *The Demonologist: The Extraordinary Career of Ed & Lorraine Warren* (NP: Graymalkin Media, 2013). Graymalkin Media has been reissuing books "by" the Warrens previously published by mainstream houses, especially since the release of *The Conjuring*. This one was originally a Prentice Hall book.

Chapter 7

Heaven is the topic of any number of books. Probably the best place to begin is with the Zoroastrians. Although dated, the best book on them remains Mary Boyce, *Zoroastrians: Their Religious Beliefs and Practices*, The Library of Religious Beliefs and Practices (Milton Park, UK: Routledge, 2001).

Aliens, being highly controversial, are difficult to locate in academically reputable sources. That's not to say that some academics don't address them (David M. Jacobs, *Secret Life: Firsthand Accounts of UFO Abductions* [New York: Simon & Schuster, 1992], Ardy Sixkiller Clarke, *Encounters with Star People: Untold Stories of American Indians* [San Antonio/Charlottesville: Anomalist Books, 2012]) but they often do so at a cost to their careers. The classic treatment of abduction was done by Harvard professor John E. Mack (*Abduction: Human Encounters with Aliens* [New York: Charles Scribner's Sons, 1994]). A general overview can be found in Lynn Schofield Clark, *From Angels to Aliens: Teenagers, the Media, and the Supernatural* (New York: Oxford University Press, 2003). More popular treatments abound as well.

Zecharia Sitchin's ideas were first presented in *The 12th Planet* (New York: Stein and Day, 1976).

The concept of Purgatory is addressed by many authors, two recent sources are Diana Walsh Pasulka, *Heaven Can Wait: Purgatory in Catholic Devotional and Popular Culture* (New York: Oxford University Press, 2014) and Greg Garrett, *Entertaining Judgment: The Afterlife in Popular Imagination* (New York: Oxford University Press, 2015).

The quote from Edgar Allan Poe is from "The Philosophy of Composition," *Graham's Magazine* 28/4, 1846, p. 165.

Books on ghosts are too numerous to mention. A few that I found particularly good are: Lisa Morton, *Ghosts: A Haunted History* (London: Reaktion Books, 2015), Roger Clarke, *Ghosts, A Natural History: 500 Years of Searching for Proof* (New York: St. Martin's Press, 2012), and Elizabeth Tucker, *Haunted Halls: Ghostlore of American College Campuses* (Jackson: University Press of Mississippi, 2007). This latter source is added as a rare example of a university press that publishes on the subject.

For the supernatural in general, see Jeffrey J. Kripal, *Authors of the Impossible: The Paranormal and the Sacred* (Chicago: University of Chicago Press, 2010) and *Mutants & Mystics: Science Fiction, Superhero Comics, and the Paranormal* (Chicago: University of Chicago Press, 2011).

The reference to the resurrection of Lazarus in John reflects the fact that none of the other Gospels mention it.

Concerning *Hellraiser*, the first movie in this franchise does not name the Cenobite leader "Pinhead." That is how he has become known subsequently, so I use the name here. One must be certain to pay the Cenobites due respect.

Filmography

The Adventures of Ichabod and Mr. Toad
  (1949)
Alien (1979)
An American Haunting (2005)
Antichrist (2009)
Apocalypse Now (1979)
The Apostle (1997)
Avatar (2009)
Black Swan (2010)
The Blob (1958)
The Blob (1988)
The Book of Eli (2010)
Book of Shadows: Blair Witch 2 (2000)
Cabin Fever (2002)
Cabin in the Woods (2012)
Cape Fear (1962)
Cape Fear (1991)
Carrie (1976)
Carrie (2013)
Cat People (1982)
Children of the Corn (1984)
Child's Play (1988)
Close Encounters of the Third Kind (1977)
Clive Barker's Hellraiser (1987)
The Conjuring (2013)
The Cross and the Switchblade (1970)
Dark Shadows (2012)
Dracula (1931)
The Evil Dead, (1981)
The Evil Dead 2, (1987)
Exodus: Gods and Kings (2014)
The Exorcism of Emily Rose (2005)
The Exorcist (1973; extended edition
  2000)
The Fog (1980)

The Fog (2005)
The Fourth Kind (2009)
Frankenstein (1931)
Halloween (1978)
The Haunting (1963)
The Headless Horseman (1922)
The Hills Have Eyes (2006)
The Innocents (1961)
Interview with the Vampire (1994)
Jaws (1975)
The Last Exorcism (2010)
The Late, Great Planet Earth (1979)
The Lazarus Effect (2015)
The Legend of Sleepy Hollow (1980)
Lost Souls (2000)
Lovely Molly (2011)
Mary Shelley's Frankenstein (1994)
The Matrix (1999)
Memento (2000)
Monty Python and the Holy Grail (1975)
Muppet Treasure Island (1996)
The Night of the Living Dead (1968)
The Ninth Gate (1999)
Noah (2014)
Nosferatu: eine Symphonie des Grauens
  (1922)
Nosferatu the Vampyre (1979)
The Omen (1976)
The Omen (2006)
The Others (2001)
Pet Sematary (1989)
*Pirates of the Caribbean: Curse of the
  Black Pearl* (2003)
*Pirates of the Caribbean: Dead Man's
  Chest* (2006)

199

Pirates of the Caribbean: At World's End (2007)
Pirates of the Caribbean: On Stranger Tides (2011)
Pirates of the Caribbean: Dead Men Tell No Tales (2017)
The Prince of Egypt (1988)
Psycho (1960)
Psycho (1998)
Pulp Fiction (1994)
Re-animator (1985)
The Reaping (2007)
Religulous (2008)
The Rite (2011)
Sharknado (2013)
The Shawshank Redemption (1994)
The Shining (1980)
The Silence of the Lambs (1991)

The Simpsons Movie (2007)
Signs (2002)
Sleepy Hollow (1999)
Star Wars (1977)
Stigmata (1999)
The Ten Commandments (1956)
Tideland (2005)
V for Vendetta (2005)
The Watcher in the Woods (1980)
White Zombie (1932)
The Wicker Man (1973)
The Wicker Man (2006)
The Witch: A New-England Folktale (2015)
Wolf Creek (2005)
The X-Files: Fight the Future (1998)
The X-Files: I Want to Believe (2008)
Zootopia (2016)

Index

Milton Keynes UK
Ingram Content Group UK Ltd.
UKHW042219281024
450376UK00022B/242